Key Themes in Media Theory

Key Themes in Media Theory

Dan Laughey

Open University Press

Open University Press
McGraw-Hill Education
McGraw-Hill House
Shoppenhangers Road
Maidenhead
Berkshire
England
SL6 2QL

email: enquiries@openup.co.uk
world wide web: www.openup.co.uk

and Two Penn Plaza, New York, NY 10121–2289, USA

First published 2007

A catalogue record of this book is available from the British Library

ISBN–10: 0335 218 13X (pb) 0335 218 148 (hb)
ISBN–13: 9780 335 218 134 (pb) 9780 335 218 141 (hb)

Library of Congress Cataloguing-in-Publication Data
CIP data applied for

Typeset by YHT Ltd, London
Printed and bound by CPI Group (UK) Ltd, Croydon, CR0 4YY
www.polskabook.pl

Contents

List of illustrations

Figures

Tables

Acknowledgements

This book has emerged from a course in 'Contemporary Media Theory' that I have taught since 2004 on the BA (Hons) Media and Popular Culture degree at Leeds Metropolitan University, UK. Thanks to all those students who I've had the pleasure to converse with – and learn from – over the years. Further thanks to my colleagues, especially Kristyn Gorton, Lance Pettitt and Neil Washbourne, who read sections of the book and provided invaluable comments. I am also indebted to Nick Couldry, David Hesmondhalgh and Brian Longhurst for their insights. Chris Cudmore and Jack Fray at Open University Press deserve credit for their editorial expertise. Thanks also to Susan Dunsmore and Suzanne Renny for copy-editing and marketing skills respectively. I'd like to acknowledge the generosity of the School of Cultural Studies at Leeds Met for arranging a period of research leave that enabled me to finish the book sooner than would have been otherwise possible. The companionship and steadfastness of my mum, dad, brothers and sister is unerring. Finally, my love to Nicky, Harry and Jamie, for sleepless nights and magical sights.

1   What is media theory?

Before we begin to answer the question 'What is media theory?', we must ask two more basic questions: what are media and what is theory?

What are media?

We could think of a list: television, film, radio, newspapers and the internet, to name but a few. But a list tells us little about what commonly defines all these media. Perhaps the solution is to define media as technologies that communicate messages to audiences in different parts of a region, country or even the world. These media are the most obvious and familiar to us, but they are more accurately described as *mass* media. Mass media mean that 'no interaction among those co-present can take place between sender and receivers' (Luhmann 2000: 2). The term 'mass', in this sense, refers to the *mass*ive reception of media such as television, film, and so on.

However, media do not have to be mass to be media. This fact draws our attention to an historical sense of a *medium* (the singular form) as an inter-vening substance or agency (Williams 1983a). Before the age of mass media, the term 'medium' referred to something or someone situated between an object (the message being sent) and a subject (the receiver of the message). As Burton (1621) remarks, 'To the Sight three things are required, the Object, the Organ, and the Medium' (quoted in Williams 1983a: 203). For example, I am looking at a computer screen as I type these words. The object is the screen and the organ is my eye(s). So what is the medium between my eyes and the screen? Answer: light. Without light, I would not be able to see what I was typing – and you would not be able to read this book. The computer is a medium of its own, of course, but it would be nothing without the medium of light. This historical sense also applies to a human medium like a clairvoyant. A human medium is possessed by a supernatural spirit that sends messages through him or her to another party. Not everyone believes in this type of medium – but many of us still read our stars. Moreover, the human medium continues to capture the imagination of contemporary popular culture, not least in films such as *The Others* (2001) and *Don't Look Now* (1973). Next time someone asks you what media studies is all about, give them a two-word answer: 'the paranormal'.

Of course, media in their historical sense are quite different from today's media. Nonetheless, this historical sense provides an important dimension to what mass media are. The supernatural, spiritual essence of media technologies lives on with every new invention. It is interesting to gauge the amazed and astonished reactions to early telegraph communications, for instance. In 1844, the American inventor, Samuel Morse, transmitted a telegraph message from Washington, DC, to Baltimore, Maryland, that was decoded into the words: *What hath God wrought?* Such was the astonishment with which it was received that the man at the other end, Alfred Vail, sent the same message back to Morse. In today's parlance, this would translate as: What has God created? The implication is that only a divine presence could have possibly enabled such a remarkable feat of communication. The radio and television were greeted with similar wonderment. With this historical sense in mind, we can confidently claim that media are not objects (newspapers, television sets, telegraph messages, and so on) but means of communication. Objects exist in our *immediate* environment – media *mediate* messages to these objects. So what are the means of communication that constitute media? This brings us to a second sense of media discussed by Raymond Williams (1983a): the technical sense. We can distinguish between word-of-mouth, print, audio, visual, analogue, digital, and so on, all of which are media in the technical sense. In this sense, the radio set which we listen to is an object; the means by which it communicates messages to us (digital or analogue) is a medium.

In addition to historical and technical senses, Williams describes a third etymological sense of the term 'media': the capitalist sense. This sense developed during the nineteenth century when media became profitable enterprises – means of making money as well as means of communication. The driving force behind the capitalist sense was commercial advertising. Early forms of mass media – such as broadsheet newspapers – relied on sales alone, which brought relatively modest financial returns, but resultant revenues from the expansion of advertising content transformed the craft of media production into a lucrative business sector.

As well as Williams's three senses, media are also importantly defined in their social and cultural senses. A common phrase used today is 'the media'. For instance, we sometimes hear celebrities say that '*the media* tells lies' or 'the *media* hunts in a pack like a feral beast' (Tony Blair), or we might say ourselves that '*the media* influences people'. Even media theorists like Niklas Luhmann use the phrase – for example, I quote: 'Whatever we know about our society, or indeed about the world in which we live, we know through *the mass media*' (Luhmann 2000: 1 – my italics). As we have already discussed, however, media is a plural form that literally means 'mediums' so it seems strange to bracket media under a single entity (i.e. *the media*). A phrase like '*the media* tells lies' literally means '*the mediums* tells lies', which is grammatical nonsense. Nonetheless, the phrase 'the media' resonates so loudly in a social and cultural sense that it cannot be – nor should it be – merely dismissed as incorrect English usage. The social and cultural senses of the term, therefore, refer to how media are perceived by us. In Western democracies such as Britain and the United States, for example, media are perceived both positively (as democratic sources of truth) and negatively (as powerful manipulators of truth). By contrast, in countries where media are wholly (e.g. China) or partly (e.g. Thailand) controlled by governments, the social and cultural senses of media may be underscored by their wider political sense – as tools of propaganda and social control.

So we have identified at least six senses of what media are (historical, technical, capitalist, social, cultural, political), notwithstanding several other senses – for example, psychological – that we have no room to consider here but will discuss later (Chapter 2 considers psychological 'media effects'). 'Media' clearly has no straightforward definition. The next question we must address is: what is theory?

What is theory?

Theory, like a virus, spreads fear and trepidation among the student population. It is almost as frightening as philosophy, which spreads fear and trepidation among the postgraduate population (not to mention one or two academics). But theory is really nothing more than a way of thinking that is more systematic and sophisticated than 'thinking' in an everyday sense.

An example might suffice. When we learn to drive a car – a rite of passage that most of us will undertake at some stage in our lives – we must think all the time about how to steer, when to brake, where to indicate left or right, and so on. However, we do not stop to think about *why* we are learning to drive a car, or why a *car* is what we are driving, or how we are operating within a particular set of rules and conventions that constitute the 'Highway Code'. After all, if we did stop to think about all these things, we would probably crash! Some of us might need to pass a 'theory test' – but this is really a practical test designed to transform us into practitioners (i.e. drivers). And then, a few months after we have passed our driving test and purchased our first car, we will start to think far less about the 'why' and 'how' questions, not to mention the 'where' and 'when' ones. Experienced drivers often talk about not needing to think about driving because it has become such a routine, familiar, everyday activity.

But to *do* theory requires us to break away from routine, familiar, everyday ways of thinking – or not thinking. To extend the current example, we need to get out of our cars and start to think with more depth and breadth. Intelligent questions are the foundations for intelligent theory, so the theorist in all of us might ask: why has the motor car become such a vital means of transportation in modern times? How does a private – yet mass – method of transport reflect our social and cultural values? What are the consequences of mass car production and consumption? What alternative forms of transport might compete with the car? Why is car transportation more popular, generally, than public transport? What would happen if each driver practised their own interpretation of the Highway Code? These questions and others start to dig into a theory of cars. The task of this book, of course, is to excavate theories of media.

What is the opposite of theory? Answer: practice. Yes, to some extent this is true, but then again, theory and practice should be treated like the contemporary husband–wife relationship – happily married but always liable to divorce. Abstract theory, in this respect, is like the lone ranger, in search of but unable to find fulfilment. Theory without practice is lonely abstraction, as was sadly demonstrated by some theorists in the 1980s who expressed 'resolute (and excessive) anti-empiricism' (Corner 1998: 150) – and who have been forgotten about ever since. Indeed, the key to unlocking the best theories lies in the practical evidence that is brought forward to support them. In short, a good theory is like a good defence in a court of law. There are no fixed rules about the type or scope of evidence that might be required, but evidence provides a bridge between theory and practice. Theory that has no foundation in practice is likely to appear disconnected or contrived. On the other hand, practice disconnected from theory is aimless and uninteresting to media scholars like us. Theoretical evidence may derive from empirical research such as surveys or interviewing, or perhaps from analysis of texts such as a popular song, film or novel, or perhaps from historical documents and accounts, including biographies and autobiographies. The type of evidence used will have a crucial bearing on how a particular theory is constructed, evaluated and – in some cases – tested out. On the whole, a theory backed by wide-ranging evidence from diverse sources will withstand the test of time longer than a theory built on shaky evidence from limited sources.

What is media theory?

We now have some sense of what media are and what theory is. So what is media theory? If we condense the discussion above, media theory can be defined as a systematic way of thinking about means of communication. These might be means of communication used historically, such as light and smoke, or mass means associated with today's electronic media technologies. Of course, this book is mostly about contemporary media theory – not theories of media history – although we will discuss theories of modernity (see Chapter 3) which, in part, offer ways of thinking historically about the development of modern civilizations. An important point about *doing* media theory is to break free from our everyday experiences, and to think about them at a critical distance, through the different perspectives that we will encounter.

How to use this book

Before we begin to tackle this media theory book, a note on how best to use it. The eight main chapters discuss distinctive themes or strands in media theory. Ideally, the chapters should be read in order (i.e. Chapters 2–9) and – even more ideally – treated as distinct topics of discussion in the context of a media theory undergraduate-level course or module. In the spirit of Michel de Certeau (as discussed in Chapter 9), however, readers are free to use this book as they see fit, regardless of authorial intentions. If you do decide to move freely over this text – which you may be doing already, oblivious to what I write now – I have a few authorial recommendations. Chapter 2 would be the best place to start for newcomers to media theory. Chapters 3, 4 and 5 should be read in order and compared with one another. These three chapters form the cornerstone of the structure–agency debate that runs through the whole of media theory. Chapters 6 and 8 are essential but can be read out of sequence with the rest of the book if required, although Chapter 8 should not be read before Chapter 3, nor Chapter 6 before Chapter 4, nor Chapter 9 before Chapter 5. Chapter 7 should not be read before Chapters 3 and 4. Chapters 7 and 9 do not follow each other in the book, but should be compared with one another where possible. Chapters 7 and 8 share similar concerns but from different theoretical perspectives. Chapter 10 is a short summary of what has gone before.

A 'Glossary' is included for reference purposes, but the definitions of key terms are necessarily brief and should not be relied upon without first consulting the relevant discussion within the main chapters of the book. Words defined in the Glossary are shown in bold on their first occurrence. Further reading lists at the end of each chapter are intended as a starting point – but only that – in the search for wider sources on media theory. The best advice is to read and research widely. It is also very important, if you are new to media theory, that you seek out and read first-hand theory – that is, the work by authors discussed throughout this book. For example, a theorist we have encountered already in this introductory chapter is called Raymond Williams, and several of Williams's theoretical works are discussed later – for example, a book called *Television: Technology and Cultural Form* (Williams 2003). Locate Williams's works in the 'Bibliography' section to the rear of this book, and then search them out in your university libraries. You may even wish to buy a book or two. Inter-library loans are an option if all else fails. Reading raw, first-hand theory can be frustrating because the terminology and writing style of some of the best-known theorists are notoriously complex. Nonetheless, reading theory close-up and discussing it with others is the key to becoming a theorist oneself – and theorists tend to get first-class honours (in theory at least). So read this book in companion with the works of media theory it discusses. There is more to media theory than can be accommodated here. This book is merely a media theory taster – a means to several ends rather than an end itself.

2 Behaviourism and media effects

Introduction

The first way of thinking about media as they developed in each of their successive forms has been to try and gauge their effect on human behaviour and well-being. This is the case from the earliest mass media to the latest forms such as video games and the internet. In each case, expressions of concern by prominent public figures have led to a perceived panic that – ironically – is partly spread by other media forms, such as the newspaper press. Occasionally, as we will see in Cantril's study of radio, panic spreads to the public at large. 'Effects' studies tend to have one of two main objectives. The first of these is a genuine social, moral and political objective to measure the power of media technologies to affect how individuals think, feel and act. The other objective – sometimes ulterior – is motivated by commercial interests and attempts to measure the effectiveness of media as vehicles for advertising and publicity campaigns. Media are often said to have effects but these can be benevolent as well as malign, depending on your point of view. There is a fine line between propaganda and publicity. Propaganda is nearly always considered an evil; on the other hand, any publicity – so the saying goes – is good publicity. This chapter is more interested in work that deals with the social and cultural, as opposed to commercial, implications of media technologies, and discussion begins with Lasswell's classic analysis of the effects of propaganda.

The question about whether or not media affect us remains an interesting one despite the fact that nearly a century of research and theoretical endeavour has been spent trying to answer just this question. Very few studies have conclusively identified or rejected the possibility of **media effects**. Part of the problem is its sheer complexity. After all, rarely are comparable institutions such as religion and law analysed in terms of their effects on individuals (McQuail 1977). These institutions, so we are led to believe, are good for us and do not harm us if we behave accordingly. Media institutions, on the other hand, are bad for us – or at best, equally cursed and blessed. Newspapers, for example, are referred to as the 'Fourth Estate' in their democratic role but as 'the gutter press' when they engage in sleazy investigative journalism. Moreover, the meaning of the term 'effects' is never straightforward. Laboratory experiments by psychologists such as Wertham to assess levels of aggression in individuals during the viewing of a violent television drama, as we shall discuss, are limited to the measuring of short-term, direct effects.

Long-term effects are much harder to measure – despite the best intentions of cultivation theory – but, if identified, would be far more significant to a theoretical understanding of media power. There is also the issue of whether media effects mostly *affect* individuals, groups, institutions, or societies and cultures more widely.

Media theories discussed in this chapter cut across the spectrum of **behaviourism**, from **direct effects** theory – sometimes called the 'hypodermic syringe model' of powerful effects – in which a (media) stimulus is followed by a straightforward (audience) response, to theories of active audiences that use media to satisfy particular needs and enable the flow of media communications from person to person. It has been stated that 'The history of mass communications research is conspicuously lacking in any clear evidence on the precise influence of the mass media' (Cumberbatch and Howitt 1989: 25). Many questions about media effects continue to be unanswered. Regardless of this state of affairs, the 'effects' debate remains alive and was revived in the 1990s, not least as a topic of media and public interest (see Barker and Petley 2001). When people who are not media students hear about an academic subject called media studies, they tend to guess that 'media power' and 'media effects' will be two of the big issues on the agenda. This points to why pioneering media studies dating back to the early twentieth century strove to learn more about these big issues. So it is with the big issues that we begin.

Lasswell's chain of communication and propaganda technique

A pioneering theoretical model of media effects is known as Lasswell's formula or **chain of communication**. According to Harold Lasswell (1971b), any act of communication – whether face-to-face or mediated – can be dissected into five processes that require separate methods of analysis, as shown in Figure 2.1.

Although Lasswell was interested in all five of these processes and their corresponding methods of analysis, his most important ideas relate to the question of effects. As Denis McQuail and Sven Windahl point out:

> The Lasswell formula shows a typical trait of early communication models: it more or less takes for granted that the communicator has some intention of influencing the receiver and, hence, that communication should be treated mainly as a persuasive process. It is also assumed that messages always have effects.
>
> (McQuail and Windahl 1993: 14)

Nonetheless, this chain of communication is an apt way of introducing not just theories of media effects but media theory more broadly. All the theories discussed in this book can fit into one or more of these five processes. Theories of behaviourism explored in this chapter, though, are mostly concerned with audience and effect analysis – and to a lesser extent content analysis of, for example, violence on television.

WHO . . .	*Control analysis*
↓	
SAYS WHAT . . .	*Content analysis*
↓	
IN WHICH CHANNEL . . .	*Media analysis*
↓	
TO WHOM . . .	*Audience analysis*
↓	
WITH WHAT EFFECT?	*Effect analysis*

Figure 2.1   Lasswell's chain of communication

Under ideal conditions, any message that is communicated by a sender will reach its intended receiver(s) along an unbroken chain and free from interference or misinterpretation. Lasswell describes an effective relay of communication as one of *total conductance* between sender and receiver. But we do not live in an ideal world. Far from it, messages that are sent via mass media are particularly prone to being altered or misunderstood along their chains of communication, meaning *modified conductance* or *no conductance* between sender and receivers. What Lasswell is describing, to put it another way, is a chain-like structure of media and word-of-mouth communications not dissimilar to a sophisticated game of Chinese Whispers.

The structure of human communication in an age of media technologies would appear at first glance to be very different from the structure of communication that operates among (non-human) animals. On the contrary, Lasswell argues that the structure of human – like animal – communication serves vital functions that help to maintain order and well-being among the communicators (i.e. senders and receivers). Like animals, human beings take on particular roles as communicators – leaders, followers, watch-keepers – that carry certain expectations in terms of behaviour and action. In order to achieve harmony and consensus, chains of communication serve three specialist functions in any given society, whether human or animal:

1   *Surveillance of the environment*: in human societies this is typically dealt with by nation-states, who assign surveillance roles to diplomats, armies and spies, for example.

2   *Correspondence with the parts of society in responding to the environment*:

this is usually communicated by specialists such as politicians, press officers and journalists via mass media.

3   *Transmission of the social heritage from one generation to the next*: this is the job of teachers and lecturers, among others.

(Lasswell 1971b: 85)

These three specialist functions of communication are evident in Lasswell's behaviourist account of propaganda, which warrants discussion at this point so as to get at the roots of his ideas about media effects. *Propaganda Technique in World War I* (first published in 1927) analyses and evaluates the effectiveness of propaganda produced, in particular, by the American, British and German state authorities during the First World War (1914–18). His conclusions are a testimony to the importance of 'mobilizing minds as well as men and money in war' (Lasswell 1971a: 195). Propaganda is only effective, however, if it can convince 'the meanest as well as the keenest intelligence' (Lasswell 1971a: 201) and it has to tap into latent public opinion within the society it aims to influence. Good propaganda technique is difficult to accomplish and even harder to maintain.

When propaganda works, though, it is an extremely effective means to win support and – in this case – win a war. Lasswell argues that the British and American were more effective than the German propagandists during the war. The following excerpt is particularly revealing:

The British were amazingly successful in the development of humanitarian war aims. The Germans aroused much resentment and suspicion abroad by talking about a war of German Kultur, and by underplaying the humanitarian ideal. The British talked about a war to protect international law and to guarantee the sanctity of treaties, and they fought against a monster, known as autocratic militarism, in the name of democracy. . . . The Germans were never able to efface the initial impression that they were the aggressors.

(Lasswell 1971a: 196, 197)

According to Lasswell, during the early years of war it was still in the balance as to how the Americans would act: join the British forces, or side with the Germans, or remain neutral. Propaganda alone did not determine the American decision to form an alliance with the British – the German invasion of Belgium, France and Russia was the ultimate deciding factor – but Lasswell suggests that the British cause won more sympathy with American state and public opinion partly due to the humanitarian aims that Britain propagated through mass media (see Figure 2.2).

Returning to Lasswell's chain of communication, it is clear how propaganda plays a vital function when its correspondence with different parts of a

Figure 2.2 WW1 British propaganda (Lord Kitchener)

society is able to affect human behaviour and action, stirring patriotism in people. In turn, propaganda can enable recruitment of civilians who will fight for the cause and – more importantly – urge other societies to become allies. Effective propaganda can therefore provide a powerful stimulus for a targeted response. For instance, it can demoralize the opposition: 'propaganda saps the stamina of the armed and civilian forces of the enemy, and smoothes the path for the mailed fist of men and metal' (Lasswell 1971a: 214). The war dance stirred the emotions of primitive tribes; the propaganda machine, likewise but on a much grander scale, is able to 'weld thousands and even millions of human beings into one amalgamated mass of hate and will and hope' (Lasswell 1971a: 221). Propaganda is considered to be a specialist and vital function in modern societies, and if we apply its *total conductance* effects to Lasswell's chain of communication, we have something approaching a behaviourist media theory of direct effects.

Propaganda continues to play a central role in today's military and political affairs, not least in the 'War on Terror' (see Chapter 7 for more on propaganda from political economy and postcolonial perspectives). A propaganda stimulus, however, is not always followed by an expected response. The British Government's dossier on weapons of mass destruction proved to be impotent propaganda when it became clear that Iraq possessed no such weapons. The fickleness of propaganda highlights a key shortcoming in Lasswell's formula – that it has 'the tendency to exaggerate the effects of, especially, mass communication' (McQuail and Windahl 1993: 14). As we can see in Figure 2.1, all the arrows point in the same direction. This means that any form of communication – including propaganda – is assumed to travel in a linear, one-way direction from sender to receiver with identifiable (intended or unintended) effects. It is also assumed that the receiver will send this communication to further receivers down the chain – like Chinese Whispers – so long as sufficient conductance occurs at the relay point. In no way is this chain of communication assumed to travel back towards senders at certain points in the sequence. In practice, though, propaganda is not a unidirectional process in which an original stimulus ends in a response. If propaganda – or any form of media communication – is to be effective, its response needs to be fed back to the sender in order to evaluate and improve upon its effectiveness next time. Regardless of weaknesses in Lasswell's chain of communication, here is a useful starting point in attempting to understand how media can affect people's lives.

Wertham: *Seduction of the Innocent*

We can see in Lasswell's version of direct effects theory that media act as communicative channels for a stimulus to receive a straightforward response. The theories of psychiatrist Fredric Wertham can be placed at the extremities of this 'direct effects' argument. The two chief targets of Wertham's vitriol in *Seduction of the Innocent* (1955) are crime comics (see Figure 2.3) and television. Particularly worrying to Wertham is the influence of these mass media on 'the minds and behaviour of children who come in contact with them' (Wertham 1955: v). He claims that 'There is at present in all media, especially as they affect children, a pattern of violence, brutality, sadism, blood-lust, shrewdness, callous disregard for human life ... The quantity of violence in all the media is stupendous' (Wertham 1955: 360). Wertham provides evidence for his theories about the malignant effects of media from a combination of content analysis and the results of psychological tests with children who visited his clinic. Before we discuss his theories, it is important to consider briefly the methods he deploys.

Most of the tests required children to look at images and stories from comics or television shows, and interpret them for the benefit of the researcher. In the Thematic Apperception Test, for example, 'the child is

Figure 2.3   Crime comic image

shown a series of pictures depicting various scenes and is asked to tell stories about them' (Wertham 1955: 57). Similarly, the Duess Test requires children to provide their own endings to stories that are told to them through the medium of comics or television. Both these tests can seriously undermine the findings that they produce because of their crude artificiality. The psychiatrist himself suspects the unscientific unreliability of the Duess Test by recommending that it be used only for children below the age of 11 and that 'one should be careful not to view the child as if he [sic] were a neurotic adult or read too much abnormality into him' (Wertham 1955: 60). There is also a counter-interpretation of these types of laboratory testing in that they have been found to encourage research subjects to provide responses that the researcher is expecting rather than responses of their own accord. How can children respond instinctively to such artificial stimuli in darkened laboratory rooms? Not all psychological tests are flawed but those that have been deployed to measure media effects have tended to suffer serious deficiencies (see Gauntlett 2005). The notorious 'Bobo' doll experiment (Bandura and Walters 1969) – in which nursery-school children were found to act more aggressively towards an inflated plastic doll after viewing a film of an adult doing the same – is unsurpassed in its artificiality and nonsensicality.

Leaving to one side the dubious reliability of Wertham's methods, let us examine five psychological problems that he identifies in relation to media effects:

1   *Passivity*: he argues that television and comics encourage passivity in children due to their low order of literacy: 'In both, the entertainment flows over the child' (Wertham 1955: 355). The saving grace for television is that it can offer some scope for active viewing if watched in the company of intelligent adults.

2   *Misconceptions*: television and comics teach children unhealthy values that they associate with the real world. For instance: 'I have found that children from three to four have learned from television that killing, especially shooting, is one of the established procedures for coping with a problem' (Wertham 1955: 372).

3   *Imitation*: children consciously copy what they learn from these media: 'That children imitate what they see on the television screen is undoubted. There have been cases where five-year-olds have shot at the screen with their father's gun to join in what they were looking at' (Wertham 1955: 379–80). Similarly, children twist each other's arms and fight with each other in ways that copy the behaviour of their favourite superheroes.

4   *Identification*: a process of subconscious identification occurs when children come into contact with these media, and this identification is often with 'the powerful villain' rather than the hero or victim: 'comic books are conditioning children to identify themselves with the strong man, however evil he may be. The hero in crime comics is not the hero unless he acts like a criminal' (Wertham 1955: 116).

5   *Desensitization*: such is the high volume of violent and pornographic images portrayed by children's media that they are now commonplace and taken for granted: 'A generation is being desensitized by

these literal horror images' (Wertham 1955: 112). Desensitization theory states that real-life acts of violence become increasingly acceptable in direct proportion to more media violence.

These are forthright views indeed! If the title is not enough – *Seduction of the Innocent* – just browsing the contents page of Wertham's book hints at the horrific vision he foresees. Chapter 13 is called 'Homicide at Home: Television and the Child'! Even if we argue that these views overstate media effects and understate the capacity of children to distinguish fantasy from reality, it cannot be denied that Wertham's ideas captured the public mood during the advent of media such as television. His ideas also spurned a small library of further studies into children and television. Some research has partly supported these ideas, such as the finding that '[Television's] introduction in several countries has coincided with rises in crime rates and in other indices of social disruption' (Howe 1977: 102) and the similarly cautious conclusion that 'television is unlikely to cause aggressive behaviour, although it could precipitate it in those few children who are emotionally disturbed' (Himmelweit et al. 1958: 20). The latter study, moreover, rejected the 'release-valve' theory that television functions positively as a harmless channel through which real-life viewer aggression can be vicariously acted out.

For every study that identifies direct effects though, many more question Wertham's account. One such study of children's television use suggests that 'It is they who use television, rather than television that uses them' (Schramm et al. 1961: 1). Another study that comprehensively reviews the literature concludes that while 'overindulgence with television, as with most other things, can bring problems, it is equally true that when it is used properly and constructively television can have many positive influences on young viewers' (Gunter and McAleer 1997: 217). Another critic responds directly to the psychiatrist's work:

> I suspect it would be a dull child indeed who could go to Dr. Wertham's clinic and not discover very quickly that most of his problematical behaviour can be explained in terms of the comic books ... to blame the comic books, as Dr. Wertham does, is simple-minded.
>
> (Warshow 1957: 206 and 210)

Despite these criticisms, the spirit of Wertham has lived on, nonetheless, in campaigns against violence and aggression on television. Campaigners in the 1980s like Mary Whitehouse in Britain and the Parents' Music Resource Center in the United States have called for television and popular music censorship respectively. More recently, 'Media Watch' organizations operating in several countries have enjoyed popular support and publicity, particularly during heightened incidents of violent crime in the 'real world'.

Having said this, Wertham's theoretical perspective has numerous limitations without doubt. One is his assumption that children view television and comics as mirrors of the real world. Even children surely have no misconceptions about the difference between, say, a television drama about downtown LA and the real streets of Los Angeles. Another limitation of his ideas is their focus on cases of juvenile delinquency in response to violent images, which he then suggests are symptomatic of a whole generation of children. If Wertham focused on the 'bigger picture', it would surely reveal that a large majority of children adopt a sensible response to what they read and watch, and rarely engage in anything but superficial troublemaking like children have done since time eternal. Moreover, the claim that children have 'innocent minds' is more of a Romanticist construction – as depicted by the poet William Blake's 'Songs of Innocence and Experience' – than a social psychological matter of fact. It can also be argued that young people are more (not less) media literate than their elders, and have more sophisticated skills at interpreting, say, television than the adults who fret and write sensational reports about media effects (see discussion of media literacy in Chapter 9). Most problematic of all, Wertham's psychological approach does not sufficiently explore wider sources of seduction that foster anti-social behaviour other than the television screen or comic book. We are left with the impression that socio-economic conditions such as dysfunctional families, inadequate housing, poverty and lack of schooling are trifles compared to the harmful effects of omnipotent mass media. Media are made scapegoats for the ills of society by Wertham, in a manner sometimes indulged in by politicians who wish to divert blame away from their policies. Wertham's views had a significant impact on theories of media effects when they were aired, but seem rather contrived and naïve now.

Cantril: *The Invasion from Mars*

While Lasswell and Wertham are interested in how media directly spread mass propaganda and effects, the social psychologist Hadley Cantril's study of mass panic tends to support an *indirect* media effects perspective. Cantril was particularly keen to assess the effects of radio on its listeners, since at the time of his research in the 1930s radio was the newest and most pervasive medium in the United States – as well as Europe. Cantril had been working on a project to explore the psychology of radio listening when an unexpected opportunity arose to investigate radio's effects on human behaviour. On the night of 30 October 1938, between 8–9pm, the day before Halloween, Columbia Broadcasting System (CBS) broadcast an adaptation of H. G. Wells's novel, *War of the Worlds*. It starred Orson Welles and a small cast of young actors. Events transpired as follows:

Long before the broadcast had ended, people all over the United States were praying, crying, fleeing frantically to escape death from the Martians ... At least six million people heard the broadcast. At least a million of them were frightened or disturbed.

(Cantril et al. 1947: 47)

Why did so many people have cause to panic when they heard this play on the radio? This is the question that Cantril and his project assistants sought to answer. Shortly after the broadcast, they interviewed 135 people who had listened in, over 100 of whom were known to have been upset by what they had heard.

The most frightening passage of the radio play involved the invasion of several American towns and cities by evil Martians riding around in giant tripod machines with hands that emitted destructive heat-rays. The moment that transformed fiction into horrific reality for a million Americans was when a radio announcer spoke fearfully in the midst of bloody battle:

ANNOUNCER: I'm speaking from the roof of Broadcasting Building, New York City. The bells you hear are ringing to warn the people to evacuate the city as the Martians approach. ... No more defenses. Our army wiped out ... artillery, air force, everything wiped out. This may be the last broadcast. ... Now the smoke's spreading faster. It's reached Times Square. People trying to run away from it, but it's no use. They're falling like flies. Now the smoke's crossing Sixth Avenue ... Fifth Avenue ... 100 yards away ... it's 50 feet.
SIGNAL TO THE ANNOUNCER IS LOST.

(quoted in Cantril et al. 1947: 30–1)

At this point, an intermission break was announced. Unfortunately, some people by now had left their radio sets and even left their homes, presumably heading in the opposite direction from New York among other places!

So why the panic? Cantril suggests five reasons following analysis of interviews, all of which indicate the high degree of realism with which the radio play was received by its audience:

1   Radio was – and still is – an accepted medium for important announcements.
2   The named speakers during the broadcast had prestige (including four Professors of Autonomy, Captains, Generals and the Secretary of the Interior).
3   All the speakers were baffled about events, despite their expertise.
4   Specific incidents were reported in specific places (e.g. smoke in Times Square).

5   The total experience (or context) of listening to the broadcast added to the tension caused by the content of the play.

The realism of the stimulus, therefore, led to a panic in response, but this conclusion did not answer the question about why some people panicked while others heard the play for what it was – light entertainment. According to Cantril's analysis, the main factor determining why some people believed the play to be a real-life news report was their lack of critical ability, in particular as they had 'failed to make adequate checks' (Cantril et al. 1947: 107) to ascertain the fact that this was fiction. Those listeners educated sufficiently to exhibit critical ability made sure-fire checks – such as turning the dial to check that other radio stations were not reporting the invasion, or consulting the radio listings in the newspaper – while those without the necessary critical ability made less rigorous checks, such as phoning an equally uneducated friend!

So it seems education was the key factor in whether listeners believed in the reality of what they were hearing or did not. Following empirical analysis, however, it was clear that 'Critical ability alone is not a sure preventive of panic. It may be overpowered by an individual's own susceptible personality' (Cantril et al. 1947: 149). Cantril wanted to know more about the social and psychological characteristics of those who experienced 'personal suscept-ibility'. His investigations found seven characteristics of susceptibility to the effects of radio and other media:

1   Social insecurity (e.g. financial depression, unemployment, political oppression).
2   Phobias (e.g. fear of heights, war, Martians, and so on).
3   Amount of worry.
4   Lack of self-confidence.
5   Fatalism (or belief in mysterious powers that predetermine one's destiny).
6   Religiosity (or belief in a particular faith).
7   Frequency of church attendance.

(Cantril et al. 1947: 130)

Personal characteristics of human behaviour, therefore, can respond to a stimulus – such as a media broadcast – in a way that is not always sufficiently compensated by competing social factors, such as educational background.

What are the underlying causes of panic? According to Cantril, panic is caused by a perceived threat to an individual's Ego. The Ego refers to the immediate life-world of an individual, and includes their personal and social values in connection with the people closest to them, such as relatives and friends (Cantril et al. 1947: 197–8). Those individuals with high enough degrees of personal susceptibility to believe that an invasion from Mars was really happening were bound to panic because their Egos faced annihilation: 'The coming of the Martians did not present a situation where the individual could preserve one value if he [*sic*] sacrificed another ... the individual stood to lose *all* his values at once' (Cantril et al. 1947: 200). In this case, the effects of radio upon the Ego proved to be harmless when – eventually – the susceptible listeners found out their folly. But radio is a vehicle for real as well as fictional stimuli, and it can play on people's fears for far more dangerous ends. As Cantril points out with respect to Nazi Germany's use of 'People's Radio Sets' at this time, 'The whole tactics of Hitler show the importance he places on providing directed relief to bewildered souls. If they are not already sufficiently bewildered, bewilderment can be manufactured by sufficient propaganda' (Cantril et al. 1947: 203). Like Lasswell, he perceives the most significant media effects in the techniques of political propaganda.

Cantril's theory of mass panic in relation to the CBS broadcast of *War of the Worlds* is empirically informed but can be criticized on various fronts. Not least, Cantril seems to exaggerate the extent to which panic was widespread across the American population in response to the broadcast. Only 12 per cent of the population listened to the play and only one in six listeners believed that they were listening to a real news event (Cantril et al. 1947: 55). This means that only 2 per cent of Americans experienced panic, which is hardly an alarming proportion of the population. Cantril's analysis is also guilty of converting statistical correlations into theoretical cause-and-effect assumptions. For example, statistics showed that individuals who worried about their financial well-being were more prone to fall victim to the effects of the radio broadcast. Here we have a correlation but this does not mean that financial concerns cause individuals to be more affected by what they hear on the radio. The fallacy of a self-fulfilling prophecy is in evidence, too, in identifying individuals who are more susceptible to fear and worry in different ways, and then showing that they are also more susceptible to panic in front of a radio set.

Nonetheless, Cantril's ideas remain compelling and it would be unfair to criticize them on the grounds of a simplistic psychological agenda that neglects to consider wider social and political forces. Importantly, he improves on Wertham's direct effects approach by analysing how media have only indirect, *mediating* effects that merely reinforce – rather than create – serious social problems such as unemployment and depression. Elsewhere he suggests that radio can be a force for good given that it is an inherently democratic medium which *broad*casts the majority view; it offers potential to provide knowledge and education to underprivileged groups in a society; and it enables all its listeners to participate in 'auditory training' (see Cantril and Allport 2004). These claims for *positive* radio effects seem highly convincing if we imagine how a pre-broadcasting democracy would have operated.

Cultivation theory

A major weakness in all these early behaviourist approaches to media effects so far considered has been their narrow focus on short-term effects. In response, the work of George Gerbner and his associates has sought to mea- sure the long-term effects of 'television's contributions to conceptions of social reality' (Gerbner et al. 1986: 37). **Cultivation theory** suggests that television – although the theory can be applied to other media too – is such an important source of information and entertainment that viewers cannot escape its gradual encroachment into their everyday lives: 'The repetitive pattern of television's mass-produced messages and images forms the main- stream of a common symbolic environment' (Gerbner et al. 1986: 18). The idea that television cultivates the minds of viewers over long periods of time applies particularly to heavy viewers and also children who have grown up with an omnipresent television (or televisions) in their homes. For children, 'continued exposure to [television's] messages is likely to reiterate, confirm, and nourish (i.e. cultivate) their values and perspectives' (Gerbner et al. 1986: 23–4). Cultivation theory involves three types of analysis:

1   *Institutional process analysis*, which is concerned with 'all major powers, roles and relationships that have a systematic and general- ized influence on how messages will be selected, formulated, and transmitted' (Gerber 1973: 559). The production and distribution of a televised sporting event can be analysed in respect of how decisions are made and power is exercised.

2   *Message system analysis*, which is basically extensive content analysis of media productions such as children's television programmes.

3   *Cultivation analysis* (see Gerbner et al. 1980), which involves longitudinal surveys of people's opinions on certain subjects with the key variable being levels of media reception (e.g. television viewing). Variations in conceptions of social reality ('the outside world') held by heavy and light viewers are measured to obtain the 'cultivation differential'.

Following analysis of several empirical studies that emerged from a wider research project called 'cultural indicators', the 'cultivation differential' was deemed to be significant – heavy television viewers think differently to light viewers about the world they live in. One example of cultivation theory in practice concerns conceptions of crime. Message system analysis of US tele- vision from 1969 until the 1980s revealed that 'Crime in prime time is at least 10 times as rampant as in the real world' (Gerbner et al. 1986: 26). Heavy exposure to the crime-ridden world of television, according to cultivation analysis, is likely to lead to a 'Mean World syndrome' effect in which viewers learn that most people should not be trusted and that crime is rampant in every neighbourhood (Gerbner et al. 1986: 28). Mean World syndrome is only likely to spread slowly over a population of television viewers but, as the authors point out, 'It takes but a few degrees shift in the average temperature to have an ice age' (Gerbner et al. 1986: 21). Furthermore, their concept of 'mainstreaming' makes the claim that media influences on people's conceptions of reality can potentially 'absorb or override differences in perspectives and behaviour that stem from other social, cultural and demographic influences' (Gerbner et al. 1986: 31). Television's mainstreaming effects may cultivate a homogenization of divergent views because the medium is intended to appeal to broad audience interests. As discussed earlier, Cantril considered radio broadcasting to be a force for democracy, but Gerbner fears that television broadcasting excludes diverse opinions and dissident voices. The mainstream institutional characteristics and interests of television, then, may over time reflect the characteristics and interests of its like-minded audience. Television provides a guide and offers a 'television answer' to the question of how to act and behave in the world outside.

These are powerful claims for television's long-term effects on how we view the world we live in. In line with earlier theories of media effects, cultivation theory aims to understand the social and psychological processes that characterize vulnerable media audiences. Emphasis has shifted, though, away from uneducated listeners or delinquent child viewers to heavy media consumers. A recent psychological account of how television is damaging children echoes Gerbner's theoretical concerns:

> Children now spend more time watching a television screen than they spend in school. At this very moment, the average 6-year-old child will have already watched for nearly one full year of their lives. In fact, most of our children now literally have more eye contact with television characters than with their own parents.
>
> (Sigman 2005: 2)

More worryingly, children under three years of age who are exposed to indiscriminate television viewing are more likely to suffer from attention deficit hyperactivity disorder (ADHD) later in childhood (Sigman 2005: 16). Evidence to support these bold assertions is by no means comprehensive but if they prove to be accurate – and we do not know just how accurate these claims are right now – the public health consequences in terms of human behaviour abnormalities are unfolding in front of our eyes.

Agenda-setting and social functions of media

A not dissimilar body of work to cultivation theory, known as the agenda-setting approach (see McCombs and Shaw 1972), also deploys extensive content analysis to show that 'Through their routine structuring of social and political reality, the news media influence the agenda of public issues around which political campaigns and voter decisions are organized' (McCombs and Gilbert 1986: 4). Like cultivation theory, the agenda-setting approach seeks to uncover long-term – not short-term – media effects. **Agenda-setting theory** has evolved from a longer theoretical tradition concerned with how public opinion is shaped by media representations of 'the world outside' (see Lipp-mann 1922). Journalists in particular influence public opinion according to the salience they give to certain news items. Newspaper stories, for example, are selected and ordered in accordance with certain news values. Those stories deemed the most newsworthy are given front-page coverage and large head-lines; less newsworthy stories are placed further back in the newspaper and given less print space. Agenda-setting theory 'asserts that audiences acquire these saliences from the news media, incorporating similar sets of weights into their own agendas' (McCombs and Gilbert 1986: 4). Four rhetorical cues affect the agenda-setting process by drawing audience attention to the salience of particular news items (McCombs and Gilbert 1986: 7–8):

1   *Frequency of repetition*: the 'rolling' news story is deemed to be salient.
2   *The prominence with which items are displayed*: headline news, by definition, is assumed to have greater significance than *smaller* news stories.
3   *The degree of conflict present in the news item*: political scandals are more newsworthy than political consensus, for example.
4   *The framing of a news item – in what context and when it appears*: summer holiday weekends are often a cue to talk about excessive teenage alcohol consumption, for instance.

The basic conclusion drawn by Maxwell McComb and other agenda-setting theorists is that any given media agenda will give rise to a public agenda over the course of time. Figure 2.4 illustrates this idea.

MEDIA AGENDA   MOST PROMINENT PUBLIC ISSUES
Patterns of news coverage

        ↓   ↓ *Transfer of*
                                              issue salience
PUBLIC AGENDA
Concerns of the public   MOST IMPORTANT PUBLIC ISSUES

Figure 2.4 Agenda-setting role of the mass media

Source: From McCombs (2004: 5)

Empirical research findings to test out the agenda-setting approach found that four months was the optimum span of time between presentation of a media agenda and it having filtered across to the public realm (Stone and McCombs 1981). Another finding from the agenda-setting approach was the salience of media *images* over *issues* for readers, in response to the editorial decisions of newspaper journalists to foreground photography. Perhaps a positive outcome of agenda setting, though, is the suggestion that news media can set the agenda in relation to political participation, 'raising the level of political interest among the general public above the threshold sufficient to assure reasonable learning about issues and candidates' (McCombs and Gilbert 1986: 11). Political apathy, the authors argue, can be remedied by exposure to a political news agenda. This is an interesting hypothesis but we might speculate sceptically that excessive political coverage is likely to 'burn out' some sections of news audiences.

Prior to agenda-setting studies, the seeds of this theoretical approach were sown by a well-known essay by Paul Lazarsfeld and Robert Merton (first published in 1948) that outlined three social functions of mass media. First, media serve a 'status conferral function': 'The mass media *confer* status on public issues, persons, organizations and social movements' (Lazarsfeld and Merton 2004: 233). Clearly, people who feature in media coverage are elevated to a certain status or standing among their audience. Fashion designers who are asked to comment on this year's designs at the Paris Fashion Week for a radio news bulletin, for example, are likely to find their status enhanced (conferred upon them) by such media appearances. A second function of media is 'the enforcement of social norms': 'The mass media may initiate organized social action by "exposing" conditions which are at variance with public moralities' (Lazarsfeld and Merton 2004: 234). One recent example of this has been the crusade against asylum seekers by several newspapers in Britain, notably the *Daily Mail*. The *Daily Mail* is one of Britain's biggest-selling news titles and – according to this social function of media – may well owe its success to such moral crusades: 'The triumphant crusade may enhance the power and prestige of the mass medium' (Lazarsfeld and Merton 2004: 235). Third and finally, media serve a 'narcotizing dysfunction' in the sense that they occupy audience time to such an extent that little time is left for organized social and political action. This idea that media make their audiences drowsy and passive is not dissimilar to Adorno's perspective on the culture industry (see Chapter 7).

Two-step flow and the phenomenistic approach

Perhaps the first major rebuttal to theories of media effects was a study of how people influence the flow of mass media messages. *Personal Influence* (1955) – using a similar anthropological approach to the Lynds' *Middletown* (1929) as discussed in Chapter 3 – reported the findings of small-group and broader survey research on how women in Decatour, Illinois, communicated with each other amid this flow of media communications. The authors, Elihu Katz and the aforementioned Lazarsfeld, begin by suggesting how Lasswell's formula fails to distinguish individuals from media institutions:

> it now has become increasingly clear that the individual person who reads something and talks about it with other people cannot be taken simply as a simile for social entities like newspapers or magazines. He himself [sic] needs to be studied in his two-fold capacity as a communicator and as a relay point in the network of mass communications.
>
> (Katz and Lazarsfeld 1955: 1)

Lasswell's chain of communication (as we discussed earlier) is based on the principle that media messages will be passed from an institutional source to person A, and from person A to person B, and so on, in a relatively straightforward sequence. On the contrary, Katz and Lazarsfeld set out to study the flow of media messages using what they call impact analysis, which compares the role of opinion leaders to the role of media in influencing individuals' decision-making processes.

We must all know one or two opinion leaders among friends and family members with whom we intermingle. They are those people who have an opinion on everything; who lead conversations as if talking came naturally; who might be otherwise called the 'movers and shakers' among their party. Katz and Lazarsfeld's study identified the impact of opinion leaders among the women of Decatour and found that 'opinion leaders seemed to be distributed in all occupational groups, and on every social and economic level' (Katz and Lazarsfeld 1955: 32). So opinion leaders are found in all walks of life and, moreover, they tend to expose themselves to media messages more so than less opinionated individuals. These findings lead the authors to a model that they refer to as the **two-step flow** in which 'ideas, often, seem to flow *from* radio and print *to* opinion leaders and *from them* to the less active sections of the population' (Katz and Lazarsfeld 1955: 32). Unlike Lasswell's formula, the 'two-step flow' model affords greater influence to individual recipients of mass communications and rejects the notion that mass media messages simply flow – like waves – over their recipients, from one sequence to the next. An opinion leader not only transfers media messages to others; he or she selects and adapts these messages in line with their own agenda. As such, opinion leaders are located between media institutions and the rest of society. Paradoxically, an opinion leader is 'a group member playing a key communications role' (Katz and Lazarsfeld 1955: 33), acting as a gatekeeper between media and the majority public.

This 'two-step flow' theory is markedly different from 'stimulus-response' theories of media effects encountered previously. Its central argument – that face-to-face, interpersonal relations intervene in the flow of media communications from transmission to reception – contrasts with earlier studies that assume media power to be directly exerted upon 'the atomized masses'. Another author who questions hypodermic syringe theories of direct effects is Joseph Klapper, who considers approaches such as the two-step flow model as heralding a shift *away* from the tendency to regard mass communication as a necessary and sufficient cause of audience effects, toward a view of the media as influences, working amid other influences, in a total situation (Klapper 1960: 5). Mass media, he argues, cannot be viewed in isolation from all the other influences that cause human beings to change their behaviour, attitudes or actions. What Klapper calls his **phenomenistic approach** is still interested in how media generate a stimulus to which audiences might respond, but now the focus is on 'the role of that stimulus in a total observed phenomenon' (Klapper 1960: 5) rather than on a laboratory approach in which a stimulus acts alone, in an artificial situation.

Klapper's phenomenistic approach proposes that media in most cases do not cause effects on their audiences but instead function as one component along a spectrum of mediating factors which 'are more likely to reinforce than to change' people's behaviour and attitudes (Klapper 1960: 8). Mediating factors incorporate a range of phenomena – such as family customs, politics and religion, as well as mass media – that influence people's opinions and attitudes (Klapper 1960: 47–52). The five main mediating factors are:

1   *An individual's predisposed opinions and how these predispositions tend to mean they use media in selective ways*: for example, an individual who dislikes sentimental melodrama is unlikely to watch soap operas on television.

2   *The group to which the individual belongs and how the predispositions of this group impact on the individual's predisposed opinions*: for example, classmates often share the same taste in music through peer-group influence.

3   *Interpersonal dissemination of media content*: the assumption here is that like-minded people talk to each other about the films they watch and the news they read about. Everyday conversations on such matters tend to limit dramatic individual changes in behaviour or opinions.

4   *Opinion leadership*: reminiscent of the 'two-step flow' model, Klapper argues that opinion leaders tend to use media messages to reinforce their predisposed opinions rather than to simply relay what these messages have to say.

5   *The role of mass media in a free enterprise society*: given the prerequisite economic imperatives to please both advertisers and audiences, media institutions tend to produce content based on successful

formulas rather than try out more innovative content and run the risk of alienating their stakeholders.

These five mediating factors identified by Klapper's phenomenistic approach – particularly the fifth one – mark a clear break from more traditional effects theories. The implication is that the only perceivable effect of mass media on its selective-viewing audience is to tell them what they already think and feel – not to change their behaviour or actions in any way. We have made a giant theoretical leap, therefore, from direct media effects (Lasswell and Wertham) to limited media effects (Katz and Lazarsfeld, Klapper) perspectives.

Uses and gratifications theory

Behaviourist media theories that cast doubt on the idea of effects provided the impetus for an antithetical approach to traditional effects research known as **uses and gratifications**. The work that emerged from this theoretical approach considers how media fulfil the needs and gratifications of their users. The assumption is that audiences use media – not vice versa. In other words, the tables have turned for theories of media effects. The underlying logic of the uses and gratifications approach amounts to 'an assessment of media consumption in audience-related terms, rather than in technological, aesthetic, ideological, or other more or less "elitist" terms' (Katz et al. 1974: 21). Audience requirements are considered to be a major intervening factor in the study of media effects and it is argued that 'media researchers ought to be studying human needs to discover how much the media do or do not contribute to their creation and satisfaction' (Katz et al. 1974: 30). We have moved from the language of 'effects' to that of 'needs'. Uses and gratifications theory has had a significant influence on theories of consumerism (see Chapter 9) but it better belongs within a discussion of behaviourism given its emphasis on the psychological dimensions of media use.

Uses and gratifications theory is concerned with the following:

1   Social and psychological origins of...
2   needs, which generate...
3   expectations of...
4   the mass media or other sources, which lead to...
5   differential patterns of media exposure, resulting in...
6   needs gratifications and...
7   other unintended consequences.

(Katz et al. 1974: 20)

According to this set of theoretical concerns, audiences go looking for certain types of media messages in order to fulfil existing needs. Certain individuals may enjoy television sitcoms (situation comedies), for example, because they help them to 'wind down' and feel good after a hard day's work. The need precedes the effect, meaning that the media effects are bound to be beneficial (sitcoms affect laughter) rather than malign. Media use is therefore goal-oriented and the audience is always active in seeking out needs gratifications. Unlike stimulus-response theories of direct effects, uses and gratifications theory does not assume media to be omnipotent and all-consuming: 'The media compete with other sources of need satisfaction' (Katz et al. 1974: 22). Music media use can be applied quite convincingly to this theoretical assumption. Music is often a soundtrack to other activities that satisfy needs, such as eating and drinking, or taking a bath, or even having sexual intercourse!

Numerous studies have tested out the idea of uses and gratifications, several of which can be found in the pioneering collection associated with this theory (see Blumler and Katz 1974). Although uses and gratifications theory has helped to correct the extremities of direct effects theories, it has been accused of being at the opposite extreme of the behaviourist spectrum, even by theorists that have adopted some of its assumptions. In particular, the approach is criticized for presupposing that media *can* satisfy needs rather than considering the possibility that media use may elude gratifications. As such, the theory 'smacks of a mere defence of the media operators' oldest argument: "We only give the people what they want"' (Carey and Kreiling 1974: 230). Moreover, uses and gratifications theory tends to 'ignore all the problems associated with the differential distribution of power and opportunity in society' (Elliott 1974: 254). There is also a more philosophical question about what exactly constitutes the 'needs' of human beings, and whether or not these needs are common to everyone or unique to individuals. We might also ask whether it is still plausible in our media-saturated world to suggest that people's needs emerge prior to media use and are not shaped in any way at the point of use. Media agendas may not necessarily set public agendas but they may at least affect them in some small measure. The uses and gratifications approach – along with Katz and Lazarsfeld's (1955) two-step flow model – represents a significant turn in behaviourist media theory but, given the shortcomings that gratifications researchers themselves have identified, it was to signal a decline in theories of behaviourism as other avenues of inquiry opened up.

Summary

This chapter has considered:

- The origins and motives of behaviourist media theory and effects research.
- Lasswell's chain of communication – 'who says what in which

channel to whom with what effect' – and its application to his analysis of war propaganda techniques.

- Direct effects perspectives, evident in Lasswell's work and in Wertham's vitriolic account of the psychological problems created by violent comics and television.
- Cantril's theory of indirect media effects that reinforce, but do not create, the social problems that are more direct causes of personal susceptibility to panic.
- Cultivation theory's analysis of long-term media effects on human behaviour, including the concept of mainstreaming.
- Theories and research into agenda-setting and social functions of media that show how public opinion and public issues are shaped by news agendas.
- Two-step flow and phenomenistic approaches that challenge theories of media effects by identifying the impact of opinion leaders and other mediating factors in affecting how media messages are received by the majority public.
- The uses and gratifications approach which claims that individuals use media in the expectation that they will fulfil inherent psychological needs.

Further reading

Barker, M. and Petley, J. (eds) (2001) *Ill Effects: The Media/Violence Debate*, 2nd edn. London: Routledge.

An edited collection of articles on a range of contemporary 'effects' issues and debates, including women's responses to violent films and – interestingly – the media-led crusade against 'trendy media studies' in the 1990s. Suitable for all media students.

Bryant, J. and Thompson, S. (2002) *Fundamentals of Media Effects*. New York: McGraw-Hill.

A useful and comprehensive introduction to media effects theory and research. Key areas of research such as media effects on health and news effects are explored in depth. Suitable for all media students.

Gauntlett, D. (2005) *Moving Experiences: Media Effects and Beyond*, 2nd edn. Eastleigh: John Libbey.

A revised edition of this polemical critique of media effects studies. Chapters on screen media and violence, pro-social media effects, and campaigns and advertising, as well as the author's own 'creative methods' approach. Suitable for all media students.

Macklin, M. C. and Carlson, L. (eds) (1999) *Advertising to Children: Concepts and Controversies.* London: Sage.

An edited collection of articles that deal with what children think about ads and societal concerns about ads aimed at children. Recommended for advanced undergraduates and postgraduates.

3   Modernity and medium theory

Introduction

In this chapter we will chart some key media theories related to the broad theme of **modernity**. Central to discussion will be the most significant and controversial contribution to our understanding of media in modern times – **medium theory**. The term 'modernity' is generally understood to refer to the social, economic, political and technological developments that have characterized the transition from traditional (pre-modern) to advanced (modern) civilizations. Figure 3.1 outlines the main features of modernity in contrast to traditional societies. However, what particular developments best capture the characteristics of modernity in any given culture or society are contested. Some theorists emphasize capitalist principles and institutions as the key factors of modernity (e.g. McGuigan 2006) while others point to the importance of secularization and instrumental rationality (e.g. Turner 1990). The history of modernity is contested too. It is sometimes aligned to the eighteenth-century Enlightenment – also known as the Age of Reason – and sometimes to the spread of Western imperialism in the sixteenth century. It has also been dated as far back as the fourth century (Kroker and Cook 1988) but, for the purposes of media theory, it suffices to situate the emergence of modernity somewhere around the second half of the fifteenth century along with the invention and expansion of the first mechanical media technology – the printing press.

Modernity (modern societies)	Pre-modernity (traditional societies)
Capitalism/Markets	Subsistence
Industrial	Agricultural
Urban	Rural
Bureaucracy	Aristocracy
Science	Religion/Superstition
Rational	Emotional
Rule of Law	Barbarism (lawlessness)
Culture	Nature
Literacy	Oral Society
Individualistic	Communal/Tribal

Figure 3.1   Characteristics of modernity and pre-modernity

Marshall Berman (1988) refers to three phases of modernity: first, the start of the sixteenth century in which 'people are just beginning to experience modern life'; second, a revolutionary age beginning in the 1790s with the French Revolution and running into the nineteenth century when 'a great modern public abruptly and dramatically comes to life'; and third, the twentieth-century globalization of modern life coupled with the rise of **modernism** as a radical art form (Berman 1988: 16–17). The second phase is especially significant to the growth of 'daily newspapers, telegraphs, telephones and other mass media, communicating on an ever wider scale' (Berman 1988: 19). It was the vast expansion of modernization in the name of industrial capitalism that heralded the culture of modernism. Modernism is not the same as modernity. Modernism refers specifically to 'the experimental art and writing of c.1890–c.1940' (Williams 1983a: 208). Modernist art, literature and criticism are centred on the idea that individual creativity is threatened by a hostile environment of oppressive politics, advanced economies, technologies and other social forces, including mass media. Although modernity and modernism have different meanings, this chapter interweaves ideas from both media theorists of modernity and modernist critics of media. This is because the art of modernism can be understood as a response to the social consequences of modernity. For media theory in general but the specialist field of medium theory in particular, the rapid development of mass media technologies is the most pressing aspect of modernity. In contrast to many other perspectives, however, medium theory assumes technology to be a powerful and mostly positive force for social change.

Innis: *The Bias of Communication*

The first medium theorist, Harold Innis, draws on historical evidence to outline a theory about what he calls the bias inherent to media technologies. Any medium of communication will be biased towards its utility either across time or space:

> Media that emphasize time are those that are durable in character, such as parchment, clay or stone. The heavy materials are suited to the development of architecture and sculpture. Media that emphasize space are apt to be less durable and light in character, such as papyrus and paper. The latter are suited to wide areas in administration and trade.
>
> (Innis 1986: 5)

It might seem odd to think about stone and paper as media of communication, but historically these materials were among the only forms of media available for communicating messages. Stone's utility was biased towards time; paper's towards space. Innis argues that empires of power – both political and economic – 'persist by overcoming the bias of media which over-emphasizes either dimension' (Innis 1986: 5). This bias needs to be overcome in order for empires to rule through a combination of centralized and decentralized power. Media biased towards *time* concerns (like stone) serve to keep economic and political power within centres of bureaucratic authority, but empires can only maintain their power by delegating some of it to external agencies. Therefore, media biased towards *space* concerns (like paper) help to decentralize and spread an empire's power. According to Innis, institutions such as governments and big businesses have used a mix of media communications to accomplish and protect their power.

Innis extends his theory of media bias to the issue of how knowledge and information are disseminated in societies. He uses historical examples to show that the *medium* through which knowledge and information is circulated has more impact on societies than the character or *content* of that knowledge or information. As such, media technologies determine human affairs to the extent that new technologies can create new ways of living: 'the advantages of a new medium will become such as to lead to the emergence of a new civilization' (Innis 1951: 34). His main evidence for this argument is the historical shift from oral to written communication that was set in motion by Johannes Gutenberg's invention of the printing press in Germany circa 1450. Prior to the printing press, the Medieval Church in Europe enjoyed a monopoly over religious information in the form of hand-written scribes that were slow and expensive to reproduce. In 1453, the first print version of the Bible – now known as the Gutenberg Bible – helped to de-stabilize this monopoly. Printing and paper technologies enabled versions of the Bible to be disseminated much more widely than previously. Ordinary, god-fearing people were encouraged to become literate (i.e. able to read written communications) and for the first time Christian beliefs could be gleaned first hand, rather than from more corruptible second-hand sources such as clergymen. The central power once exercised by the Church via time-biased media was consequentially weakened by the spatial bias of print media that led to a vast decentralization of power to Christian people.

Innis's theory finds support from at least two noteworthy studies that followed him. First, Walter J. Ong (1993) suggests that literate cultures which emerged in the wake of print technologies developed different sensory experiences than traditional, oral cultures. For instance, oral memory by necessity was highly sophisticated and frequently drawn on. By contrast, the ability to read and 'write down' information – to produce a material record of that information – reduced the necessity for and capacity of human memory exertions. Less reliance on human memory is inextricably linked to the decentralizing power of space-biased print media. Second, Benedict Anderson

(1991) argues that the printing press helped to develop what he calls 'print-languages' which assembled the vernacular of different dialects into the accepted linguistic code of a nation. In turn, print technology and capitalist economics 'created the possibility of a new form of imagined community' (Anderson 1991: 46) in which local communities became united through a common language and national identity. Innis is not without his critics, however. The idea that media technologies *in themselves* determine social, political, economic and religious change – that they have a life of their own beyond the human beings that invent and use them – is far from convincing. Elizabeth L. Eisenstein's (1979) far more comprehensive history of the printing press is highly critical of 'the sweeping and sensational claims made by Innis and McLuhan' (Eisenstein 1979: 171) that, she argues, lack historical context. The second name mentioned by Eisenstein is Innis's best-known student, Marshall McLuhan, whose even more emphatic claim that technology revolutionizes society is considered now.

McLuhan: the medium is the message

McLuhan is perhaps the only media theorist to have become a media celebrity. During the height of his fame he even played a cameo role in Woody Allen's acclaimed film, *Annie Hall* (1977). Beginning with Innis's ideas about the impact of the printing press on information monopolies, McLuhan's medium theory states that any advanced modern society is shaped by the various media technologies that are available to it. Media have powerful effects on societies. Moreover, media become extensions of ourselves; extensions of our human senses. What matters, then, is not the content of these media technologies but the technologies themselves. Take television, for instance. It matters not in the least whether we refer to a soap opera, a news bulletin, a serial drama, a documentary, and so forth. What matters is the medium, not the message, because 'the "message" of any medium or technology is the change of scale or pace or pattern that it introduces into human affairs' (McLuhan 1964: 8). In other words, the messages contained in any medium are inseparable from the medium's human consequences, and it is these consequences that matter most. Therefore, ' "the medium is the message" because it is the medium that shapes and controls the scale and form of human association and action' (McLuhan 1964: 9). Television, then, is an electrical medium that transmits sequences of audio-visual material across vast distances (and sometimes across nations) to its viewers. Televisual images and sounds are the messages sent out by television. What those images show or those sounds emit are inconsequential to the grander scheme of things in which television transformed patterns of leisure, domestic life, education and – for those employed by television and its related industries – work.

We can best understand McLuhan's medium theory by examining how it compares the properties of different media. McLuhan's principal distinction is between 'hot media' and 'cold media'. Hot media require low levels of audience participation because they 'extend one single sense in "high definition"' and are 'well filled with data' (McLuhan 1964: 22). A typical photograph, for example, requires little effort in defining what it represents. A cartoon, in comparison, is a cold medium because – with less visual data – it requires higher levels of sensory participation (i.e. eye work) in order to be defined. A similar distinction can be drawn between film and television. Film is a hotter medium than television because its richer visual resolution requires lower audience participation. The celluloid and projection technologies of film, McLuhan claims, provide high-definition visual data in comparison to the scan lines transmitted through television. Even high-definition television (HDTV), while hotter than standard television images, cannot compete with the heat of 35-millimetre movie images. You have to work harder as a television *viewer* than a film *spectator*. Some other hot and cold media comparisons are listed in Figure 3.2.

HOT media	versus	COLD media
Photograph		Cartoon
Film		Television
Radio		Telephone
Tabloid newspaper		Broadsheet newspaper
Lecture		Seminar/Tutorial class

Figure 3.2 Hot and cold media

McLuhan argues that this distinction in the properties of different media technologies effectively shapes how we use and learn from them. Hot media tend to function as easily forgotten and highly disposable entertainment forms; cold media, by contrast, afford greater capacity for learning because they require higher levels of sensory participation, concentration and literacy skills. This distinction is thoughtful but – to be critical – does not always allow for clear-cut examples. The internet, for instance, requires higher levels of participation (including computer literacy skills) than television in one sense, but in another sense – speed of information – it requires less participation. If I want to know the news headlines, the internet is likely to involve the least participation in terms of time because television news headlines only appear at intervals (every 15 minutes on rolling news channels typically). The internet is therefore a hotter medium than television in some sense and a cooler medium in another.

McLuhan's emphasis on (hot or cold) medium over message, format over content can appear somewhat abstract and is certainly open to debate. Before we address some criticisms of medium theory, though, we should consider McLuhan's argument in a wider historical context. We tend to take television for granted today, but it is a relatively recent media technology that only became widespread in developed countries during the middle of the twentieth century, and in many developing countries a good deal later. The impact television made on human actions and behaviour – as we discussed in the previous chapter – is still difficult to measure, and could only really have been felt by a particular generation of people who witnessed its advent and subsequently adopted it. So imagine an event like the one that occurred on September 11th 2001. Two planes crash into the twin towers of the World Trade Center. How did the vast majority of the world's population experience this event? Of course, they watched the shocking images on television. But what if an event similar to 9/11 had occurred in 1801 rather than 2001? The event (and the message sent out by its terrorist perpetrators) would have still been shocking to hear about, but 'hear about it' – through word-of-mouth or, if we were wealthy and educated, reading about it in a newspaper – is all we could have done, because in 1801 television and other electrical media did not exist. The medium is the message here in the sense that the medium through which a message is sent to its receiver dictates the power of that message. Today's media technologies are, on the whole but with a few exceptions, hotter than yesteryear's cool technologies.

Like Innis's theory of media bias, McLuhan's medium theory can only be understood through an historical lens. Medium theory is inseparable from the processes of modernity undergone by advanced industrial societies. McLuhan refers to three eras of media history within the wider context of modernity (see Table 3.1).

Table 3.1 McLuhan's media history of modernity

Era	Type of medium	Dominant medium	Time period (approximate)
Tribal	Oral (word-of-mouth)	Speech/song	Before 1500
Detribalization	Mechanical	Print	1500–1900
Retribalization	Electrical	Television	After 1900

Prior to the invention of the printing press, a tribal era holds sway. Human beings communicate with each other through media of speech and song. Oral literacy is the only type required. Gutenberg's invention, as discussed earlier, changes the course of media history and sets the wheels in motion for modernity. Print media – books, pamphlets, letters – begin to dominate human communications and more traditional notions of literary (reading and writing skills) become a requirement for social progress. As individuals and groups turn to the written word for cool instruction and education, an era of detribalization sets in. It is no longer necessary for people to live, speak, listen and be governed in the intimacy of tribal gatherings now that print media can be mass-produced and widely distributed. Detribalization brings with it, however, new forms of decentralized power and authority. Centres of power hoard new mechanical technologies in order to determine the content of books and other print media destined for 'the masses'. Before the French Revolution, print media disseminated by aristocratic powers succeeded in homogenizing France: 'Frenchmen were the same kind of people from north to south' (McLuhan 1964: 14). French culture and language were standardized throughout the nation from their Parisian stronghold.

Since the turn of the twentieth century, however, an era of retribalization has evolved in tandem with the electrical age of media communications. Telephone, television and the internet, for instance, are shrinking the world and bringing people closer together via audio and visual media. This is the inspiration behind another well-known phrase coined by McLuhan: 'the global village' (McLuhan and Fiore 2001). We no longer live in tribal villages in the literal sense, but in the metaphorical sense electrical media have expanded our horizons to such an extent that we feel a vicarious intimacy with people and places all over the world. The advent of the internet and email communications has helped to revive McLuhan's medium theory and specifically his ideas about an era of retribalization in today's global village. eBay, for example, is a McLuhan-esque web venture – The World's Online Marketplace – with its own virtual community (tribe) of buyers and sellers located in over thirty different countries. MySpace also resembles a global village in which users spatially distant from each other can converge – in a virtual sense – around common tastes and interests. Nonetheless, medium theory has undergone sustained criticism and McLuhan has as many opponents as exponents (see discussion of Williams later in this chapter). Particularly problematic is the assumption that media and communications technologies revolutionize all parts of social and economic life. This contradicts a theory of social exclusion which incorporates the idea that less affluent societies and social classes do not gain the same access to or benefit from technologies enjoyed by those who can afford to invest in them. eBay might be a boon to business enterprise in the 'markets' within which it operates, but it does nothing to improve the lives of would-be entrepreneurs in parts of the world without the necessary communications infrastructure.

One of McLuhan's exponents, Neil Postman (1987), begins with a sympathetic rendition of medium theory but applies it to a far more cynical picture of contemporary media influence. In contrast to the Age of Exposition – meaning 'thorough explanation' – so helpfully forged by print media, Postman argues that the invention of the electric telegraph in the United

States in 1837 signalled (no pun intended!) a new era – the Age of Show Business. The telegraph provided far faster communication across greater distances than any medium had done before. While McLuhan suggests that the telegraph catapulted society into a phase of mighty progress and advancement, Postman suggests that it attacked the literate culture nurtured by print media in 'introducing on a large scale irrelevance, impotence, and incoherence' (Postman 1987: 66). Unlike print communications such as letters, telegraphic messages tended to lack context or detail, did not answer complex questions or dilemmas, were often addressed to a general audience of no one in particular, and did not sufficiently afford the right to reply. Along with telegraphy, another new technology that became known as photography, likewise, brought with it an idiosyncratic series of responses: 'For countless Americans, seeing, not reading, became the basis for believing' (Postman 1987: 76). The Age of Show Business had arrived as image and sound-bite overcame the more cultured Age of Print. Like children, we have learnt to enjoy visual rather than textual pleasures and now live in a 'peek a boo world' that resists intellectual substance. Moreover, children are now more like adults. The past dominance of print media such as books required a schooling period for children in their intellectual development, but the Age of Show Business is equally accessible to child and adult alike, hence the disappearance of childhood (Postman 1983).

The main object of scorn for Postman is not telegraphy or photography but their offspring, television. Such is television's influence on contemporary life that it has created a new epistemology. 'Epistemology' is a complex term meaning a theory of knowledge, and more specifically, how we come to know about things that claim to be true. Television is 'an instrument that directs not only our knowledge of the world, but our knowledge of *ways of knowing* as well' (Postman 1987: 80). Television's epistemology is defined by its overriding feature as a medium – it is for our *vision* more so than any other human sense. And its audience sees countless images without any coherent structure (commercial breaks, for example) that function primarily as infantile entertainment. Television entertains even when the intention is to inform, such as during news bulletins:

> The problem is not that television presents us with entertaining subject matter but that all subject matter is presented as entertaining ... Everything about a news show tells us this – the good looks and amiability of the cast, their pleasant banter, the exciting music that opens and closes the show ... They are not assembling the news to be read, or broadcasting it to be heard. They are televising the news to be seen. They must follow where the medium leads.
>
> (Postman 1987: 89–90)

Television news values are based on the drama of spectacle; by contrast, the values of news print media can still be based on sustained, intellectual debate and dialogue. Postman fears that electrical technologies like television are effectively leading to 'culture-death'. Elsewhere, the author has suggested that the United States has become the first 'Technopoly', meaning it is the first nation that has submitted 'all forms of cultural life to the sovereignty of technique and technology' (Postman 1993: 52).

Benjamin: art and mechanical reproduction

Writing long before McLuhan and Innis, Walter Benjamin in his classic essay 'The Work of Art in the Age of Mechanical Reproduction' (first published in 1936) draws a similarly optimistic theory about the revolutionary qualities of media technologies. Benjamin considers that mechanical technologies, especially photography and film, have 'transformed the entire nature of art' (Benjamin 1973a: 220) rather than diminished it. This transformation is due to their reproducibility. Mass reproduction of art meant that, for example, great paintings such as the 'Mona Lisa' could be seen in a replica (i.e. photographic or filmic) form by millions of ordinary people – not just by a privileged class who owned or could afford to access these works of art. Reproduction comes at a price, however: 'Even the most perfect reproduction of a work of art is lacking in one element: its presence in time and space, its unique existence at the place where it happens to be' (Benjamin 1973a: 214). Original works of art contain this missing element, which explains why they take on an 'aura' – a mystical sense of authenticity that makes them special and extremely sought after. This sense of aura is threatened, though, when an original work of art is reproduced on a mass scale (see Figure 3.3). The 'Mona Lisa' original is unlikely to be a first sighting of Leonardo da Vinci's painting for visitors to the Musée du Louvre in Paris today. The fascination has worn off to some extent. On the other hand, those people lucky enough to see the painting up close in the pre-mechanical age would have no doubt been awestruck in expectation at what they might see.

Benjamin's theory of aura is based on the claim that 'the existence of the work of art with reference to its aura is never entirely separated from its ritual function' (1973a: 217). Original artistic productions are therefore experienced in ritual contexts, which means they acquire a set of customs and traditions associated with their existence. For example, paintings are experienced in art galleries; music is heard at concerts. By contrast, reproduced art – distributed through media technologies such as television or magazines – is freed from customary ritual and instead serves an exhibition function: 'With the emancipation of the various art practices from ritual go increasing opportunities for the exhibition of their products' (Benjamin 1973a: 218–19).

Figure 3.3   Mona Lisa reproduced in an ad

Beethoven's Fifth Symphony, for instance, is no longer tied to the ritual of the concert hall – where a ticket might cost a month's wages – when it can be exhibited in the living room via CD or MP3. This transition from ritual to exhibition marks a simultaneous transition, moreover, from original use value (or 'cult value') to reproducible 'exhibition value'. What Benjamin means is that the use value of a mechanically-produced, original art work (its ownership value) is less significant than its exhibition value (its value as a commodity that can be distributed and sold in multiple copies). By the same token, an original Hollywood film recording is worth nothing in comparison to an original da Vinci painting, but the mass reproducibility of a Hollywood film – its exhibition value – can be very lucrative indeed.

What are the consequences of mass reproduction of art in modernity? According to Benjamin, art and cultural products more generally have become increasingly political. Freed from ritual contexts of aura and freed from the ownership of powerful elites, contemporary art forms such as popular music – in all its recording formats – are produced and consumed by millions of people, sometimes to express oppositional politics in the face of oppressive regimes. Bertolt Brecht, the famous playwright and friend of Benjamin, produced and directed films for political ends. Informed by Benjamin's theories, he developed his own theories about the political purpose of art – particularly theatre and film – which in turn informed his friend (see Benjamin 1973b). Armed with new technologies, Brecht intended to change the way in which audiences responded to plays and films. His theory of alienation stated that audiences should be encouraged to become actively involved in what they watched; to think about and analyse situations; to take sides and hone opinions on controversial topics; and not to feel sympathy or empathy for characters or predicaments. Of course, Brecht had a political axe to grind – he was a communist whose Marxist sympathies are expressed in plays such as *Mother Courage and Her Children* (1949) – but through alienation, he sought to foster intellectual detachment in audiences so that they could make their own, informed political judgements (see Brecht 1979). The Marxist beliefs of Brecht and Benjamin were taboo in Germany during the rise of Hitler and fascism. Both men were forced to curtail their intellectual activities and, ultimately, had to flee their native country for fear of imprisonment and possible execution. Brecht escaped to the United States but Benjamin lost his life in 1940 while in exile in France.

A later adaptation of Benjamin's theories is John Berger's *Ways of Seeing* (1972). Berger's argument is that today's flood of publicity and advertising images share much in common – their layout, motifs and messages – with eighteenth-century oil paintings. The major difference is that while oil paintings were once addressed to the 'spectator-owner', advertising images are addressed to the 'spectator-buyer':

> The oil painting was addressed to those who made money out of the market. Publicity is addressed to those who constitute the market, to the spectator-buyer who is also the consumer-producer from whom profits are made twice over – as worker and then as buyer. The only places relatively free of publicity are the quarters of the very rich; their money is theirs to keep.
>
> (Berger 1972: 142)

As this quote suggests, Berger has a dimmer view of publicity images than Benjamin's view of photography as a radical art form. Nonetheless, there is a political dimension to mass-reproduced advertisements, albeit a sinister one that favours those in power: 'Publicity turns consumption into a substitute for democracy. The choice of what one eats (or wears or drives) takes the place of a significant political choice. Publicity helps to mask and compensate for all that is undemocratic within society' (Berger 1972: 149). While Third World countries see publicity images as symbols of free choice and democracy, the truth according to Berger is that advertising restricts choice and disengages Western people from serious political issues. Technology as a flagship feature of modernity is being used in dystopian rather than progressive, utopian ways. Brecht's revolutionary art is being directly challenged, then, by a profit-driven media culture of advertising, plugging and endorsements that deals more in candy and catharsis than intellect and politics (see discussion of Adorno in Chapter 7 for a similarly pessimistic account of technology from a political economy perspective).

The Leavises and the Lynds

Theories of modernity such as McLuhan's medium theory are indebted to a related but slightly different phenomenon known as 'modernism'. As discussed earlier, modernism is a literary and aesthetic tradition particularly associated with the late nineteenth and early twentieth centuries. Modernism, in stark contrast to medium theory, expresses cynicism about modernity and technology. Brecht's plays are modernist in their attack on fascism and rampant capitalist greed. Typically, a golden age of high morality and humanity is evoked in modernist art and juxtaposed with the barbarism of the present. Two key exponents of modernist criticism are F. R. Leavis and Q. D. Leavis, probably the most famous of all intellectual couples.

F. R. Leavis's modernist theories are based on the premise of an elite **minority culture** that he identifies as having emerged to counter the threat of banal, mass-produced entertainment:

> In any period it is upon a very small minority that the discerning appreciation of art and literature depends … Upon this minority depends our power of profiting by the finest human experience of the past; they keep alive the subtlest and most perishable parts of tradition. Upon them depend the implicit standards that order the finer living of an age.
>
> (F. R. Leavis 1930: 3, 5)

For F. R. Leavis, an elite group of educated cultural critics is paramount for the provision of moral guidance to mass civilization. Hollywood films, for the majority of their unthinking audience, 'involve surrender, under conditions of hypnotic receptivity, to the cheapest emotional appeals' (F. R. Leavis 1930: 10). This quote smacks of media effects, but it is rooted in a broader cultural theory about the forces of modernity. Cinema, radio, best-selling novels, large-circulation newspapers and magazines are, according to Q. D. Leavis (1932: 193), 'standardizing forces' that threaten intellectual culture. Popular films and novels work to the same formula: they 'must promise romance or fail' (Q. D. Leavis 1932: 320). The Leavises are concerned with the 'levelling down' – or what is known these days as the 'dumbing down' – of popular culture via mass media. The authentic, poetic voice of what T. S. Eliot (1951) – another modernist – called the 'individual talent' has been usurped by the profit-seeking motives of capitalist-driven media corporations.

One of these profit-driven corporations under attack from the Leavises was Lord Northcliffe's popular newspaper press. The rise of Northcliffe's popular press in early twentieth-century Britain – evidenced by the *Daily Mail*, one of the first million-selling newspapers – may have given the public what they wanted, but not what was good for them. Northcliffe's news values were about eye-catching presentation and entertainment, as opposed to the serious politics and foreign affairs covered by broadsheet newspapers in the nineteenth century. While 'The old journalist was controlled by a sense of the dignity of his [*sic*] profession', by contrast 'the modern "cynical", cheaply sophisticated journalist who gives the public what it wants is, and considers himself, a businessman, and he has precisely the same code and outlook as the next man who is out to sell his goods' (Q. D. Leavis 1932: 181). This business-like style of the new journalism was grounded in sensational human interest and crime stories that appealed, the Leavises argued, to the base emotions of uneducated readers. Economic interests held sway over moral standards. Northcliffe was the first press baron to set advertising rates in proportion to circulation figures. Following the success of the *Daily Mail*, Northcliffe took control of several other newspapers including *The Times* during an inter-war period that witnessed intense concentration of press ownership. This led to the decline of provisional newspapers and – to prove the Leavises' point – increased standardization of editorial content and decision-making in the interests of sales and advertising revenue.

The cheap values represented by Britain's commercial press were symptomatic of wider American cultural and economic influences. The fear of Americanization as a pervasive feature of modernity is perceived by F. R. Leavis in the pages of a book written by anthropologists Robert and Helen Lynd called *Middletown* (1929):

> There we see in detail how the automobile (to take one instance) has, in a few years, radically affected religion, broken up the family, and revolutionized social custom. Change has been so catastrophic that the generations find it hard to adjust themselves to each other, and parents are helpless to deal with their children.
>
> (F. R. Leavis 1930: 6)

The implication is that Americanization in all its cultural and media forms – automobiles, Hollywood films, and so on – will drift across the Atlantic to

Britain and beyond (see Hebdige 1989). The book being referred to is an ethnographic account of everyday life during the 1920s in a place given the pseudonym 'Middletown', which was in fact the small city of Muncie, Indiana, in the United States. Rather than simply detailing the customs and habits of Middletown at a given period in history, though, the Lynds compared their own research with similar ethnographic data gathered in the same town during the year 1890. Interestingly, Lynd and Lynd are able to compare an age when mass media had only a limited presence in the lives of Middletown's residents (i.e. 1890) with a period of history 35 years later when the impact of radio, cinema and phonograph – as well as the expansion of print media – were growing in prominence within American culture. According to the authors, these new mass media were re-making leisure in Middletown by standardizing people's pastimes and outlooks on the world beyond their community. Unlike life in 1890, Middletown leisure pursuits in the 1920s were more passive and less creative. Organizational forms of leisure such as sports and music clubs were being superseded by the lure of movies and automobiles.

The advent of media technologies in Middletown had ultimately shifted people's leisure-time from public to semi-public or private activities. Popular leisure pursuits such as travelling in cars and listening to the radio had a 'decentralizing tendency' in drifting away from community-based clubs and organizations in favour of 'individual, family or small group affairs' (Lynd and Lynd 1929: 265). In addition to this 'decentralizing tendency', media were impacting in two other important and interrelated ways in the lives of Middletown's inhabitants. At the same time that technologies such as radio were affecting a standardization of habits and opinions, by letting in the outside world they also had the beneficial effect of 'rolling back the horizons' and 'lifting Middletown out of the humdrum of everyday' (Lynd and Lynd 1929: 269, 271). McLuhan's retribalized global village, it would appear, was at least tangible in a small, 1920s American city. The authors suggest that media influences on Middletown are considerable, stating that 'these space-binding leisure-time inventions imported from without – automobile, motion picture, and radio – [are] reshaping the city' (Lynd and Lynd 1929: 271). To some extent this 'reshaping of the city' is a positive development in that it enables individuals to educate themselves in politics and world affairs. On the negative side, though, external influences are diluting the local character of places like Middletown. In 1890, it was better able to display its peculiarities, but by the 1920s, Middletown – both the place and the people – was being reshaped into an American city like any other. It seems like McLuhan failed to account for this dark side of the global village. The modernist fears of the Leavises are largely realized, therefore, in the Lynds's account of how forces of modernity – particularly new media and communications technologies – are threatening traditions and standardizing people's lives.

Riesman and Hoggart: other-directed character and its uses of literacy

Modernity's darker side is also evidenced in theories of mass media and culture, including two seminal works from either side of the Atlantic: David Riesman's *The Lonely Crowd* (first published in 1950) and Richard Hoggart's *The Uses of Literacy* (first published in 1957). Both books are concerned with the consequences of widespread public literacy brought on by both mass media technologies and an ostensibly progressive facet of modernity, namely the expansion of education. Riesman identifies three types of 'direction' in the character of American people that have evolved during the course of modernity:

1   *Tradition-direction*: this condition was typical in early America. Lack of social mobility means that individuals remain tied to fixed clans and castes (social classes), and behavioural conformity is a social expectation.

2   *Inner-direction*: increased personal mobility, expansion of wealth and new employment opportunities characterize this type. Direction is 'inner' because an individual's role in society is 'implanted early in life by elders' (Riesman 1961: 15).

3   *Other-direction*: this type of direction is prevalent in contemporary America. Inner-directed patterns of discipline and family values are displaced as individuals become directed towards 'others' of their own age and background (i.e. peers) as well as the influences of media and popular culture.

Other-directed character 'types' are indicative of a young generation of metropolitan, middle-class Americans – well-educated and highly literate – working in service and financial industries. However, within the realm of leisure and consumption, Riesman considers the other-directed to be inferior to the inner-directed character. Inner-directedness is guided by didactic training and good practice, such as playing a game of chess. With other-directedness, on the other hand, 'mass media serve as tutors' and effectively replace parents, teachers and other elders (Riesman 1961: 290). Instead of productive leisure pursuits, emphasis is directed towards what Riesman calls 'consumership' – which film to watch, which album to buy.

Being a good consumer is vital for other-directed individuals in securing peer-group approval. Other-directed types exhibit 'an exceptional sensitivity to the actions and wishes of others' (Riesman 1961: 22) which leads to behavioural conformity. Unlike tradition-directed conformity that was an expectation instilled from positions of authority, however, other-directed conformity is a social contract that people accept voluntarily. Elsewhere, Riesman's theory of other-directed character is evidenced in research on teenage popular music consumption (Riesman 1990). He analysed interviews with teenagers about their music tastes and drew a distinction between a majority and a minority audience. Differences in how the two groups listened to and talked about popular music are shown in Figure 3.4.

Majority	Minority
Pop bands and star singers	Underground /'hot' jazz
Passive	Active
Peer-group conformity	Peer-group rejection
Commercial tastes	Alternative (non-commercial) tastes
Conservative	Rebellious
Value-free judgement	High standards of technical judgement

Figure 3.4   Majority and minority audiences for popular music

As we can see from these differences, the majority of teenagers listen to popular music in an other-directed manner: 'The functions of music for this group are *social* – the music gives them something to talk or kid about with friends' (Riesman 1990: 8). For young people keen to join the majority audience along with their peers 'the fear is to be caught liking what the others have decided not to like' (Riesman 1990: 12). In stark contrast, the minority audience is critical of both the majority attitude and expresses a 'resentment of the image of the teenager provided by the mass media' (Riesman 1990: 10). Although the comparison is not strictly a fair one, we can nevertheless see similarities in Riesman's minority audience and the minority culture expounded by the Leavises in the fight against standardized mass entertainment.

Hoggart, like Riesman, examines popular music and its impact on vulnerable people, and more specifically, the working-class youth of Britain (especially industrial northern England). The increasingly literate and wealthy, but poorly educated, young in 1930s Britain remain 'substantially without a sense of the past' (Hoggart 1958: 190). If some youth groups 'still sing some of the songs their grandparents sang' (Hoggart 1958: 158), this is only due to their being directly taught them; not due to their having sought to learn of them. It is behind this backdrop that Hoggart outlines his theory of cultural classlessness. The working classes – along with more affluent groups – are 'becoming culturally classless' because mass media such as popular songs 'cannot reach an audience of the size they need by cutting across class boundaries' (Hoggart 1958: 342). Mass media are quite literally *broad*casted. For instance, mass-produced songs cause 'weak communalism' (Hoggart

1958: 228) and threaten working-class traditions. Hoggart suggests that while older forms of communal singing were 'both personal and public', in newer forms such as crooning 'there is a huge, public effect ... The singer is reaching millions but pretends that he is reaching only "you"' (Hoggart 1958: 227). The uses of literacy are being wasted on these sentimental, phoney, 'candy floss' forms of mass entertainment. More recently, Hoggart (2004) has continued this theme of mass media contributing to a mass, culturally deprived society without a true sense of identity and belonging. In another work, he outlines his solution: 'Broadcasting will be on a local scale; it will be something people take part in, not something that they are simply given' (Hoggart 1972: 88). Hoggart's remedy is a retreat from advanced modernity back to a nostalgic age of class traditions – a blend of cultural pessimism and conservatism where elders hold sway over peer-group and media influences, akin to Riesman's theory of inner-directedness.

Williams: technology and cultural form

Medium theory is criticized most often for its **technological determinism**. Raymond Williams – particularly in *Television: Technology and Cultural Form* (first published in 1974) – has been one of the most ardent critics of this concept, which he defines as follows:

> The basic assumption of technological determinism is that a new technology – a printing press or a communications satellite – 'emerges' from technical study and experiment. It then changes the society or the sector into which it has 'emerged'. 'We' adapt to it, because it is the new modern way.
>
> (Williams 1983b: 129)

The deterministic approach states that technologies have an autonomous power to 'create new societies or new human conditions' (Williams 2003: 6) notwithstanding the fact that they are invented, produced and used by human beings. In the case of medium theory, McLuhan insists that the introduction of any new medium will shape how people live their lives. Williams argues against such an idea by showing how 'a technical invention as such has comparatively little social significance' until it has been adapted to existing social and economic conditions (Williams 1983b: 129–30). For instance, the printing press may have been invented in the fifteenth century but 'The rise in reading, and in quality, was in fact steady' (Williams 1965: 181) and it was not until over three hundred years after the Gutenberg invention that literacy had become widespread enough in Britain to identify a middle-class reading public. Working-class literacy, by contrast, was only

achieved much later as a foremost consequence of social and political processes – namely, the 1870 Education Act that introduced compulsory
schooling – as opposed to technological ones.

Unlike McLuhan's account which he attacks as 'wholly unhistorical and
asocial' (Williams 2003: 131), Williams draws on a series of historical examples of inventions in media communications to show how each technology
was always foreseen for a previously devised purpose before it was discovered.
Moreover, the effects of each media technology were anticipated before that
technology came into use: 'In no way is this a history of communications
systems creating a new society or new social conditions' (Williams 2003: 12).
Rather than focus on the *causes* of technologies – as does McLuhan – Williams
addresses what *causes them*. In the main, technologies of all kinds, and not
just media ones, develop for commercial, political and military purposes. In
the case of railways and telegraphy (the predecessor of telephony), both
developed in the USA and Britain for commercial reasons, to drive industrial
development by enabling the efficient transportation of raw materials to
factories and distributing the finished products across nations. These two
technologies combined to ignite what the renowned social historian Asa
Briggs calls a communications revolution: 'Railways and telegraphs ... were
directly related to each other. There was, indeed, a continuing link between
physical and electrical communication' (Briggs 1966: 8). McLuhan also
mentions the role of railways in industrialization, but is surely wrong to argue
that these technologies created new societies 'quite independent of the
freight or content of the railway medium' (McLuhan 1964: 8). The railway
medium, on the contrary, contained a message such as 'coal' that fuelled the
fires to create steel, textiles and other essential materials for the Industrial
Revolution.

At first it might seem strange to compare the railway medium with those
technologies more familiarly referred to as 'media' today, such as television.
Williams, however, attempts to make these comparisons by showing how the
history of communications follows the same pattern in different societies:
business and transport communications develop first, caused mostly by economic demands, and then there emerge forms of information and entertainment communications, caused mostly by social and cultural demands. So
television was slow to develop in comparison with, say, the telephone,
because it did not initially demonstrate obvious economic benefits. In contrast to medium theory, then, technologies are shown by Williams to develop
as an outcome of human needs and intentions. Technologies do not emerge
from the isolation of a laboratory and then determine the needs that humans
require. Television, argues Williams, was invented due to social demand – as
well as political and economic demands – and the use to which it was put was
intended before the first television sets were sold.

Like the radio, Williams suggests that demand for television resulted from a social tendency which he terms 'mobile privatization'. This concept refers to 'an at-once mobile and home-centred way of living' (Williams 2003: 19) that became commonly experienced in late industrial societies during the first half of the twentieth century. People are increasingly living as 'private small-family units' or as 'self-enclosed individuals' but at the same time 'there is a quite unprecedented mobility of such restricted privacies' (Williams 1983b: 188). For instance, the family home becomes increasingly privatized and self-sufficient as people's working and living conditions – and wages – improve, but this privacy and self-sufficiency are dependent on external factors such as job opportunities and social welfare. From this state of affairs results 'the need and form of a new kind of "communication": news from "outside", from otherwise inaccessible sources' (Williams 2003: 20–1). It was this need for a continuous 'flow' of communication that television fulfilled. Another example of mobile privatization is car traffic. From the outside, 'traffic flows and their regulation are clearly a social order of a determined kind' in which technology appears to determine and dehumanize our lives, but this is 'not at all how it feels inside the [car] shell, with people you want to be with, going where you want to go' within the privatized, 'conditioned atmosphere and internal music of this windowed shell' (Williams 1983b: 188–9). Williams's theory of mobile privatization is simultaneously about regulation and self-determination; containment and freedom; technology and cultural form. As such, mobile privatization is able to overcome 'the unholy alliance' (Williams 1983b: 143) in the great debate about modernity – on the one hand, medium theory and its flawed technological determinism; and on the other hand, the Leavisite tradition of modernist criticism and its cultural pessimism with respect to the 'levelling down' effects of mass communications technologies.

Habermas: media and the public sphere

How have media changed the character of public opinion through the course of modernity? This is the question addressed by Jürgen Habermas in *The Structural Transformation of the Public Sphere* (first published in 1962). Habermas argues that a bourgeois (middle-class) **public sphere** of intellectuals that helped to supplant medieval aristocracies and served an important political function in the eighteenth and early nineteenth centuries in countries such as Britain, France and Germany has become obsolete during the phase of late modernity or advanced capitalism. No longer is it possible for a public sphere made up of private citizens to engage in critical debate likely to have repercussions for contemporary politics, art, and so on. However, in the coffee houses and social clubs of eighteenth-century London and Paris – among other centres of power and struggle – such critical debate and its political consequences were wide-ranging. This bourgeois public sphere of academics, shopkeepers and others collectively generated ideas and policies in critical dialogue with aristocratic counterparts – often circulated through self-produced periodicals, sometimes known as 'moral weeklies' – that effectively steered the course of politics, art, science and morality in the world outside and beyond. Institutions of the public sphere, such as coffee houses and clubs, had three criteria in common: all participants were treated as equals and status was disregarded; debate was focused on issues rarely questioned by the powerful nobility; and 'everyone had to *be able* to participate' (Habermas 1989: 37) in this inclusive arena of discussion. Unfortunately according to Habermas, from the 1830s onwards, the political influence of the bourgeois public sphere weakened as a result of its small-circulation periodicals suffering direct competition from the large-circulation commercial press.

The decline of the bourgeois public sphere was partly due to the rise of mass media along with wider trends in the concentration of economic capital. Newspaper presses merged and bought out one another, combining their economic and technological prowess to reinforce and strengthen their market share. In nineteenth-century Britain this resulted in rapid concentration of media power (see Curran and Seaton 2003). Trends in the media industry were not peculiar to wider trends in different sectors – textiles, steel, food, financial and other sectors all experienced takeovers and mergers that concentrated capital in the hands of a few wealthy industrialists. For Habermas, this advanced capitalist phase of modernity effectively transformed the public sphere from a culture-debating to a culture-consuming one. As the author notes, 'rational-critical debate had a tendency to be replaced by consumption, and the web of public communication unravelled into acts of individuated reception' (Habermas 1989: 161). Television, radio and other mass media – as the Lynds observed – separated the private from the public sphere by detrimentally affecting participation in organized forms of leisure and social (including political) activities. Political debate still receives airtime across today's media but such debate has lost its critical edge and no longer speaks to public concerns because the umbilical cord that formerly connected private individuals to the public sphere has been severed. As such, 'The world fashioned by the mass media is a public sphere in appearance only' (Habermas 1989: 171) and far removed from the golden age of a culture-debating public sphere. Today's mediated political debates function as 'a tranquillizing substitute for action' (Habermas 1989: 264) in which participants carefully hone their self-presentations so as to manage public opinion about their political positions.

For Habermas, two main factors that have diluted the public sphere and dragged it into the 'levelling-down' pit of the mass media are advertising and public relations. Figure 3.5 outlines how Habermas distinguishes between three phases of news print production that developed chronologically in

Type of news medium	Emphasis in content	Main gatekeeper/ influence
1. Information pamphlet (e.g. newsletter)	Factual news	Non-specific
2. Critical journal/periodical (e.g. moral weekly)	Editorial comment/literary and political dialogue	Editor/writers (the bourgeois public sphere)
3. Consumer title (e.g. popular newspaper)	Advertising/public relations	Publisher/owners

Figure 3.5   Habermas's history of news print production

European countries, although these phases did not apply to the development of news print media in the United States, which from the outset was an advertising-driven, commercial enterprise.

The popular, consumer-oriented press was 'released from the pressure to take sides ideologically' (Habermas 1989: 184) by the all-important profit motive, although Habermas points out that such a profit motive itself amounted to the declaration of a political stance that pandered to existing commercial interests and stood in opposition to the 'hard talk' of the critical bourgeois press. Consumer titles enjoyed substantial profits through advertising revenue and effectively allowed the public sphere – once an important arena of debate between private individuals and the nobility – to be invaded by privileged individuals (such as advertisers) with privileged private interests to publicize.

The public sphere as a platform for advertising also became, a little later, a platform for public relations and what Habermas refers to as the psychological techniques of opinion management. Public relations, like advertising, aims to achieve publicity – and subsequent profit through sales or public support – for particular private interests. However, public relations is more effective than advertising because it disguises itself as editorial penned by the ostensible integrity of 'learned' journalists:

> The sender of the message hides his business intentions in the role of someone interested in the public welfare. The influencing of consumers borrows its connotations from the classic idea of a public of private people putting their reason to use and exploits its legitimations for its own ends. The accepted functions of the public sphere are integrated into the competition of organized private interests.
>
> (Habermas 1989: 193)

The bourgeois public sphere – 'a public of private people putting their reason to use' – is therefore cynically reconstructed for the benefit of private commercial interests. Public relations is a process of legitimating such interests for the public good. Like Riesman's notion of other-directedness, Habermas considers modern-day consumers to be hoodwinked into 'constant consumption training' (Habermas 1989: 192) that shapes public opinion into a soft exchange of views – about the latest washing-up liquid, or the new-release video game, or the next generation of mobile phones – instead of hard, serious discussion about the politics and policies of the day. Moreover, media-inflected public relations and advertising are leading to a 'refeudalization of the public sphere' (Habermas 1989: 195) because governments follow the example of private enterprises by addressing their citizens as consumers. These consumers suffer from 'the false consciousness that as critically reflecting people they contribute responsibly to public opinion' (Habermas 1989: 194) when in fact they are merely puppets being pulled by the strings of businesspeople and politicians. It is these powerful individuals with privileged access to the mediated public sphere of contemporary developed societies who represent a modern-day aristocracy (media barons no less) bestowed with great public authority like the feudal lords of medieval times.

Habermas's theory of the public sphere has been questioned by critics, especially in the way it romanticizes a golden age of bourgeois intellectuals before the advent of mass media and culture. Four criticisms cited by one critic are that Habermas equates the bourgeois public sphere with popular opinion, which is unconvincing in relation to historical evidence; that he assumes the public sphere granted access to all, when, in fact, eighteenth-century bourgeois society excluded a majority of poor and ill-educated people as well as women; that he has a simplistic view on contemporary media consumers as manipulated individuals; and that his model for more democratic public affairs in modern, diverse societies is vague and unworkable (Thompson 1995b). It could be argued that Habermas also fails to appreciate the wide-scale distribution or reproducibility (in Benjamin's terms) of moral and political debate across modern-day press and television – a far cry from the relatively inaccessible bourgeois public sphere.

Nonetheless, Habermas has identified a problem in how mass media represent – or rather, misrepresent – public opinion and public interests which can be traced back to an earlier period in our contemporary history. A team of sociologists and anthropologists in Britain, known as Mass-Observation, echoed Habermas's views on the refeudalization of the public sphere back in the late 1930s. They argued that 'People want inside information, they want to get behind the news' and that 'a growing number of people want less stories and more facts' about social life (Madge and Harrisson 1939: 7 and 10):

> The present position of the Intellectual Few is a relic of the times
> when the mass of the population consisted of serfs who could neither

read nor write. Then a few people at the top could easily impose their beliefs and rule on the multitude … in many ways there is as much intellectual serfdom as ever.

(Madge and Harrisson 1939: 11)

Mass-Observation compared fact and 'objective reality' – which they tried to capture using social survey and observational methods – with the mass media and party politics, both of which were elitist institutions out of touch with the concerns of everyday people. In contrast to these elitist institutions, 'Mass-Observation shares the interests of most people in the actual, in what happens from day to day' (Madge and Harrisson 1937: 30). The reports and directive replies that were compiled and published by Mass-Observation aimed to represent an alternative public sphere whose voice could not be heard by a hostile, media-driven sphere of phoney public relations and propaganda. Elsewhere, Habermas (1985) has argued that the 'project of modernity' has so far failed because its social and cultural force has only been realized in one aspect: that is, its aesthetic form (modern art). Modern science and morality remain incomplete forms precisely because the public arena in which to debate and evaluate them is yet to be retrieved.

Summary

This chapter has considered:

- What modernity means, its social and historical context, and its relationship to modernism.
- Medium theory (Innis, McLuhan) and its revolutionary claims about the influence of media and communications technologies on social life.
- The reproducibility of mechanical technologies such as film (Benjamin) and their political function in modern societies.
- Modernist criticism of mass culture, also known as cultural pessimism (e.g. the Leavises).
- Theories of mass literacy (Riesman, Hoggart) that point to the unhealthy influence of mass media and modernity.
- Critiques of medium theory that emphasize the social, economic and political factors that determine technological use – and reject the idea of technological determinism (Williams).
- The decline of a culture-debating public sphere and its replacement by a culture-consuming, mass-mediated public sphere in late modernity (Habermas).

Further reading

Curran, J. and Seaton, J. (2003) *Power Without Responsibility: The Press and Broadcasting in Britain*, 6th edn. London: Routledge.

Now in its sixth edition, this comprehensive overview of British media history is a tried-and-tested resource for all students interested in the relationship between media and processes of modernity such as industrialization and public regulation.

Garnham, N. (2000) *Emancipation, the Media and Modernity: Arguments About the Media and Social Theory*. Oxford: Oxford University Press.

A polemical account of the relationship between media, modernity and Enlightenment thought. Chapters on media histories, media as technologies, and media and politics. Recommended for advanced undergraduates and postgraduates.

Levinson, P. (1999) *Digital McLuhan: A Guide to the Information Millennium*. London: Routledge.

This book discusses McLuhan's ideas about media and their impact on our lives, as well as the author's updating of these ideas to shed light on our present-day digital age. Recommended for advanced undergraduates and postgraduates.

Morley, D. (2007) *Media, Modernity and Technology: The Geography of the New*. Abingdon: Routledge.

A diverse selection of essays from Morley on geographical and anthropological approaches to media technologies in modern life, including a fascinating approach to television as a visible object rather than a medium. Accessible to all media students, although some essays are better suited to advanced undergraduates and postgraduates.

4   Structuralism and semiotics

Introduction

This chapter focuses on structuralist theories of media and the method of **semiotics** that emerged from theoretical themes which underpin **structuralism**. The work of a linguist, Ferdinand de Saussure, will begin our discussion. Central to Saussure's theory of language is the distinction between synchronic and diachronic forms of analysis. Synchronic analysis explores language as a system at a given moment in time. It is a 'snapshot' form of analysis. Diachronic analysis, on the other hand, explores a language system as it evolves over a period of time. Etymology is a type of diachronic analysis. By contrast:

> Structuralism as a whole is necessarily synchronic; it is concerned to study particular systems or structures under artificial and ahistorical conditions, neglecting the systems or structures out of which they have emerged in the hope of explaining their present functioning.
>
> (Sturrock 1979: 9)

Unlike theories of modernity, structuralism is oblivious to history in its search for what language means and represents here and now. Semiotics is the method that serves this purpose. Semiotics analyses language as a whole system that structures its individual parts into distinct units of meaning. These units of meaning are referred to as signs. Since the system is constantly changing – new signs emerge, old signs become obsolete – what semiotics does is freeze the moment in order to analyse the system at work. Structuralism is the theoretical framework that seeks to understand how systems work to structure their individual parts at any given moment in time.

Language is the system *par excellence*, but inextricably linked to language are social, cultural, political and economic systems. Societies, like languages, structure their individual parts (i.e. citizens) precisely through processes of differentiation. Our social lives are structured by powerful agents of the social system such as governments. Media institutions are also powerful agents of the social system, but at the same time these agents are structured by the system too. As we will discuss in relation to structuralist theories of myth, ideology and hegemony, it is possible to theorize media texts (especially news) and the institutions that produce them as meaning-makers. The ways in which we perceive our social and cultural lives are shaped to a great extent by what we see on television or read in newspapers or hear on the radio. Media – among other meaning systems – structure our lives. Of course, we do not simply accept what we see on television or read in the newspapers or hear on the radio. As Hall (1980) notes, we 'decode' media texts in different ways – sometimes we agree, sometimes we disagree. Nonetheless, the power to decide what stories, ideas, tastes and values are offered to us via media communications is structured unequally in favour of some interests (the ruling ones) rather than others (the interests of the silent majority). Hebdige's subcultural theory reminds us that ideological and hegemonic power can be met with resistance, but for Foucault resistance is banal because we have internalized the power structures that oppress us.

Saussure and Barthes: language and myth

Before we can begin to understand structuralist theories of media, it is first necessary to probe in greater depth the theory of **language** outlined by Saussure's *Course in General Linguistics* (first published in 1916). Saussure dismissed the notion that language simply reflects reality and instead suggested that language operates within its own system. This system *constructs* meanings within a language – meanings do not evolve in any natural or unique way. He called this approach semiology, which means the study of signs, but we will use the more common term for this approach, known as semiotics. A sign (word) such as 'rat', for instance, has two properties: a sound and an idea. But there is no connection between the sound and the idea: 'the choice of a given slice of sound to name a given idea is completely arbitrary' (Saussure 1966: 113). Even a sign like 'sizzle' – which some would cite as an example of onomatopoeia – has no meaning in relation to its sound, according to Saussure's theory of language. Working as a system, the signs (i.e. words) that form a language are able to signify ideas precisely because they are different from other signs: 'Language is a system of interdependent terms in which the value of each term results solely from the simultaneous presence of the others' (Saussure 1966: 114). So language is structured through difference, and different ideas depend on different sounds, or 'the phonic differences that make it possible to distinguish this word from all others, for differences carry signification' (Saussure 1966: 118).

For example, we can only understand the word 'rat' as a unit of meaning in the English language because its sound – as well as the idea or thing it signifies – differs from that of other words, such as 'mouse' or 'cat'. If 'rat' was the word used to signify all of these 'real' things (i.e. mouse and cat as well as rat), its meaning would be imprecise and the whole system of language would have effectively failed to signify. However, in Latin there is only one term – 'mus' – to refer to both a rat and a mouse. Latin speakers, historically, have not distinguished between the two creatures because they are 'indifferent' to Latin cultures. Likewise, Eskimos have several different words to describe 'snow' whereas English speakers only use one. As Umberto Eco rightly demonstrates in support of Saussure, 'any cultural phenomenon is *also* a sign phenomenon' (Eco 1973: 61). Cultural meanings are therefore specific to language systems that operate within the rules of semiotics.

Saussure shows, therefore, that any single sign (or word) in a language system is inextricably linked with the system as a whole. A word's 'content is really fixed only by the concurrence of everything that exists around it' (Saussure 1966: 115). In order to illustrate this, he makes a distinction between the *langue* (the whole system or structure) and the *parole* (specific utterances within this system) of a given language. An utterance (*parole*) can only signify meaning effectively in its relation to the whole system of a language (*langue*). The analogy to a game of chess is a good one:

> Each individual move in chess is selected from the whole system of possible chess moves. So we could call the system of possible chess moves the *langue* of chess. Any individual move in a game of chess would be *parole*, the selection of a move from the whole set of possible moves in the *langue* of chess.
>
> (Bignell 2002: 8)

This distinction between *langue* and *parole* can be applied not only to the formal properties of a language (linguistics) but also to uses of language in social contexts. As Figure 4.1 shows, language usage is structured by a system that works along two axes: the *syntagmatic* (meanings which exist at a specific moment in time) and the *paradigmatic* (meanings which could be used to substitute existing ones). The examples in Figure 4.1 prove Saussure's point that changes in the paradigmatic features of a language system alter the whole structure of meaning as carried by the syntagmatic features, and vice versa.

Following Saussure, Roland Barthes's theory of **myth** is indebted to his predecessor's claim that a word's idea (its signified element) and its sound (its signifier element) are unconnected but together make up the total meaning of that word (its sign), which can only be understood in relation to all other signs – as in the relationship between *langue* and *parole*. However, Barthes extends Saussure's theory of language systems by applying it to the systems by which societies and cultures develop 'myths'. Societies and cultures, like languages, are considered to be structured by a 'whole' system that determines their individual parts. Of course, language as a system is also fundamental to how societies or cultures persist. But Barthes suggests that purely linguistic meanings are radically changed by social and cultural practices.

Barthes's most important work in this respect is *Mythologies* (first

PARADIGMATIC DIMENSION

(vertical substitutions of meaning)

	Politicians		suffered	defeat
The	**Media**	have	**expressed**	**anger**
	Courts		enjoyed	success

SYNTAGMATIC DIMENSION (horizontal substitutions of meaning)

Figure 4.1   Syntagmatic and paradigmatic dimensions of semiotics

published in 1957). Here he develops Saussure's notion that meanings do not simply refer to real things. Furthermore, meanings can develop beyond their linguistic properties and take on the status of myths. Saussure suggested that the meaning of any term in a language system consists of a signifier plus a signified to give a sign (Figure 4.2).

SIGNIFIER (sound/phonetic quality) + SIGNIFIED (idea) = SIGN (total meaning)

Figure 4.2   Saussure's semiotic theory of language

Barthes, on the other hand, introduces an extra dimension to this equation (Figure 4.3).

Language   { SIGNIFIER + SIGNIFIED = SIGN

Myth   {

SIGNIFIER + SIGNIFIED = SIGN

Figure 4.3   Barthes's semiotic theory of language and myth

Source: Barthes (1993: 115)

Language – the first order of signification in Barthes's model – is therefore capable of generating a second order of signification called myth. This is the basis for Barthes's approach to semiotics. In Figure 4.3 we can see how a sign (i.e. an idea plus a sound) such as 'rat', which operates in a first order of signification, becomes a signifier within a second-order 'myth' system of signification. In the case of rat, therefore, its sign in the 'language' order of signification defines it as, say, 'a small rodent with a pointed snout'. However, its sign in the 'myth' order of signification would be extended to what rat means in particular social and cultural contexts. In English-speaking, Western countries such as Britain, rat as a myth signifies dirt, disease, the darkness of underground sewers and cellars. Most of the mythical meanings that we attach to 'rat' are negative, because most of us dislike or even fear the 'real' creature which the word signifies. The distinction between language and myth is sometimes equated to the distinction between denotation and connotation. Denotation is similar to a dictionary definition of a sign; connotation, by contrast, refers to the wider social and cultural meanings (myths) attached to a sign. Rat denotes rodent; it connotes much, much more (dirt, disease, and so on).

How does Barthes's semiotic – or structuralist – theory of myth apply to media? If we consider media to be an important – perhaps *the* most important – element within a social and cultural system of signs that are capable of generating myths, then clearly television, the internet and other mass communications can help to nurture some myths and not others. Barthes's best-known example of myth-making derives from a medium. He analyses the front cover of an issue of *Paris-Match*, a French magazine, which depicts a black boy in military outfit looking upwards and saluting what is assumed to be the French flag. Barthes reads this image (i.e. sign) as language and myth. On the level of language, the image denotes a black boy giving a French salute. Far more can be read into what this image *connotes* though. As a myth, Barthes suggests that the image signifies 'that France is a great Empire, that all her sons, without any colour discrimination, faithfully serve under her flag' (Barthes 1993: 116). The image of the proud black soldier connotes a myth that France is a multicultural land of opportunity far from an oppressive colonizer of foreign peoples. Clearly, the meanings signified by this image as language and myth are only *made* possible in how they compare with the vast range of other meanings that an image like this might depict if it was configured differently. If the boy in the image is white and not black, the image's meaning is radically changed.

Barthes applies his theory of myth to several 'mythologies' associated with his native French culture, such as wine and Citroen cars. We can apply his theory to contemporary media mythologies, although we would need to stretch our imagination and thought processes in the same way that Barthes did. For instance, BBC News 24 occasionally broadcasts a pre-recorded trailer just before headlines appear 'on the hour'. In the order of a language system, the moving images shown denote foreign correspondents 'on location' in various parts of the world, reporting on different kinds of news stories (environmental, political, financial, and so on). A timer counts down the seconds from 30 to 0 in anticipation of the headlines that will immediately follow once the trailer has finished. But we can read this sequence of images on the more sophisticated order of a myth system. From this reading we can appreciate how the BBC News 24 channel – and its journalists – takes on connotations of a professional organization dedicated to fast, concise, global news coverage. BBC foreign correspondents are eyewitnesses to international affairs in a not dissimilar way that Britain has its metaphorical eyes on the world. We seek out evil, we search out poverty and disease – 'we' the BBC, like the country we represent, are a force for good, and a picture of fine health compared to the tyranny and misfortune of others. The timer, moreover, connotes punctuality and recency (i.e. BBC news values). News does not occur on the hour – in reality, it can occur at any time – but news is always made fresh by headlines 'on the hour' to reinforce the myth that news is always 'new'. A timer that began counting down the seconds from 30 *minutes* to zero, rather than 30 seconds, would generate very different meanings (and myths) about BBC News 24. Instead of pandering to breaking news or the headline stories, we might read this news channel as dedicated to programming that deals with in-depth debate and dialogue.

The need to 'stretch one's imagination' when identifying media mythologies points to a weakness with semiotics as a method and the structuralist theory it informs. Far from a science, semiotics is a highly sub-jective method of reading social and cultural myths that depends entirely on 'the analytical brilliance of the semiotician' (Couldry 2000a: 75). Moreover, as well as being unable to account for historical changes in language and myth, given its focus on synchronicity, semiotics is only able to analyse one par-ticular text in isolation. What Nick Couldry calls the 'total textual environ-ment' (Couldry 2000a: 73) – the multitude of media texts and technologies that we interact with on a daily basis – cannot be penetrated by semiotic analysis. Moreover, semiotics as a method of textual analysis is easily abused to make claims about how media texts signify meanings in everyday use. Angela McRobbie acknowledges that while semiotics can 'read' ideologies in media texts, it cannot account for the views of readers/audiences and there-fore cannot 'understand the complex and contested social processes which accompany the construction of new images [and texts]' (McRobbie 1994: 165). Similarly in relation to semiotic analysis of music texts, Tia DeNora rightly interprets 'an epistemologically naïve move' in 'a tacit shift in many semiotic "readings" of music ... from description of musical material and its social allocation to the theorization of that material's "wider" significance and cultural impact' (DeNora 2000: 28). Semiotics, given that it can only ever be one person's interpretation of what they read, hear or see, is certainly not a substitute for empirical audience research.

Hall: Encoding/Decoding, ideology and hegemony

While he does not theorize **ideology** in any great depth, Barthes is nonetheless clear that myths contain ideological meanings. Myth and ideology in
their structuralist senses are synonymous. For Barthes, the ideology of French
colonialism is expounded in the proud salute of the black soldier. It is only by
deconstructing a myth, or reading a myth's hidden meanings, that its
ideology – the values and beliefs it upholds – can be exposed. The concept of
'ideology' has been theorized to a greater extent by structuralist Marxists who
followed Barthes, such as Louis Althusser and Stuart Hall. Althusser (1971)
argued that individuals in capitalist societies are governed by ideological state
apparatuses (ISAs), including schools, legal systems, religious institutions,
media communications, and so on. These ISAs espouse the ideologies of
powerful political institutions, such as governments and armies, in implicit –
not explicit – ways, and sometimes without knowing it. As such, individuals
'internalize' ruling capitalist ideologies, unaware that their lives are repressed
by the very institutions that represent and serve them (and perhaps even
employ them). As Hall notes, Althusser's approach was more sophisticated
than the classical Marxist notion of top-down 'false consciousness' which
suggests that ideology is imposed 'from above' by elite powers upon the
unknowing masses (see discussion of Adorno in Chapter 7, for a version of
classical Marxism). ISAs point to a 'more linguistic or "discursive" conception
of ideology' (Hall 1996a: 30) that is reproduced by various institutional
practices and structures. Ellis Cashmore (1994) applies Althusser's theory of
ISAs to television by suggesting that viewers are given a partial view of the
world that fits with state interests, even when television is not explicitly state-
controlled.

　　Although Althusser's ideas can be applied to media, the ideas of Hall
rework structuralist theories of ideology into a more systematic theory of
media in their social and cultural functions. Hall also criticizes Althusser for
assuming that ideology, although internalized, always functions to reproduce
state capitalist values: 'how does one account for subversive ideas or for
ideological struggle?' (Hall 1996a: 30). As such, Hall defines ideology in a
discursive sense as 'ideas, meanings, conceptions, theories, beliefs, etc. and
the form of consciousness which are appropriate to them' (Hall 1977: 320).
Hall, along with other theorists associated with the Birmingham Centre for
Contemporary Cultural Studies (CCCS) such as Dick Hebdige and David
Morley, investigated the relationship between media and ideology through
semiotic analysis of systems of signification in texts such as television news
bulletins.

　　Hall's aim is to rediscover ideology as a concept that can reveal the
'politics of signification' engaged in by media institutions. His starting point

is to attack behaviourist theories of media. Models of 'effects' such as Lass-well's formula theorize the communication process in terms of its reliability (see Chapter 2). If messages are not received as intended, this is deemed to be a failure of communication in a technical or behavioural sense. According to 'effects' perspectives, messages are not received correctly if the channels of communication from sender to recipient are distorted by electrical or human error. The meanings of messages themselves, however, are assumed to be distortion-free and universally transferable. But Hall argues that behaviourist models are flawed because they fail to situate media communications within existing social, economic and political structures. The meanings of messages, then, are able to be distorted and interpreted differently than intended according to the positions of producers (senders) and audiences (recipients) within these existing structures:

> Meaning is a social production, a practice. The world has to be *made to mean*. Language and symbolization is the means by which mean-ing is produced. This approach dethroned the referential notion of language, which had sustained previous content analysis, where the meaning of a particular term or sentence could be validated simply by looking at what, in the real world, it referenced.
>
> (Hall 1982: 67)

Content analysis – a favoured method of cultivation theory (see Chapter 2) – is rendered meaningless by this structuralist perspective on meaning as social production. Like Saussure and Barthes, Hall states that meaning is a discursive process that operates within a language system (what he terms 'a set of codes') loaded with ideological signification.

Media institutions and the texts they generate are important ideological dimensions through which we make sense of the world. Hall deploys semiotics to understand the sense-making process by which media transmit messages to their audiences. Language is *encoded* (made to mean something) by those with 'the means of meaning production' (i.e. producers) and is then *decoded* (made to mean something) by audiences (Hall 1982: 68). Hall extends this semiotic theory of meaning construction to a model of media production and reception which is commonly known as the Encoding/Decoding model (see Figure 4.4). Unlike the behaviourist approach to communication, Hall's Encoding/Decoding approach does not assume a direct correspondence between the meaning intended by a sender and how that meaning is inter-preted by a recipient: 'The codes of encoding and decoding may not be per-fectly symmetrical' (Hall 1980: 131). Hall is interested in how media represent – and misrepresent – what they mean rather than simply reflect those meanings on to their audiences. While encoding and decoding are separate processes, they are not arbitrary however. Encoding – at the phase of

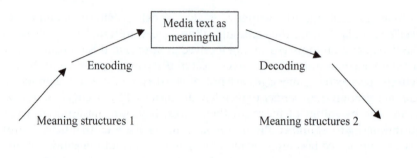

Figure 4.4   The Encoding/Decoding model

Source: Adapted from Hall (1980: 130)

production – operates within a set of *professional codes* such as technical competence and high-budget production values. These professional codes generate preferred meanings that 'have the institutional/political/ideological order imprinted in them and have themselves become institutionalized' (Hall 1980: 134). Television is the medium that Hall is most interested in. In Britain, for example, the BBC operates a professional code in line with their public service ethos. One characteristic of this code relates to political impartiality – the BBC is not allowed to take sides in party politics, otherwise it would be breaking its code and being unprofessional. The preferred meanings encoded by BBC news channels, therefore, include political impartiality. The assumption is that audiences will not decode partial political points of view if – as seems likely – they adopt the BBC's preferred meanings in their news broadcasts.

While Hall argues that preferred meanings have considerable weight in determining how messages are decoded, they are not *determinate*. This returns us to a basic – but crucial – theory of structuralism that informs the Encoding/Decoding model: 'In a "determinate" moment the structure employs a code and yields a "message"; at another determinate moment the "message", via its decodings, issues into the structure of social practices' (Hall 1980: 130). It is precisely because encoding and decoding are distinct, determinate moments that explains why the meaning structures of media messages do not reflect reality in an objective sense. Rather, in the case of television, messages 'can only be signified within the aural-visual forms of the televisual discourse' (Hall 1980: 129). A news event such as a state funeral, for instance, cannot represent the experience of actually being in attendance at the funeral – it can only signify what the experience is 'really' like through the meaning structures (rules and conventions) of the televisual message. Media – like language systems – are therefore structured through a set of rules, codes and values that make them highly prone to ideological constructions of meaning, or what Barthes refers to as myths. Television is a primary myth-maker – constructer of ideology – according to Hall. Processes of editing, selection, camera operation and arrangement are all important aspects of encoding, in the sense of determining preferred meanings (Hall 1975). BBC news bulletins – like those of all news institutions – are loaded with the ideology of professionalism. What news stories are selected, how each of them are edited, and how they are arranged in a particular order (of importance) are just some of the ways in which the ideology of media professionalism is constructed. Ideologies of newsworthiness do not correspond to an objective set of criteria. On the contrary, newsworthiness is highly subjective and differs from institution to institution, and from country to country. Nonetheless, wherever newsworthiness is practised (on the BBC, CNN, Al Jazeera, and so on), it exerts its preferred meanings upon its audience.

Encoded ideologies such as media professionalism and newsworthiness, however, do not determine meaning structures at the reception phase. Hall (1980) identifies three categories of decoding through which audiences make meaning of media messages. First and in keeping with the professional code, an audience member may adopt a *dominant code* which accepts the preferred meanings intended by the encoders (i.e. media producers). A second possibility is that an audience member adopts a *negotiated code* which accepts some preferred meanings of a media production but opposes others. On a general level, the encoded meanings may be understood and endorsed; but on a more specific, local level these meanings and the rules within which they operate may be discarded, as audience members consider their own positions to be exceptions to the general rule. For example, a parent may adopt a negotiated code when decoding a television show about how to care for babies. He may agree that, in general, the best advice is to lay a baby on its back when placing her in a cot, but disagree in the case of his own son who only ever goes to sleep on his front. Third and finally, an audience member may completely disagree with the preferred meanings of media producers (both on a general and local level), in which case they adopt an *oppositional code* and 'decode the message in a *globally* contrary way' (Hall 1980: 137–8). For example, a news story might be encoded with an ideological message about how 'yobbish' youths are becoming more troublesome and anti-social than previous generations of young people. An oppositional code is adopted at the moment of decoding, however, by someone with historical knowledge of how young people have committed crimes and been stigmatized by societies (including mass media institutions) since time immemorial.

Hall's Encoding/Decoding model is an attempt to rediscover and rescue ideology from its conception as an omnipotent, oppressive force wielded by the ruling classes upon the masses in the classical Marxist tradition of political economy theory (as we will discuss in Chapter 7). However, in a later work (Hall 1996a), he refers to the 'problem of ideology' as a concept. Can it still withstand application in contemporary, democratic societies where media institutions appear free from the power of states and commercial forces? He acknowledges that Marxist theories of ideology tend to overemphasize 'negative and distorted features' of bourgeois capitalist ideas and values (Hall 1996a: 28). Nevertheless, he remains sympathetic to Marx's original formulation of ideology and particularly to the related concept of **hegemony** formulated by Antonio Gramsci. Unlike many Marxist conceptions of ideology (such as that of Adorno), Marx did not suggest that ideology amounts to mass deception but rather to a situation where individuals within capitalist social systems can only gain a limited impression of the consequences of such systems, given ideological constraints imposed by ruling power elites. The best revision of Marx's ideas, argues Hall, is by Gramsci who contends that 'in particular historical situations, ideas "organize human masses, and create the terrain on which men [sic] move, acquire consciousness of their position, struggle, etc."' (Hall 1996a: 41, quoting Gramsci 1971). Social, economic and political ideas create struggle, and 'ideological struggle is a part of the general social struggle for mastery and leadership – in short, for hegemony' (Hall 1996a: 43).

Gramsci's theory of hegemony marks a fundamental shift from orthodox structuralism to a more discursive form of post-structuralism with which Hall, among others (see also discussion of Foucault in this chapter), has identified. Hegemony, unlike orthodox approaches to myth and ideology, is about a dialogue between those parts of a society with and without the power to signify their values and intentions:

> [H]egemony is understood as accomplished, not without the due measure of legal and legitimate compulsion, but principally by means of winning consent of those classes and groups who were subordinated within it ... This approach could also be used to demonstrate how media institutions could be articulated to the production and reproduction of the dominant ideologies, while at the same time being 'free' of direct compulsion, and 'independent' of any direct attempt by the powerful to nobble them.
>
> (Hall 1982: 85–6)

In other words, hegemony is a 'give and take' form of power. Hegemony works to permit dissenting voices and oppositional politics, but to suppress the force of dissent and opposition by actively seeking out support from all parts of a society. Media are argued by Hall to encode their products in the interests of dominant hegemonic forces, such as governments: 'The professional code operates *within* the "hegemony" of the dominant code' (Hall 1980: 136). Even if media institutions do not intend to collude with the forces of hegemony that operate in their countries or regions, they are likely to do so unwittingly because hegemony – unlike more orthodox versions of ideology – is a function of existing social structures and practices; not an intention of individuals. Unlike behaviourists such as Katz and Lazarsfeld, who argued that media have no direct effects other than to reflect the consensus opinion among people, Gramsci and Hall would argue that media – in their propensity to serve a hegemonic function for the good of those in power – effectively manufacture consent (see discussion of Herman and Chomsky in Chapter 7 for a political economy approach to hegemony).

Glasgow Media Group: the ideology of news

Structural Marxist theories about the ideological function of media have been tested out using the types of empirical methods associated with media effects research. Perhaps the most substantial and innovative examples of this research were undertaken by the Glasgow Media Group (GMG) in Britain from the mid-1970s to the mid-1990s. Its findings suggest that Hall's Encoding/Decoding model affords the audience too much scope for alternative decodings of television productions:

> although there are variations in audience 'readings' of media reports, there are pervasive common themes in the meanings conveyed to the public ... even though people may 'resist' the dominant message of a programme, it may still have the power to convey facts and to influence their ideas, assumptions, and attitudes.
>
> (Eldridge et al. 1997: 160)

John Eldridge et al. have tended to theorize media – television news organizations in particular – as influential shapers of public opinion. Rather than take the 'effects' approach associated with behaviourism, though, the GMG has re-articulated the debate in terms of the power of media to serve the interests of dominant ideologies. Media are ideological in the sense that they present 'a way of seeing and understanding the world which favours some interests over others' (GMG 1982: 3).

Early studies by the GMG (1976; 1980; 1982) centred on television news reports. Extensive textual and image analysis – inspired by Barthes's ideas about denotative and connotative levels of signification – revealed that 'news is not a neutral product ... it is a sequence of socially manufactured messages, which carry many of the culturally dominant assumptions of our society' (GMG 1976: 1). The GMG aimed to 'unpack the coding of television news' and 'reveal the structures of the cultural framework which underpins the production of apparently neutral news' (GMG 1976: 1). News presents itself as 'truth' and 'fact' under the guise of impartiality, as Hall argues, but GMG researchers set out to deconstruct what they called its ideology of truth and neutrality. Analysis of news programming was coupled with participant observation of newsroom practices at the two main news broadcasters in Britain, the BBC and ITN (Independent Television News). The ideological functions of television news are laid bare in the case of reports on industrial strikes by trade unions. Analysis revealed that these reports tended to represent bosses as rational, civilized individuals who were often invited to the studio for interviews, while trade union officials and ordinary workers were represented as emotive members of the baying crowd. In its worst forms, such media **representation** can construct a biased perspective in favour of dominant ideological interests (i.e. those of bosses) and 'the laying of blame for society's industrial and economic problems at the door of the workforce' (GMG 1976: 267). While the workforce is never directly criticized by 'neutral' news presenters and journalists, its side of the argument is presented in a less favourable light by being ignored, sensationalized or juxtaposed with negative images of violent confrontation on picket lines – confrontation that it is often provoked by police and other state authorities.

Akin to Hall, the GMG's argument is that the structural qualities of television news productions determine the ways in which they are interpreted as much as the content of specific news stories. News media therefore possess 'the power to tell people the *order* in which to think about events and issues' (GMG 1982: 1). As well as industrial disputes, the GMG's later studies examined media representations of AIDS (Kitzinger 1993; Miller and Williams 1993), child abuse (Eldridge et al. 1997) and the women's peace movement (Eldridge 1995) among other topics. In each case, news reports were deconstructed to reveal an ideological bias in the way media represented certain groups (police, politicians, doctors, and so on) in comparison to others (social workers, gay people, feminists, and so on). While the GMG's research has achieved the status of a long and established tradition in media studies, its theoretical framework has been criticized in at least two respects. First, it could be argued that the ideological force of media is most pervasive and least noticeable in their capacity to be impartial, as suggested by Hall's professional code. This would problematize the GMG's claim about the ideological function of biased news reporting because

> [the] ideological effectivity of the news is greatest in those areas
> where the operation of the particular signifying conventions which

constitute the news and seem to secure impartiality ... conceal the operation of another, ideologically loaded set of signifying conventions.

(Bennett 1982: 304)

In other words, the ideological bias of news reporting is powerful precisely because it is concealed under a veil of impartiality that not even the most perceptive textual analysis could detect. A second criticism of the GMG has been its lack of sustained audience research to test whether the ideological functions of media representations actually affect viewers' opinions at the point of reception and thereafter. This leaves the GMG open to an elitist fallacy given the underlying assumption – by not analysing audience responses – that media researchers and theorists can *see* what the rest of us cannot.

Williamson: the ideology of ads

Structuralist theories of ideology have also been applied to the meanings of advertisements. As well as selling goods, ads create structures of meaning, and 'in providing us with a structure in which we, and those goods, are inter-changeable, they are selling us ourselves' (Williamson 1978: 13). Informed by structural Marxism, Judith Williamson analyses how ads structure the ways we identify with ourselves in relation to the goods they sell to us. She agrees with Althusser's idea that ideology is 'internalized' in individuals through subtle or subliminal techniques on the part of ISAs. The advertising industry, Williamson suggests, is a highly pervasive ISA in advanced capitalist societies. One such function served by the ideology of ads is to mask the reality of stark class differences in such societies – ads assume that we all have equal access to wealth and luxury. Not everyone can afford a Versace dress but ads – and advertisers – take insufficient account of different consumer needs and expenditure. Williamson does not attempt to measure the effects of adver-tising on people's spending habits. This kind of research – typical of the behaviourist approach – would be worthwhile to some extent but would tell us little about how advertising structures our values, tastes, ideas and expectations. Instead, Williamson's semiotic analysis of visual signs in ads reveals their hidden ideological meanings and intentions, and their ideolo-gical power to structure our lives.

How do ads signify their ideology? Williamson's answer to this question forms her main theoretical argument, which is that ads construct ideological meaning 'not on the level of the overt signified but via the signifiers' (Wil-liamson 1978: 24). She states that 'the signifier of the overt meaning in an advertisement has a function of its own, a place in the process of creating another, less obvious meaning' (Williamson 1978: 19). In other words, beneath the surface images (i.e. signifiers) contained in any ad can be deciphered hidden meanings using the method of semiotics. So ads make their meaning through a play on the meaning of signifiers rather than what is being signified (i.e. the obvious product meaning). Perfume ads are a good example because they cannot give any 'real' meaning or information about the products they are selling. How can smell be signified without a sample of perfume being attached? In the absence of sufficient 'signifieds', then, perfume products are sold as 'unique, distinctive' consumables through less overt 'signifiers' – images that are attached to those products. Perfume becomes associated with a particular style or 'look' rather than – as it ought to be associated – with a particular smell. These signifiers that work their meaning beneath the surface messages of ads are drawn from what Williamson calls a 'referent system', akin to systems of signification that operate on the basis of differentiation (see discussion of Saussure). Referent systems make connections with images that are auxiliary to those of the product being advertised. There are, in fact, only superficial differences between one perfume product and another (even if one is ten times more expensive than another!), but referent systems are sophisticated enough to carve out and manufacture differentiation even so. As such, referent systems constitute the ideological dimension of ads.

Nonetheless, the ideology of ads can only work its ulterior motives – to mask class differences, to present a world of glamour and happiness, and so on – at the moment in which they are received by consumers. Williamson explains that the reason why the ideological meaning buried in an ad is so elusive and invisible to us is because 'we constantly re-create it. It works *through* us, not at us' (Williamson 1978: 41). As consumers, we are lured into accepting the ideology of ads because they afford us an active role in deciphering their hidden meanings. However, this 'activity' afforded to us is a phoney activity that sucks us into an ideological vacuum wherein we are prevented from seeing a real world – outside referent systems – of inequalities and hardship. One way that we re-create and, moreover, appear to embrace the ideology of ads is by falsely decoding them as personal invitations to improve ourselves. Ads appear, through their signifiers, to address us as individuals, but although we might sense that ads are addressed to lots of people – not just you or I – we are still inclined to accept the invitation: 'You have to exchange yourself with the person "spoken to", the spectator the ad creates for itself ... The "you" in ads is always transmitted plural, but we receive it as singular' (Williamson 1978: 50). Ads provide consumers with an activity, but in partaking in this activity – substituting yourself for 'you' – we are internalizing its preferred ideology, which is that you 'yourself' can be like the ideal 'you' represented in the ad. So while 'we can "consciously work" in "producing" a meaning ... we do not produce a genuine "meaning" but consume a predetermined "solution"' (Williamson 1978: 75). Ads pretend to empower us but only in ways that they would wish us to be empowered.

They wish us to think 'I am empowered enough to convince myself that I am like the woman in that ad with men flocking around her as she sits in that expensive sports car, which I can also afford and am seriously thinking of buying ... if I can arrange another high-cost loan with my bank!' The 'ideal' types in ads, moreover, are stereotypes that conform to dominant ideological representations of what 'success' and 'happiness' look like (see Qualter 1997). The 'people' represented by ads are typically white, affluent, relatively young and physically attractive but these shiny, happy people are hardly a typical cross-section of society.

Morley: the *Nationwide* audience

The work of David Morley, by contrast to Williamson's study of ads and the GMG's research on television news, has sought to apply structuralist theories of ideological meanings in media texts – particularly Hall's Encoding/ Decoding model – to empirical research on media audiences. Echoing Hall and Williamson, Morley suggests in *The Nationwide Audience* (first published in 1980) that 'audiences, like the producers of messages, must also undertake a specific kind of "work" in order to read meaningfully what is transmitted' (Morley and Brunsdon 1999: 125). Moreover, media can only reproduce the dominant ideology of powerful institutions by articulating this ideology to audiences at their level of common sense. He states: 'I would want to insist on the active nature of readings and of cultural production. Too often the audience subject is reduced to the status of an automated puppet pulled by the strings of the text' (Morley and Brunsdon 1999: 273). This audience-centred approach to structuralist theory was tested out by the author in a research project that interviewed groups of people about their responses to viewing two episodes of *Nationwide*, a long-running BBC current affairs television programme that was popular in Britain between 1969 and 1984. These groups were selected according to occupational status and their opinions of what they viewed were applied to the three categories of decoding outlined in Hall's Encoding/Decoding model.

Morley's findings are interesting, even though – as he later recognizes (Morley 1992) – the somewhat contrived method of grouping people's pre-supposed ideological positions on the basis of their occupations alone must question the validity of these findings. What Morley found, however, to some extent met but in other ways contradicted expectations. Those groups who tended to decode the stories and debates presented by *Nationwide* using a dominant code (i.e. the preferred meaning suggested by the programme's representation of these stories and debates) included bank managers – who it might be expected would accept the ideological consensus worked by the professional code at the encoding stage given their middle-class status – but also working-class apprentices (semi-skilled manual workers) whose subordinate position in existing social and economic structures might suggest that they were more than likely to disagree with dominant or preferred meanings. Moreover, those groups who tended to decode *Nationwide* using a negotiated code (accepting some preferred meanings but opposing others) included trade union officials and university art students, who it might be assumed would be more hostile (i.e. oppositional) to the capitalist-driven, dominant ideologies reinforced by the programme. While some groups decoded *Nationwide* along expected class lines, other groups confounded expectations. Moreover, a group of black further education students did not understand the programme's content, which would suggest the need for a further category of decoding – a rejection code.

Morley's subsequent critique of the Encoding/Decoding model is perhaps more significant than what he found initially by testing it out. He argues that 'in the case of each of the major categories of decoding (dominant, negotiated or oppositional) we can discern different varieties and inflections of what, for purposes of gross comparison only, is termed the same "code"' (Morley 1992: 118). There are three problems with the model that arise from its theoretical foundations in structuralism and semiotics. First, as referred to in the quote above, decoding suggests a single, universal form of audience interpretation of media texts which is surely too simplistic and fails to account for more subtle nuances in how we read the different meanings that a television programme or pop song might *convey to us*. The complexities of audience interpretations are tackled in a later study (see Morley 1986). Second, there is the issue of intentionality or what literary critics would term 'the intentional fallacy'. Morley notes that the Encoding/Decoding framework is too liable to confuse the ideological meanings of texts with the ideological motivations of producers or authors. Texts themselves are often difficult to interpret in terms of their political, economic or ideological bias without implicating producers with the self-same biases. And third, Morley criticizes the notion of preferred meanings that generate 'preferred readings'. Certain media texts, such as party political broadcasts and possibly news bulletins, can be deemed to present a preferred reading that corresponds more or less with that of the dominant ideology of ruling interests – politicians and big business owners, for example. However, it is much harder to identify the preferred reading of a fictional text such as a romantic film or pop song. Morley asks: 'is the preferred reading a property of the text, the analyst or the audience?' (1992: 122).

In order to bridge this institution–text–audience split in the ideological transfer of meaning, Morley suggests an alternative approach: genre theory (Morley 1992: 126–30; see also Morley 1980). Genre theory derives from the work of Stephen Neale who claims that 'genres are not to be seen as forms of textual codifications, but as systems of orientations, expectations and conventions that circulate between industry, text and subject' (Neale 1980: 19). So media genres characterized by certain expectations and conventions – horror films, house music, reality TV, and so on – are defined as such by a combination of the institutions that produce them, the texts that constitute them, and the audiences that receive them. Genres ensure that audience expectations and prejudgements about a given media text are generally satisfied by industry production techniques. Genres, unlike the individual texts which make up their parts, are categorized by sets of rules determining how they signify meaning that must be governed by both producers and audiences in order for those genre categories to withstand signification. However, genres are not ideologically neutral in the way they generate this semiotic harmony between producers and audiences. On the contrary, certain genres demand different forms of 'cultural competence' (Morley 1992) that tend to result in one genre becoming associated with a different class of audience in comparison to another. In crude terms, working-class women are more likely to become culturally adept at watching soap operas, while middle-class men locate cultural competence in financial news programming. Morley's discussion of cultural competence in relation to genre theory is not dissimilar to the concept of cultural capital (see discussion of Bourdieu in Chapter 9).

Hebdige: *Subculture*

The most systematic attempt to analyse oppositional forms of decoding in media and cultural texts is Dick Hebdige's subcultural theory. Hebdige deployed semiotics to analyse how texts and products are used in subversive ways by youth subcultures such as punks and mods in order to articulate their resistance to dominant ideologies in society such as education and housing policies. Subcultures operate through a system of oppositional codes that offend the majority, threaten the status quo and contradict the 'myth of consensus' suggested by dominant codes (Hebdige 1979: 18). Like Hall, Hebdige applies hegemony theory to his structuralist approach, but his concern is more with how a dominant hegemony can be challenged and threatened rather than with how it maintains its hold over society. What does he mean by a 'subculture'? Essentially, a subculture is an underground set of practices – usually working-class in character – that try to resist surveillance by the dominant culture (e.g. police) as well as incorporation into mainstream cultures. A subculture ceases to exist when it becomes incorporated, manufactured and packaged by commercial interests. Punks' use of dog collars, bought from pet shops, cease to retain their subcultural value when they can be purchased for twice the price in High Street shops, for example.

According to Hebdige, subcultures resist surveillance and incorporation by creating their own internal logic of identity and cohesion. Two structuralist concepts underpin this claim: theories of homology and *bricolage*. Referring to Willis's (1978) theoretical conception, homology is defined as 'the symbolic fit between the values and lifestyles of a group, its subjective experience and the musical forms it uses to express or reinforce its focal concerns' (Hebdige 1979: 113). Music is only one media and cultural form, though, in which subcultures reinforce their concerns, fit together their values and experiences. Table 4.1 suggests some others, including the system of language (what Hebdige calls 'argot') adopted by a subculture to reinforce its unity.

Table 4.1   Homologies of youth subcultures

	Teds	Mods	Punks	Ravers
Music	Rock 'n' Roll	Ska/reggae	Heavy rock	Acid house
Clothes	Suits	Smart casual	Homemade	Baggy casual
Objects	Cigars	Scooters	Dog collars	Whistles
Drugs	Tobacco	LSD	Dope	Ecstasy
Argot/slang	'Spiv'	'About town'	'Piss off'	'Buzzin''

Each subculture, therefore, becomes associated with a cultural inventory of signs and symbols that 'fit' with its identities and concerns. This model harps back to Saussure's syntagmatic and paradigmatic dimensions (see Figure 4.1). Through homologies, therefore, subcultures develop exclusive, sophisticated systems of signification that protect them from censure or exploitation by outsiders. However, we can see that any single change in the syntagmatic features of a subculture would affect the whole paradigmatic fit of meanings and therefore break down its homological unity. As soon as the scooter becomes a mass-produced fashion object not solely used by the mod subculture, the whole homological unity of mods is fractured.

Related to homology is the concept of *bricolage* (first used by Claude Lévi-Strauss, a well-known structural anthropologist) and its sister term, appropriation. *Bricolage* and appropriation refer to the way in which symbolic objects are invested with subcultural meanings that are borrowed from different contexts and oppose their original functions. Dog collars had their original meaning – that is, as a pet-restraining device – opposed and appropriated by punks to fit with their own style and values. Similarly, 'the teddy boy's theft and transformation of the Edwardian style revived in the early 1950s by Savile Row for wealthy young men about town can be construed as an act of *bricolage*' (Hebdige 1979: 104). Black subcultures such as Rastafarians and rude boys had a particularly powerful influence on the *bricolage* practices of white working-class youth subcultures in Britain during the post-war period. Rasta haircuts, fashions, reggae and cannabis use were all appropriated by white subcultures such as mods in order to express their resistance to dominant white, middle-class ideologies. This is akin to playing with Barthes's interpretations of cultural myths to suit the interests of one's own subculture while opposing the interests of the dominant culture. Mass media texts and the institutions that produce them are clearly outside the reference systems in which subcultures make their oppositional meanings. The most effective way to escape the ideological function of media, according to Hebdige's subcultural theory, is to ignore them and seek out cultural forms untarnished by media exposure.

Despite the ongoing currency of 'subculture', concepts of homology and *bricolage* informed by theories of structuralism have undergone significant critiques and revisions since Hebdige's account (see, for example, Clarke 1990; Muggleton 2000). This is partly because new media, information and manufacturing technologies have simultaneously widened and restricted the scope of opportunities for subcultures to evolve. Faster and more sophisticated production techniques enable the latest 'subcultural' music, fashion, argot, and so on to be delivered direct from 'the street' into multinational retail outlets in such short time that a subculture is strangled of its authenticity before it can get to its feet. Commercial incorporation is more ruthless now than in the days of mods and punks. Genre theory (see discussion of Morley) has been cited as an alternative to subcultural theory given its twin concerns with cultural production and (subcultural) consumption (Hesmondhalgh 2005). This would seem to offer a way forward in understanding how the internet provides new opportunities for subcultural networks such as Goths to form and disseminate their values and experiences among themselves (Hodkinson 2002). Indeed, the internet has served as a subcultural medium of consumption, albeit under the constant shadow of 'offline' production interests. For example, some resistant consumer practices – such as illegal music file-sharing – have become serious threats to dominant economic interests, such as major record companies. Whether or not unlawful music uploading and downloading is a subcultural practice in its strictest sense is open to debate, but it has certainly enabled consumers to wrestle authority from producers by forcing the music industry to explore alternative styles of music and forms of distribution (see Chapter 9 for further discussion of consumer authority in a non-subcultural sense).

Foucault: discourse and disciplinary society

The work of Michel Foucault is wide-ranging and not specifically concerned with media, so for the purposes of this book we will only focus on his theory of **discourse** in relation to surveillance and what he called 'panopticism'. In *The Archaeology of Knowledge* (first published in 1972), Foucault (1989) argues that discourse functions to make certain ideas and values *present* while others are made *absent*. Discourse is an exclusionary mechanism that allocates power and knowledge to those whose ideas are included and made present at a given moment in time, but at the same time exerts power and knowledge over the excluded/absent. Foucault defines discourse – much like Saussure's definition of language – as a system of signification governed by rules that structure the ways in which we classify and divide its different meanings. He differs from orthodox structuralism, though, by investigating how discourse evolves and changes through history (diachronic rather than synchronic analysis) in the shape of discursive practices (see White 1979). The historical dividing of meanings and practices into different classifications (e.g. good versus evil) ensures 'the infinite continuity of discourse and its secret presence to itself in the interplay of a constantly recurring absence' (Foucault 1989: 25). People can gain power over time, for example, by articulating a discourse of goodness and comparing their own ideas with an absent discourse of evil that exists elsewhere. As such, discourse disperses power and knowledge by dividing and differentiating itself into what Foucault (1989) calls discursive formations.

An example of what he means by discursive formations is found in *Discipline and Punish* (first published in 1975):

> Generally speaking, all the authorities exercising individual control function according to a double mode; that of binary division and branding (mad/sane; dangerous/harmless; normal/abnormal); and that of coercive assignment, of differential distribution (who he [*sic*] is; where he must be; how he is to be characterized; how he is to be recognized; how a constant surveillance is to be exercised over him in an individual way, etc.).
>
> (Foucault 1995: 199)

The power to decide, say, what is criminal or lawful is exercised by those authorities who speak the discourse of law and construct discursive formations out of it. This is what Foucault means by 'binary division and branding'. The other half of the double mode that exercises control over individuals – the technique of discipline through coercion – is surveillance, the best example of which for Foucault is Jeremy Bentham's design for the 'panopticon'. Designed to be the ultimate prison, the panopticon consisted of a central watchtower in which prison officers could observe the inmates in their cells situated along several 'corridor-like' wings extended out from the watchtower. The cells housing the prisoners appear to those who watch over them 'like so many cages, so many small theatres, in which each actor is alone, perfectly individualized and constantly visible. The panoptic mechanism arranges spatial unities that make it possible to see constantly and to recognize immediately' (Foucault 1995: 200). Moreover, the panopticon's all-seeing power extends to situations in which the watchtower is unmanned. Inmates act and behave in a disciplined manner, as if they are being observed all the time, given their uncertainty as to whether they are or are not because they cannot see into the watchtower. As such, panopticism is both an externalized and an internalized power mechanism: 'Disciplinary power ... is exercised through its invisibility; at the same time it imposes on those whom it subjects a principle of compulsory visibility' (Foucault 1995: 187). Like Foucault's theory of discourse, panopticism disperses power in such a way that it becomes instilled into individuals' consciousness until they accept the discursive formations exercised upon them (good versus evil, lawful versus criminal, and so on).

What has all this to do with media theory? Perhaps most importantly, Foucault argues that the panoptic mechanism of surveillance and its 'infinitesimal distribution of the power relations' extends beyond prison walls to what he calls the 'disciplinary society' (Foucault 1995: 216). As such, panopticism can be considered a function of media as well as prisons and other powerful social institutions. Television in particular has the power to make visible certain kinds of ideas and forms of behaviour to the exclusion of others. The powerful discourse of media – like the discourse of crime and punishment – classifies certain forms of knowledge as 'true' and others as 'false'. For example, health advice from medical 'experts' on television is classified as the truth in interplay with other, 'false' sources of medical knowledge – such as alternative medicines. At first, this seems awfully similar to the ideological function of media as theorized by Hall, Williamson and the GMG, among others. However, unlike ideology or hegemony which are forms of power external to individuals, Foucault conceives discourse as dispersed internally *into* individuals. There is no manufacture of consent, and there are no oppositional or resistant codes that individuals can adopt against a dominant culture, because power has been distributed everywhere into our hearts and minds. Media institutions – like hospitals, schools and other state apparatuses – disperse and distribute power through discourses that we cannot help but internalize and accept as 'the truth'. *Big Brother* (2000–) and the reality television genre could be theorized as a panoptic media discourse that includes and excludes certain types of participants. However, an Orwellian 'Big Brother' watching over us – the BBC is nicknamed 'Big Brother' by those who see its public service values as excessively paternal – does not fit with Foucault's theory of discourse as infinitesimally distributed. Rather, we are all 'little brothers' – or 'little sisters' – partaking in surveillance of ourselves and each other, regardless of what Big Brother might be doing.

Summary

This chapter has considered:

- Saussure's theory of language – 'differences carry signification' – that underpins structuralism and semiotics.
- Barthes's theory of myth that develops Saussure's ideas and shows how signs operate within wider social and cultural – not just linguistic – structures.
- Theories of ideology and hegemony in relation to the production and reception of media texts – with particular reference to the Encoding/Decoding model (Hall) and its subsequent application to media audience research (Morley).
- The ideology of news (GMG) and ads (Williamson) – and how the meaning structures of these media texts represent ruling political and commercial interests.
- Hebdige's subcultural theory, including concepts of homology and *bricolage* as forms of resistance to dominant cultural structures.
- Foucault's theory of discourse in relation to the disciplinary mechanisms of panopticism, and how this theory applies to media surveillance.

Further reading

Bignell, J. (2002) *Media Semiotics: An Introduction*, 2nd edn. Manchester: Manchester University Press.

Semiotics is clearly explained and then thoughtfully applied to examples from ads, magazines, newspapers, reality TV, cinema and interactive media. Accessible to all media students.

Hall, S. (ed.) (1997) *Representation: Cultural Representations and Signifying Practices*. London: Sage and The Open University.

Even if somewhat dated, this edited collection of articles remains seminal to structuralist theories of representation, developed through semiotic, sociological, Foucauldian and gender perspectives. Suitable for all media students.

Morley, D. and Chen, K-H. (eds) (1996) *Stuart Hall: Critical Dialogues in Cultural Studies*. London: Routledge.

This edited collection of articles charts and evaluates the wide variety of Hall's work, from questions of ideology and hegemony to postmodernism and postcolonial theory (note that this book is also useful in relation to post-colonial perspectives discussed in Chapter 7). Recommended for advanced undergraduates and postgraduates.

Tudor, A. (1999) *Decoding Culture: Theory and Method in Cultural Studies.* London: Sage.

A thoroughly critical analysis of structuralism, post-structuralism and the CCCS tradition of media and cultural theory. Suitable for all media students.

5   Interactionism and structuration

Introduction

This chapter focuses on theories of **interactionism**. Interactionism is a strand of theory about the way we, individually and in groups, act in our relation to others in specific social environments (see Atkinson and Housley 2003). Interactionist media theory derives from the sociological tradition of symbolic interactionism that has its origins in the Chicago School from where Erving Goffman, the first theorist we will discuss, plied his trade. According to another Chicago School theorist, Herbert Blumer, interactionism is founded on three basic premises:

1   'human beings act toward things on the basis of the meanings that the things have for them' (Blumer 1969: 2): actions and meanings are therefore self-generated in everyday situations – not in any way determined by structures of production, as structuralists would generally argue.
2   'the meaning of such things is derived from, or arises out of, the social interaction that one has with one's fellows' (Blumer 1969: 2): actions and meanings are self-generated, but only after they emerge in social relations with others. In short, no one lives in an autonomous social vacuum.
3   'meanings are handled in, and modified through, an interpretative process used by the person in dealing with the things he [sic] encounters' (Blumer 1969: 2): this process of interpretation requires that one can generate meanings (as in premise 1) and also 'select, check, suspend, regroup, and transform the meanings' (Blumer 1969: 5) according to one's actions and situations.

Unlike behaviourist and structuralist theories that tend to emphasize the power of media texts and technologies to determine our meanings of the social world, interactionist media theory considers the dynamic relations between producers, texts, technologies and interpretative audiences. This marks a particular shift in focus from structuralism. Whereas structuralists aim to identify how we are located within media structures, interactionists are more interested in how media interact with the structures of our lives. This is a complex concern in modern societies. Over the course of the past century, the means by which we can communicate and interact with others have proliferated wholesale. Long gone are the days when face-to-face interaction was the only means to see, hear or talk to others. It has become a cliché to observe how people phone their neighbours or email their work colleagues when it would make more sense – at least to a traditionalist – to take the short walk to meet them personally. All the perspectives discussed in this chapter are concerned with this dynamic interaction mix in which we are all engaged. Media are defined as social phenomena that contribute to – rather than psychologically influence or ideologically structure – our social environment and consciousness. Labelling and moral panic theories, for example, do not claim that media *per se* construct fear and panic in society, but that media are a significant component in collective, interpretative processes that together generate societal reaction to deviance. Societal reaction is self-generated – not imposed by external or internalized power structures. Media are part of society – not ideologically opposed to certain social trends. However, Giddens's **structuration theory** is an attempt to marry structuralism and interactionism by claiming that social structure (institutional power, including media power) and social action (individual agency, including mediated interaction) are not diametrically opposed, but interact and overlap with each other.

Goffman: self-presentation

Goffman is probably the best-known theorist of social interaction. His interactionist theories, however, are mostly concerned with face-to-face (i.e. physically co-present) rather than mediated interactions. His analysis of everyday conversations is mostly restricted to one-to-one or group *gatherings* rather than, say, telephone conversations. Nonetheless, Goffman's work can be and has been applied to mediated forms of interaction in diverse ways, several examples of which are discussed later in this chapter. Moreover, in his later work Goffman shows a marked interest in how social interaction rituals are performed and reproduced across the media of radio, television and advertising. Two of these later works we will examine in detail – *Gender Advertisements* (1979) and *Forms of Talk* (1981) – but first we must understand Goffman's theory of **self-presentation**, which informs these later works and is widely referred to across several disciplines (sociology, anthropology, literary studies and social psychology as well as media, communication and cultural studies).

Goffman's self-presentation thesis is first outlined in *The Presentation of Self in Everyday Life* (first published in 1959). By self-presentation, Goffman means the techniques deployed by individuals and groups to perform an expression of themselves to others. This expression is usually intended to form a favourable and amicable impression – it is human nature, after all, to be liked as well as wanting to like. Moreover, 'When an individual or performer plays the same part to the same audience on different occasions, a social relationship is likely to arise' (Goffman 1990: 27). The key word here is 'performer'. Goffman's model for understanding everyday social interactions is the theatrical stage. His is a dramaturgical theory of interactionism. Human beings are therefore analogous to 'real' actors, which implies that they are highly skilled agents of interaction and communication. This implication is warranted, and Goffman's interactionist perspective affords far more autonomy and power to individuals than do behaviourist or structuralist theories. As well as individual performers, there are self-presentational 'teams': 'if performers are concerned with maintaining a line they will select as teammates those who can be trusted to perform properly' (Goffman 1990: 95). Team roles are allocated to individuals, usually by a team director who oversees the smooth running of the performance. An example of a 'team' in this sense would be public relations executives who work with individuals and companies to manage their media performances (i.e. their public reputation). Promotion and crisis management are akin to what Goffman (1990) calls the arts of impression management. These days, PR is essential for anyone or anything on the public stage and in the public eye. However, individuals and teams can only control *expressions* of themselves through self-presentation techniques – *impressions*, on the other hand, may be managed but are never entirely controlled. As he states famously, 'Performers can stop giving expressions but cannot stop giving them off' (Goffman 1990: 111).

Given this state of affairs, Goffman divides the stage-managed regions within which self-presentation is performed into two parts: 'front' and 'back'. An individual's front refers to their capacity – through appearance, manner and social setting – to control the way in which they present themselves to others. Front is 'the expressive equipment of a standard kind intentionally or unwittingly employed by the individual during his [*sic*] performance' (Goffman 1990: 32). It should be noted from this quote that one's front region is not always *consciously* performed and controlled because its expressions are often taken-for-granted. For example, thanking someone for saving your life would be an intended expression of gratitude, while thanking a checkout operator for returning your change is more likely to be expressed unwittingly, as a routine social norm and rule of etiquette. By contrast, an individual's back is the region in which they withdraw from social performances and drop their front. Like the backstage region of a theatre, one's back is ideally concealed from view but always has the potential to be revealed in all its undesirable guises. An individual at a job interview, for example, can exhibit a favourable front (smart clothes, well-combed hair) that they have prepared in 'backstage' settings such as bathrooms, but find other facets of their back region behaviour (casual body language, stuttering speech) intruding on the situation when unprepared to answer that stickler of a question, 'WHY DO YOU WANT THIS JOB?'

How do front and back regions apply to media? To answer this question, we need to assess two of Goffman's more 'media-friendly' accounts of self-presentation. In both these accounts he argues that the dramaturgical character of everyday interactions is reproduced in, and accentuated by, media interactions. Performers on radio and television both represent and amplify certain social roles, norms and conventions familiar to their audiences. Goffman's first engagement with media forms of interaction is his analysis of radio and television talk, which he compares to that of 'ordinary talk' that is performed in physically co-present situations. Radio announcers in particular, by which he means 'live' announcers such as newsreaders or DJs, aim 'to produce the effect of a spontaneous, fluent flow of words – if not a forceful, pleasing personality – under conditions that lay speakers would be unable to manage' (Goffman 1981: 198). These media performers must adopt a front that accommodates the diversity of their audiences and avoids alienating or offending them: 'the audience must be addressed as though it were the public-at-large' (Goffman 1981: 242). However, radio and television announcers must work hard to conceal aspects of back region behaviour, given the multitude of people they must seek to please, who are also witnesses to their every word or action. Four kinds of speech faults are identified by Goffman as particularly applicable to radio talk: influencies (stutters or restarts), slips (incorrect phrasing or words being mixed up), boners (misinterpretation of words) and gaffes (unintended mistakes in choice of words or actions).

Goffman provides some examples of gaffes in radio talk. This from a BBC DJ: 'Here's an all time favourite made popular by the famous Miss Jessie Matthews several years back, *Dancing on the Ceiling*. This one surely deserves to be on every British Hit List' (cited in Goffman 1981: 250). Clearly had the DJ said 'every British Hit *Singles* List' his meaning could not have been radically misinterpreted to suggest that this particular crime of British culture should be targeted by the SAS. Here is another gaffe, following a technical fault in broadcasting: 'Announcer: Due to circumstances beyond our control, we bring you a recorded programme featuring the Beatles' (cited in Goffman 1981: 261). This is surely one of the few occasions when the Beatles have been effectively rendered second-rate, albeit unintentionally. At first, these gaffes might appear to be merely trivial asides and certainly not the stuff of grand theoretical ideas. However, what Goffman achieves in analysing these speech faults in radio talk is a sense of intimacy between producers (performers) and audiences that sows the seeds for a theoretical understanding of how production and reception practices interact with each other (see Scannell 1991; Tolson 2005, on media talk). Producers do not merely 'encode' their media productions according to institutional or professional codes (see discussion of Hall in Chapter 4), but do so in the service of assumptions they make about audiences. Radio announcers, for instance, broadcast 'self-constructed talk projected under the demands, gaze, and responsiveness of listeners who aren't there' (Goffman 1981: 241), while audiences 'are not only personally offended by faults, but ... actively seek out faults that might be offensive to someone' (Goffman 1981: 247). So although not physically able to interact, media producers and audiences encounter perceptions of each other – expressions and impressions – in dynamic interactions that construct what is produced, how and why it is produced.

This dynamic relationship between ordinary, 'real' actors and media performers or productions is evidenced in a second study by Goffman of gender representations in magazine advertisements. His notion of 'display' is akin to the 'front' and 'back' components of self-presentation. Displays 'establish the terms of contact, the mode or style or formula for the dealings that are to ensue between the persons providing the display and the persons perceiving it' (Goffman 1979: 1). Performers and audiences together construct the meanings enacted by a display, whether this occurs in face-to-face or mediated situations. Therefore, displays usually 'have a dialogic character of a statement–reply kind' (Goffman 1979: 1). This dialogue is a ritual feature of social interactions in both co-present and mediated situations. For example, photographic images of celebrities in public circulation – in the form of, say, advertising images – strike up a dynamic relationship with audiences in that these images constitute what it means to achieve success. As such,

> Celebrities not only link their own private lives to the public domain, but also can link the lives of private persons to it. For persons in the public eye ... seem to acquire as one of their powers the capacity to be a contagious high point.
>
> (Goffman 1979: 11)

This high point is what private individuals might aspire to. Body image is a clear example of how we interact with mediated celebrities. One author refers to 'countless images of idealized bodies' on television that 'serve as a common resource for judging the adequacy of self and others' (Glassner 1990: 215), and contribute to wider social interest in fitness and dieting. Being famous – already a social ritual indicating successful achievement – is reinforced by mediated displays of celebrity.

Moreover, mediated forms of display such as gender display in magazine ads tend to reproduce conventionalized images of interaction rituals in social life (i.e. the real world). Stereotypical gender roles are represented in order for the meanings of ads to be instantly recognized by audiences who are familiar with these social rituals on display. However, stereotypes *in themselves* are not the only significant techniques of gender display. As important are the construction of typical social situations, such as a man eating his meal while a woman does the cooking. It should be noted here that application of

Goffman's notion of gender display is limited to ads or other media that represent human figures in realist (i.e. real-like) situations. These realist – and gendered – situations invite audiences to witness and become involved in the conventionalized rituals being portrayed. Goffman refers to six conventionalized portrayals of gender display in ads:

1   *Relative size*: men in ads are usually bigger – both in terms of size and height – than women. While men are, on the whole, biologically bigger and taller than women, ads 'transform what would otherwise be a statistical tendency into a near certitude' (Goffman 1979: 28). In line with social rituals, taller and bigger figures tend to represent greater power than smaller and shorter ones. So men are usually seen in superior relation to women through relative size.

2   *The feminine touch*: this is typically represented as soft and gentle (a woman's hand caresses an object such as a perfume bottle) but the masculine touch is rarely depicted in ads – presumably lest, with all its masculine strength, it might break something!

3   *Function ranking*: in this portrayal a man 'is likely to perform the executive role' (Goffman 1979: 32) while a woman assists. For example, men usually drive cars while good-looking women assist in conversational exchange.

4   *The family*: this is usually depicted in ads according to a hierarchy which is governed by a combination of age and gender rituals. The father is usually the dominant figure in terms of size and position within the group, while the youngest daughter is usually the least noticeable and the lowest positioned.

5   *The ritualization of subordination*: acts of subordination in gender displays are usually performed by women in the service of men, or younger men in the service of their seniors. Women lie down on sofas, for example, while men stand behind them and aim sexually suggestive looks their way.

6   *Licensed withdrawal*: women more than men tend to find themselves withdrawn into situations in which they are solitary and appear vulnerable, and in which the 'absent man' – of whom the consumer may be implicated – is assumed to provide the missing protective role.

What Goffman argues in relation to these six conventionalized portrayals of gender display, then, is that they are not solely produced through media stereotyping but through a dynamic relationship between social (i.e. real) and constructed (i.e. mediated) interaction rituals. Moreover, meanings are not structured separately during the phases of production and reception – as structural Marxists like Hall might suppose – but in the interaction between producers (those constructing displays) and audiences (who receive these displays in reference to social rituals). As such, there are neither media effects of the stimulus–response kind nor any ideological functions of media, but rather reconstructed media displays of 'standardization, exaggeration, and simplification that characterize rituals in general' (Goffman 1979: 84). So media such as ads represent a contrived version of social rituals, norms and conventions – like women being subordinate to men – that already exist in 'real', social situations. This is what Goffman calls 'hyper-ritualization', in which media tend to ritualize forms of interaction that are already rituals in the social world. In this sense, mediated interactions – and our interactions with media – merely reproduce, artificially, what we learn and recognize about our lives through face-to-face interactions. Interestingly, in the internet age, Goffman's discussion of hyper-ritualized mediated self-presentation has renewed resonance. However, internet-mediated interaction becomes an alternative to, rather than accentuation of, face-to-face interaction on profile websites such as MySpace. MySpace users perform their online profiles in intimate – almost *imm*ediate – interaction with other profiles, but as well as expanding opportunities for personal relationships such as internet dating (see Gibbs et al. 2006), profile websites provide spaces for carefully honed 'online fronts' to perform sinister self-presentations such as paedophilia.

Meyrowitz: *No Sense of Place*

Goffman's interactionist theory of self-presentation has been combined with McLuhan's medium theory (as discussed in Chapter 3) by Joshua Meyrowitz to formulate ideas about how media might affect social change. In *No Sense of Place* (1985), Meyrowitz argues that 'electronic media, especially television, have had a tremendous impact on Americans' sense of place' (Meyrowitz 1985: 308). While Goffman tends to think of social situations in physical places, Meyrowitz argues that television has brought different social situations in different physical places into a shared domain – that is, everyone's living rooms and the public eye. As he states, 'The telephone, radio and television make the boundaries of all social spaces more permeable' (Meyrowitz 1994: 67). This is very different from the impact of print media on society. Echoing McLuhan, Meyrowitz argues that print media such as books and newspapers have, historically, retained the link between social situations and a sense of place. Individuals who were highly literate could gain access to knowledge and information from which illiterate people were excluded. Moreover, skilled users of print media tended to build social networks with like-minded, intelligent others rather than with people who could not read or write. With the advent of television, telephone and radio, however, Meyrowitz claims that access to knowledge and information is shared by all, regardless of literacy skills. So electronic media help to blur class, age and other social differences. For example, a modern-day child watching a television news bulletin can learn about sexually transmitted diseases. In the age of print media, that child would have had to be able to read as well as access the right books in order to learn about these 'adult' issues – information of this kind was far less easily *placed* then than now.

Meyrowitz (1985) draws on Goffman's notion of front and backstage behaviour to show how media can affect social situations and the social networks with which individuals identify. While print media have tended to segregate groups of people according to education and socio-economic class, electronic media tend to merge these groups together. For example, television viewers can be educated and informed in backstage settings such as their homes, and then use their new-found knowledge in front regions such as workplaces. According to Meyrowitz, the middle-class and the ghetto family inhabit the same social networks of information and knowledge, so their sense of physical separation – the fact that they live in different places – is insignificant compared to their sense of mediated togetherness. This is the basis for Meyrowitz's theory of **placelessness**, in which he proposes that people are no longer defined by physical boundaries or places (where we are) but rather by networks of information and knowledge (what we know) – facilitated by new media technologies – that have no sense of place. As such, television and other electronic media can be regarded as important resources for social and political change in pursuit of banishing social inequalities:

> it is not surprising that the widespread rejection of traditional child and adult, male and female, and leader and follower roles should have begun in the later 1960s among the first generation of Americans to have been exposed to television before learning to read.
>
> (Meyrowitz 1985: 309)

Unlike Bourdieu (as discussed in Chapter 9) who argues that cultural capital – what one knows through education and upbringing – is closely linked to socio-economic class, Meyrowitz's more radical argument is that electronic media have helped to transform their audience, whether rich or poor, into equally informed and educated citizens. Issues of technological, educational and social exclusion are strangely absent from Meyrowitz's argument, however, which is clearly problematic.

While front and back region behaviour are kept apart for beneficial ends in the case of social climbers among media audiences, those who perform in the public eye of electronic media find the maintenance of a front and its separation from backstage behaviour impossible to manage. There is simply no escape – no safe haven – from surveillance in the form of television cameras and microphones. Electronic media have led to back region behaviour being witnessed by millions, as was the case when President Nixon underwent a very public trial during the Watergate scandals. Meyrowitz states: 'The disclosure of authorities' backstage behaviour leads to shock and public demand for increased attention to ethics and standards' (1985: 169). While ordinary people make their backstage an increasingly important region in which to develop effective front region behaviour in the electronic age, media personalities cannot avoid revealing some of their back region during the front they present in public life. Meyrowitz suggests that electronic media have changed the dynamics of public performances in such a way that a new type – what he calls 'middle-region behaviour' – has evolved. The watchful eye of television, for example, makes it almost impossible for public performers such as politicians and celebrities to separate their front (public) from their backstage (private) lives. So rather than the traditional theatre experience eluded to by Goffman, Meyrowitz suggests that media audiences adopt a side-stage view of performances in which they witness both front and backstage behaviours in public figures. By extension, in 'revealing previously backstage areas to audiences, television has served as an instrument of demystification' (Meyrowitz 1985: 309). Media personalities are forced to be more honest and publicly accountable about their private as well as their public lives; they are forced to practise what they preach . . . and preach what they practise.

Horton and Wohl: personae and para-social interaction

An early account of mediated interaction by Donald Horton and R. Richard Wohl, 'Mass Communication and Para-Social Interaction' (first published in 1956), derives from the Chicago School tradition of interactionist sociology along with Goffman's early work. Two important theoretical concepts are explored by Horton and Wohl which have had a significant bearing on subsequent theories of media production and reception. The first is what they call **para-social interaction**. Different but not dissimilar to ordinary social interaction of the face-to-face kind, para-social interaction refers to the *apparent* familiarity between media personalities and audiences that can be established through routine use of radio and television, particularly chat shows and other formats which include a studio audience. This familiarity can become a substitute for or may complement more traditional sources of familiarity, such as interactions between family members, relatives and friends. An 'illusion of intimacy' (Horton and Wohl 2004: 375) can be fostered in the performance features of these media, such as their conversational style and – in the case of television – the capacity to view close-up shots. Studio audiences also play an important function in coaching wider audience attitudes. A studio audience 'exemplifies to the home audience an enthusiastic and "correct" response' (Horton and Wohl 2004: 377), such as when to laugh or cheer. Para-social interaction is perhaps at its most intense in television talent shows such as *American Idol* (2002–) and *The X-Factor* (2004–), in which heartthrobs sing while screaming fans (in the studio and, presumably, at home) pour out their emotion – and hold up banners or pick up phones to register their love and approval. Horton and Wohl tend to share the view of behaviourists that media have quite direct and powerful effects on audiences, although their value-free judgements on para-social interaction do not assume negative effects.

A second concept inextricably linked with para-social interaction is that of 'personae'. Personae are what Horton and Wohl call the personalities or performers that build up intimate, para-social relations with audiences via the media of radio and television. The important characteristic of personae is that they provide 'a continuing relationship' for audiences and that their 'character and pattern of action remain basically unchanged in a world of otherwise disturbing change' (Horton and Wohl 2004: 375). In this sense, para-social interactions with personae provide ordinary individuals with an escapist outlet away from the fears and uncertainties of a 'real world' subject to all the implications of modernity (see Chapter 3). Personae must work hard, though, in order to receive the affection and affiliation of a nation: 'Every attempt possible is made to strengthen the illusion of reciprocity and rapport in order to offset the inherent impersonality of the media themselves' (Horton and Wohl 2004: 378). Expert performances of self-presentation are the stimulus for para-social intimacy – not media technologies, as Meyrowitz and medium theorists might argue. Personae deploy various tricks and techniques, such as mingling with studio audiences, expressing feelings from 'the heart' in close-up, and mixing sincerity with comedy, so as to invite para-social relations with individuals whom they cannot see or hear. According to Horton and Wohl, these invitations are usually granted by individuals, particularly those who feel lonely or unloved due to unfortunate personal circumstances. It could be argued that this is hardly a convincing conception of the fallibility of media audiences. Moreover, Horton and Wohl's article can be criticized for making a crude distinction between social (i.e. real) and para-social (less real) interactions (Handleman 2003). As we shall encounter in Chapter 8, postmodern theory would reject such a distinction because media create new senses of reality that are divorced from traditional ones associated with face-to-face interaction. Having said this, Horton and Wohl's ideas have had a weighty bearing on later theories of celebrity and mediated interaction, including the work we will discuss next.

Thompson: mediated quasi-interaction

Influenced by Horton and Wohl's concept of para-social interaction, a more sophisticated interactionist theory is John B. Thompson's notion of **mediated quasi-interaction**. Thompson's earlier work (see Thompson 1990) engages with theories of ideology that are closer aligned to structuralism (see Chapter 4) than interactionism, but subsequently he has argued that 'the notion of ideology still has a useful role to play in the analysis of the media, but only in so far as it is linked more closely to the conditions of reception of media products' (Thompson 1994: 28). Like Meyrowitz, Thompson is influenced by the ideas of McLuhan as well as Goffman, but it is fair to say that Thompson's perspective runs closer to that of Goffman. Rather than consider media technologies as either a threat to social values and traditions, or a revolutionary means of changing sensory experience, Thompson argues that they help to maintain and renew our sense of identity, tradition and belonging (see Thompson 1996). Far from transmitting dominant ideologies from the ruling groups to the masses, he suggests that 'media products, which have been disconnected from their contexts of production, are re-embedded in particular locales and adapted to the material and cultural conditions of reception' (Thompson 1994: 44). Audience interactions with media, therefore, are not passive or 'para-social' but are better understood as a constitutive feature of everyday life that carry opportunities and threats for both audiences and producers. Interactions with media should also be understood in relation to other types of social interaction such as face-to-face conversations because 'people undertake mediated interactions together as a form of social interaction' (Scollon 1998: 29). This is especially important given that we are often engaged in both mediated and face-to-face interactions at the same time when, say, we listen to music or watch television while chatting to friends, having a meal with them, or even making love to them.

Our everyday encounters with media, especially television, are what Thompson calls 'mediated quasi-interaction'. This form of interaction can be distinguished from two other forms which are dialogical in character: face-to-face interaction, on the one hand; and, on the other, mediated interaction such as a telephone conversation or email correspondence. The term 'quasi-interaction' is used because although there is a process of interaction between media producers and audiences, mediated quasi-interaction 'does not have the degree of reciprocity and interpersonal specificity of other forms of interaction, whether mediated or face-to-face' (Thompson 1995a: 84). Interacting via email or in face-to-face conversations allows us to change or modify each other's thoughts, feelings and actions, but interactions between, say, television presenters and viewers do not allow for instantaneous exchanges of opinion. Interactive media technologies have improved the speed and effectiveness through which audiences can feed back their opinions to media producers, but even the most advanced technological developments cannot alter the basic one-way, monological flow of interaction that characterizes television as a medium. Mediated quasi-interaction is applied by Thompson to Goffman's self-presentation theory. While face-to-face and mediated forms of interaction require participants to present front region and conceal back region behaviour in equal measure, mediated quasi-interaction demands greater shows of self-presentation on the part of producers than audiences. Producers present 'fronts' – such as pristine newsrooms and polished acting – that are usually maintained effectively, but on occasions we witness elements of back region behaviour, such as gaffes and technical faults, which break the illusion of smoothness and professionalism. On the other hand, media audiences are invisible and inaudible to producers and performers. So back region behaviour is never an issue for individuals in mediated quasi-interaction with distant others.

Although audiences do not need to manage self-presentations in the same way as producers at the point of reception, they play an important interactive role in the wider dissemination of media messages after their reception. For example, a music video might be seen by a relatively small proportion of the people who eventually find out about it through word-of-mouth. This process in which individuals describe, praise and criticize what they receive through media in subsequent face-to-face or mediated interactions is what Thompson calls 'discursive elaboration' (Thompson 1995a: 110). Audiences can also react to media messages with concerted forms of responsive action. Such forms can be concerted but uncoordinated – such as a news story about the healthy effects of aspirin causing rapid sales increases – but they can also be coordinated and collectively participated in, as we have witnessed in recent times when disturbing images of the Iraq war stir people to march through Western cities in protest at American and British foreign policies. As Thompson notes:

> the media are actively involved in constituting the social world. By making images and information available to individuals located in distant locales, the media shape and influence the course of events and, indeed, create events that would not have existed in their absence.
>
> (Thompson 1995a: 117)

Mediated quasi-interaction has the effect of bringing global events and issues close to home. The process by which television and other global media technologies are interpreted by audiences in their local contexts of reception is referred to as 'space–time interpolation' (Thompson 1995a: 93). Audiences become space–time travellers, astutely incorporating spatially and temporally distant actions into their everyday interactions with others. For example, our mediated experiences of horrific murders on television or the internet can be shocking and disturbing if we are not familiar with such experiences ourselves, but they can become re-embedded into local experiences as topics of conversation that might lead to a change of opinion or action on our behalf.

Audiences are only one half of the mediated quasi-interaction equation, however. 'Action at a distance' (Thompson 1995a: 100) is perhaps a more pressing matter for those caught in the glare of media exposure than for their audiences. As mentioned earlier, media performers and producers are at a disadvantage because they have to manage their front and back region behaviour to a much greater degree. Thompson refers to four types of acting for distant others: recipient address, mediated everyday activity, media events (see also Dayan and Katz 1992), and fictionalized action. The latter two are carefully rehearsed forms of action at a distance which tend to separate front from back region behaviour and therefore limit the scope for mistakes, although even rehearsed and recorded material can backfire on occasions. The other two forms are more open-ended. First, recipient address – for example, when live newsreaders address the audience directly or, if interviewing someone, indirectly – is a common type of action for performers, but it provides ample scope for back to interfere with front region behaviour. The speech faults identified by Goffman earlier in this chapter can break the illusion of polished, professional action sought by producers in the mediated quasi-interaction mix. Politicians being interviewed by news presenters on television must be careful not to 'lose their cool' if questioned persistently about an issue which they wish to avoid discussing, but at the same time they must be 'on guard' not to express opinions that contradict the 'party line' – they must be effective team members in the Goffmanian sense. The risks associated with mediated quasi-interactions that address mass audiences require performers to undergo extensive media and public relations training. Politicians use spin doctors to advise them on which sound-bites to use – and which to avoid – before they expose themselves to the potential pitfalls of, say, a television debate.

Second, and perhaps more prone to backstage discrepancies, is mediated everyday activity. Here, 'the very possibility of being filmed and made visible to television viewers may transform the ways in which individuals act and interact in the contexts of daily life' (Thompson 1995a: 105). Mediated everyday activity can include Foucauldian situations in which 'actors' are unaware – as well as aware – that they are being filmed but nevertheless act in a certain way in case they *might be* being filmed, such as soldiers on the battlefield. It can also include situations that are deliberately constructed for media purposes, in which a politician, for example, shakes hands with a political correspondent before being interviewed. These situations may appear relatively 'safe' for actors, but mistakes can and do occur. For example, in 1993, the British Prime Minister, John Major, referred to some of his Conservative colleagues as 'bastards' in private conversation with ITN political editor, Michael Brunson, unaware that his comments had been recorded on a stray microphone while they waited to enter a television studio for an interview (see Thompson 2000: 66, 278). His comments became headline news and added to a series of setbacks – including stories of political sleaze and scandal uncovered by investigative journalism – that plagued the Major Government during its term in office. Backstage discrepancies in mediated everyday activity have more serious implications than unmediated kinds too, precisely because 'a message fixed in some medium – an intimate letter, a recorded conversation, a revealing photo, etc. – may provide an incriminating form of evidence' (Thompson 2000: 69). For example, secret email systems are commonplace in highly-sensitive centres of public interest such as government offices. In acting for distant others, then, Thompson shows how media encourage those who produce and perform for a distant public to be accountable for their words and actions. Media audiences, in turn, act upon what they see and hear in mediated quasi-interactions for mostly democratic, positive ends.

Labelling theory and moral panics

Along with an interactionist tradition of media theory that tends to focus on everyday social interactions or rituals, there is a similar tradition of interactionism that takes its theoretical ideas from the study of deviance or what some might call 'criminal activity'. Howard S. Becker's *Outsiders* (first published in 1963) considers deviance to be a social construction used by certain groups in order to exclude and criminalize others:

> *social groups create deviance by making the rules whose infraction constitutes deviance* ... From this point of view, deviance is *not* a quality of the act the person commits, but rather a consequence of the application by others of rules and sanctions to an 'offender'. The deviant is one to whom that label has successfully been applied; deviant behaviour is behaviour that people so label.
>
> (Becker 1991: 9)

Similar in some ways to Foucault's theory of discourse, this approach is nonetheless fundamentally different because discourse in Becker's sense is socially created – not dispersed and manifested in society via powerful institutions of the state. So an act of deviance, such as a child using an expletive, is only labelled deviant if others in that social context of interaction (i.e. adults) classify it as 'not normal' behaviour, in which case *they* create the label. On the other hand, one adult using an expletive among other adults might be construed as perfectly normal behaviour and not worthy of a deviant label. Becker applied his ideas about deviance, known as **labelling theory**, to various deviant groups such as marijuana users and jazz musicians. The jazz musicians he studied, for instance, rejected the various labels – some derogatory, some complimentary – which non-musicians gave to them and distanced themselves from commercial forms of jazz that could be heard on record or the radio. Indeed, these musicians acknowledged the deviance associated with them by applying labels of their own to others. As one musician says, 'outside of show people and professional people, everybody's a fucking square. They don't know anything' (Becker 1951: 140). Deviance becomes a vicious circle – once labels are attached to a deviant group, the deviance is accentuated by group reactions that in turn label the 'labellers', which provokes further social condemnation of the group.

Becker's labelling theory helps us to understand broader types of interaction between mainstream and deviant cultures but, in its original formulation, it had little to say about the social role of media in labelling processes. Nonetheless, it is not difficult to find examples of how media partake in the social creation of labels that classify certain individuals or groups as deviant, such as asylum seekers and single-parent families. One of the most significant attempts to adapt the interactionist framework of labelling theory to media practices is Stan Cohen's *Folk Devils and Moral Panics* (first published in 1972). The concept of a **moral panic** is defined as a situation wherein

> A condition, episode, person or group of persons emerges to become defined as a threat to societal values and interests; its nature is presented in a stylized and stereotypical fashion by the mass media; the moral barricades are manned by editors, bishops, politicians and other right-thinking people.
>
> (Cohen 2002: 1)

We sometimes hear the phrase 'moral crusade' used when, for instance, a newspaper begins a campaign against some 'social ill' like drugs or soccer hooliganism. Media crusades amounting to misrepresentation of drug and hooligan cultures have been critically analysed by Young (1971a; 1971b; 1973) and Hall (1978) among others. Moral panics have been provoked in particular by youth cultures and subcultures of the kind that Hebdige semiotically analysed (see Chapter 4). In contrast to Hebdige's structuralist approach, however, Cohen suggests that subcultures are not primarily deviant because of their political resistance to the social system, but because societal – including media – reaction has labelled them as 'folk devils': 'visible reminders of what we should not be' (Cohen 2002: 2). Folk devils are the personifications of moral panics, labelled as villains by 'right-thinking people' as well as the police and legal system, but hailed as martyrs by fellow outsiders.

Cohen applies his theory of moral panics to the mods and rockers – two opposing groups of working-class youth who came into conflict with each other at English seaside resorts in the mid-1960s. Cohen argues that media did not merely *report*, in an objective way, the crowd disturbances that occurred between the two groups, but actually helped to *construct* social reaction to the 'deviance' of the mods and rockers by sensationalizing the level of violence and disruption that occurred on the beaches and promenades of Brighton and other seaside towns. Tabloid newspapers in particular used dramatic phrases such as 'orgy of destruction' and 'screaming mob' (Cohen 2002: 20). These mediated messages, in close interaction with public opinion, contributed to increased concern about the threat posed by the mods and rockers to societal rules and norms. This process is known as 'deviance amplification' (Figure 5.1).

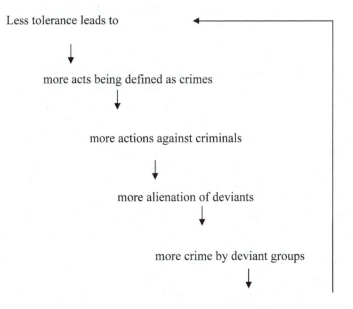

Figure 5.1 Deviancy amplification model

Source: See Wilkins (1964: 90)

As we can see in Figure 5.1, the defining and labelling of deviance have a spiralling effect in alienating and criminalizing those deviants or folk devils.

In the case of the mods and rockers, media had a fundamental impact on their deviance amplification. Stereotypical phrases associated with these youth cultures – 'thugs', 'hooligans', 'menaces' – were freely highlighted in bold news headlines to reinforce pre-existing perceptions and beliefs held by 'normal' (i.e. white, middle-aged, middle-class) folk. The manufacture of news stories as a means of constructing and amplifying definitions of deviance from conformity is discussed by Cohen and others elsewhere (Cohen and Young 1973; see also Schlesinger 1978).

Deviance amplification via mass media may increase societal concern and trigger widespread moral panic (see Figure 5.2), but – as with Becker's jazz musicians – it also bestows credibility and helps to recruit members to the groups being labelled as deviant. When the line between insiders and outsiders is clearly drawn, there are always similarly disaffected individuals who wish to identify with what the wider society would call 'outsiders' but what they identify as 'insiders'. Likewise if tabloid newspapers label you as a 'thug', you might not like it but you're also likely to gain rather a following among 'would-be-you' devotees. Cohen (2002: 135–9) shows how media effectively provided pre-publicity for the mods and rockers – individuals scattered the length and breadth of Britain could pick up the *Daily Mirror* to learn when and where to meet up for a confrontation. Moreover, the presence of cameras and photographers provided a metaphorical public platform for mods and rockers to engage in role-playing behaviour. Pleasantly surprised by the amount of media attention being given to them, the mods and rockers would 'play up' their image of rebelliousness, and therefore effectively play the stereotypical roles created for them by mass media – as well as other 'right-thinking' elements of mainstream culture. Media also contributed to an accentuation in the differences between the two youth subcultures. Cohen notes that 'the antagonism between the two groups was not initially very marked' (2002: 139), partly explained by the fact that the mods and rockers lived in the same working-class neighbourhoods, but subsequent media representations that juxtaposed aspects of the mod subculture (scooters, the smart-casual image, the Beatles and Kinks motifs) with those of the rocker subculture (motorbikes, the Hell's Angel image, the Rolling Stones and Elvis motifs) cut deeper into differences and indirectly helped to stir up conflict.

Although moral panic theory was initially applied to deviant youth cultural activities of various kinds, it has since been applied to societal and media reaction to AIDS (Watney 1997), 'video nasties' (Petley 1997), and paedophilia (Critcher 2003) – topical issues that emphasize how deviance is by no means exclusively a 'youth' problem. The theory has undergone criticism and revision, however. One criticism we might cite is a tendency to overemphasize the power of media in determining how people – including 'right-thinking' politicians and policy-makers – react to particular issues and events. There is no straightforward connection between media and public opinion.

Journalists tend to justify their journalism in the way it mirrors 'the public interest' but sometimes sensationalist stories can appear absurd and unprofessional, evidenced by a drop in a newspaper's circulation figures, for instance. Thornton (1995) has also questioned whether moral panics necessarily result in deviance amplification and criminalization, given that more recent youth cultures – particularly rave and dance cultures – have actively sought to spread panic as a means of publicizing their hedonistic values and presenting their side of the argument on the health consequences of ecstasy use. It seems that moral panics in practice are more complex and not always driven by tabloid journalists and other moral crusaders, but this in turn makes Cohen's theory of moral panics all the more intriguing to develop and refine.

Figure 5.2 Newspaper front page

Giddens: structuration theory

Most of the theories of interactionism discussed so far in this chapter have dealt with questions of action and agency above those of structure and institutional power. Goffman, we can see, is interested in micro-social forms of action and behaviour rather than the macro-structural forces (governments, capitalist economics, legal institutions) that arguably shape these micro-social contexts of action. Meyrowitz's theory of placelessness is determined by the social consequences of media technologies but says little about the economic and political motives that may underpin technological developments (see discussion of Williams in Chapter 3). Thompson's notion of mediated quasi-interaction is institutionally structured, of course, but what matters most is how, *in practice*, such interaction empowers audiences by always having the potential to reveal backstage discrepancies in the rich and powerful (politicians, celebrities) who perform through media. Labelling theory and the concept of moral panic are socially created by me and you as well as media and other institutions – in comparison, ideological and discursive power structures are redundant. Interactionism is, to some extent, the antithesis of Marxist structuralism.

It is important to end this chapter, however, by discussing Anthony Giddens's theory of structuration that seeks to reconcile the differences between interactionism and structuralism. Here Giddens refers to the duality of structure and structured forms of action – hence the hybrid term 'structuration'. Like Bourdieu (see Chapter 9), Giddens aims to accommodate what have traditionally been interpreted as polar opposites – institutional structures and individual agency – into a combined model of social theory. He argues that everyday actions, such as shopping or going to school, both produce and reproduce social structures: 'we have to try to see how [individual] practices followed in a given range of contexts are embedded in wider reaches of time and space – in brief, we have to attempt to discover their relation to institutionalized practices' (Giddens 1984: 298). Central to Giddens's theory of structuration is the notion of 'time–space distanciation'. He argues that structural changes in power that arose through several facets of globalization – monetary exchange, technological developments and widespread political democracy – have led to a corresponding change in our sense of time and space. In pre-modern societies space and time were unified in the sense that people tended to interact in proximity with others, but one major consequence of modernity is our capacity to live and work across spatial and temporal dimensions that are separated from one another. This is not dissimilar to Thompson's and Meyrowitz's social theories of the media, nor should this come as a surprise because Giddens has influenced and been influenced by their work.

Where Giddens differs from more explicitly *media* theorists of interaction, however, is in his view that everyday actions are structurally constrained by actors themselves. Media technologies are implicated in this argument too. In contributing to the stretching of time–space, mediated experiences enable the 'intrusion of distant events into everyday consciousness' (Giddens 1991: 27) that can lead to feelings of insecurity and 'reality inversion', in which media representations of news events such as a military coup in Thailand (as happened in September 2006) can appear more 'real' than the actual events themselves. For Giddens, mediated experiences serve as 'external conditions of action' (Giddens 1991: 175) that make us reflect upon and rethink our own self-narratives in relation to others – including people we will never meet or know personally. Time–space distanciation also impacts on our sense of trust. Trust in pre-modern societies was easily established through face-to-face interactions, but in late modern societies there has evolved a process of dis-embedding or 'the "lifting out" of social relations from local contexts of interaction and their restructuring across indefinite spans of time-space' (Giddens 1990: 21). We tend to place a great deal of trust in what Giddens calls 'abstract systems' – such as food safety inspectorates, health services, transport networks, as well as media organizations – that purport to offer professional expertise but do not openly reveal how this expertise is proven and practised (Giddens 1990). In our everyday interactions with these abstract systems, and by placing trust in them, we are reproducing the institutional structures that legitimate these abstract systems. As Giddens notes, 'everyone in modern systems is a lay person in virtually all aspects of social activity' (1991: 195). However, late modernity – despite its ostensible orderliness, sophistication and 'nanny-state' protectiveness – continues to be characterized by a lack of trust in others, personal insecurity, the management of risk and a turning-in to the self – what Giddens means by 'self-identity'.

Self-identity is similar in some ways to Goffman's theory of self-presentation. However, Giddens applies the concept to everyday practices that only partly express individual agency but at the same time express the *structuration* of individual agency: 'The reflexive project of the self, which consists in the sustaining of coherent, yet continuously revised, biographical narratives, takes place in the context of multiple choice as filtered through abstract systems' (Giddens 1991: 5). The reflexivity of individuals – 'not what we are, but what we make of ourselves' (Giddens 1991: 75) – offers at least potential for agency through displays of creativity, productivity and positive self-evaluation. Modern-day individuals exhibit reflexive and flexible bodies that are adept in, for example, communicating to others via laptop and mobile phone simultaneously while travelling faster than the speed of sound on a jumbo jet. And yet the reflexive project of the self serves to reproduce – rather than produce new – existing social structures that tend to constrain individuals. Actions are pre-determined by what has gone before and, once practised, effectively set the parameters for actions that ensue. Narcissism is a symptomatic trait of self-identity in the phase of modernity. Consumer capitalism perpetuates the flawed project of self-love which encourages individualism and discourages 'giving to others' (Giddens 1991: 173). Media celebrities provide role models for our own physical appearance. Some of us invest vast amounts of money on cosmetic products and surgery in order to love ourselves even more, and in order to be loved by others. We should trust our 'natural' appearances but abstract systems such as women's magazines and makeover television programmes lead us to self-doubt and anxiety. The narcissistic personality that features in so many people's self-identities is surely testimony to the power not of structure or agency but of structuration, as we constantly re-produce our individualistic roles in society rather than collectively working to change them.

Summary

This chapter has considered:

- What interactionism and theories of social interaction mean in relation to media.
- Goffman's self-presentation theory, his concepts of 'front' and 'back' in relation to how individuals and teams manage their media performances, and his argument that conventionalized media interactions reconstruct and accentuate existing social interaction rituals.
- Meyrowitz's theory of placelessness which claims that media technologies provide access to information and knowledge for all, that mediated togetherness transcends physical separation, and that media help to demystify the private and public lives of media personalities.
- Concepts of personae and para-social interaction, and the 'illusion of intimacy' that they foster between media performers and audiences (Horton and Wohl).
- Thompson's theory of mediated quasi-interaction, and his concepts of 'discursive elaboration' and 'action at a distance' as they relate to processes of globalization and public accountability respectively.
- Labelling and moral panic theories that implicate media as important sources of societal reaction to the classification and amplification of certain groups' deviancy, and also consider how deviant groups label themselves in response.

- Giddens's theory of structuration which claims that everyday actions reproduce existing social structures, including those structures routinely enacted by media (e.g. consumer capitalism and its embodiment in practices of narcissism) that contribute to self-identity.

Further reading

Critcher, C. (2003) *Moral Panics and the Media*. Buckingham: Open University Press.

A useful introduction to different theories of moral panics and how media play a key role in provoking them. Case studies on AIDS, ecstasy and rave culture, video nasties, child abuse and paedophilia. Suitable for all media students.

Dayan, D. and Katz, E. (1992) *Media Events: The Live Broadcasting of History*. Cambridge, MA: Harvard University Press.

Despite its age, this is still an important ethnographic – and partly interactionist – contribution to how public events are scripted, performed, celebrated and shamanized by media. Includes discussion of the Olympic Games and the wedding of Prince Charles and Lady Diana among other 'media events'. Suitable for all media students.

Moores, S. (2005) *Media/Theory: Thinking about Media and Communications*. Abingdon: Routledge.

A comprehensive discussion of media interactionist and structuration perspectives among others. The chapters on cyclicity, interaction and identity are particularly useful. Recommended for advanced undergraduates and postgraduates.

Scannell, P. (1996) *Radio, Television and Everyday Life: A Phenomenological Approach*. Oxford: Blackwell.

Broadcasting media are analysed in terms of their 'sociable' dimension to address the daily thoughts and feelings of audiences. Chapters included on intentionality, identity and eventfulness. Recommended for advanced undergraduates and postgraduates.

6 Feminisms and gender

Introduction

This chapter will discuss a range of work in feminist media theory, which can be distinguished from other theories of media given 'Its unconditional focus on analysing *gender* as a mechanism that structures material and symbolic worlds and our experiences of them' (van Zoonen 1991: 33). I have used the plural term, **feminisms**, in the chapter heading because the different theoretical perspectives we will encounter would be misleadingly huddled together under an umbrella term like 'feminism'. A typical inventory of perspectives – several of which we shall discuss in relation to media theory – would include 'liberal feminism, socialist feminism, radical or revolutionary feminism, lesbian feminism, black feminism, postmodern feminism, first-, second- or third-wave feminisms to name just a few' (Boyle 2005: 29). Even the history of feminism is now so long and complex that it is generally divided into three 'waves'. First-wave feminism refers to the early feminists, including the Suffrage Movement that fought to secure the vote for women. Then in the 1960s came second-wave feminism, including the Women's Liberation Movement that campaigned for equal rights on issues such as employment, marital relationships and sexual orientation. Second-wave feminism, though, is often regarded as less about raw power and more about the power of representation: 'women recognised the need to challenge the dominant ideological definitions of femininity' (Whelehan 1995: 5). What it means 'to be a woman' becomes the central issue.

Perhaps the pioneering voice of the **second wave** was Betty Friedan. In *The Feminine Mystique* (first published in 1963) she writes about a 15-year period after the Second World War in the United States (circa 1945–60) when the 'suburban housewife' became the feminine ideal upon which American women were expected to build their lives. This 'happy housewife heroine' was a myth perpetuated by media and socially accepted to be the 'image of a good woman' (Friedan 1992: 30). From a young age, women were expected to sacrifice their career, independence, skills and qualifications for the benefit of their 'nuclear family'. Friedan's account helped to stir a feminist revolt against this feminine mystique that raged throughout the 1960s and 1970s, and is still engaged in today. But second-wave feminism has been challenged since the 1990s by **postfeminism** and the **third wave**. Postfeminism and third-wave feminism are not synonymous perspectives – as discussed later in the chapter – but they both reject the rigid gender politics of the second wave, and instead see gender identities as less fixed and personally empowering. These new perspectives followed in the wake of Judith Butler's (1990; 1999) seminal work on gender performativity. As we shall discuss, Butler explores the concept of 'gender' not – in the way it appears – as a natural or biological phenomenon, but as a performance that is socially and culturally constituted. This reminds us of a basic distinction between sex and gender: **sex** is an outcome of nature (we are born male or female); **gender**, on the other hand, is an outcome of culture and society (we grow up in accordance with masculine or feminine norms). In this sense, mass media play an important role in representing gender and the feminist pursuit of gender equality – a role that they have often played badly.

Radical feminism

Second-wave feminism, as we will see in this chapter, accommodates a diverse range of feminist perspectives, each with their own peculiar slant on the problems of **patriarchy**, but all sharing the same anti-patriarchal values and the same goal of equality between the sexes. The most militant form of second-wave feminism is often referred to as 'radical feminism' – a body of theory particularly associated in a media theory context with anti-pornography campaigns and concerns about the 'effects' of sex-role stereotyping. Andrea Dworkin's well-known attack on pornography along with polemic statements such as 'Men are rapists, batterers, plunderers, killers' (Dworkin 1981: 48) position her within radical feminism. Along with feminist lawyer Catherine MacKinnon, Dworkin actively campaigned against the pornography industry by claiming that it violated the civil rights of women. Dworkin argued that pornographic representations of women socialized men into acts of rape and sexual violence in their real lives. Pornography perpetuates the masculine-inflected ideology that women are prostitutes subject to men's sexual domination. Pornography and prostitution are synonymous for Dworkin, who claims that 'The pleasure of the male requires the annihilation of women's sexual integrity' (Dworkin 1981: 47). A graphic illustration of male pleasure in pornography is the close-up focus on a woman's bodily parts, which affords a malign sexual power to the voyeur, and disregards the whole character (i.e. body) of the woman herself. These degrading images of women are underpinned by the ideological implication that 'physical possession of the female is the natural right of the male' (Dworkin 1981: 203). Dworkin's and MacKinnon's ideas continue to fuel debate in contemporary feminist scholarship a decade or two after their conception (see Cornell 2000).

　　Dworkin and MacKinnon tried – but ultimately failed – to amend the United States Constitution on freedom of speech in order to introduce censorship on pornographic materials. Their anti-pornography campaign has also been rejected by other second-wave feminists, as well as third-wave feminists and postfeminists (discussed later in this chapter). Liesbet van Zoonen, for instance, questions 'why pornography should be treated as a separate phenomenon, given a wider cultural tradition of representing women as objects of the male gaze' (van Zoonen 1994: 21). A clear theoretical weakness of Dworkin's argument is that it adopts a hypodermic needle model of media effects in assuming that pornography will, in some way, cause male sexual violence against women. Also prone to a behaviourist fallacy is the radical perspective of Gaye Tuchman, who argues that women are 'symbolically annihilated' by television's portrayal of unhealthy sex-role stereotyping and female under-representation. Tuchman argues that mass media such as television act as 'agents of socialization' (Tuchman 1978: 37) in encouraging female viewers to think about marriage ahead of their careers. Echoes of a naïve behaviourism can be heard in her claim that 'Mass-media stereotypes of women as housewives may impede the employment of women by limiting their horizons' (Tuchman 1978: 7). It is one thing to argue that mass media foster traditional sex-role stereotypes, but it is a much less convincing argument which claims that these stereotypes may affect the long-term attitudes and life-courses of women who witness them.

Unfortunately, radical feminism – the least supported perspective among feminists – is the inspiration behind the 'feminist stereotype' that mass media most often foster (van Zoonen 1994). Feminists are often represented by journalists and other 'right-thinking' spokespeople as deviants (see discussion of labelling theory and moral panics in Chapter 5). Feminists are 'lesbians', 'dykes', 'man-eaters', 'man-haters', 'loners', 'extremists', 'physically revolting' – the list goes on. It goes without saying that these media representations of feminism are false and stirred up by the traditional moralist view that feminists are a threat to social order, family life and human reproduction. Moreover, few women celebrities are outspoken feminists. Germaine Greer is an exception to this rule, but her appearance on the British reality TV show *Celebrity Big Brother* (2001–) contributed little to the contemporary feminist cause. Declaring feminist values is considered a dangerous career move, perhaps even more so today than in the 1970s when feminism was at least represented as both a threat to patriarchal order *and* a fashionable, worthwhile pursuit.

Mulvey: the male gaze

Laura Mulvey's article entitled 'Visual pleasure and narrative cinema' (first published in 1975) marks a shift away from radical and behaviourist models of feminism. Rather than seek to identify 'effects', Mulvey draws on Freudian psychoanalysis and structuralism to argue that mainstream Hollywood narrative films represent women characters as passive objects of male sexual desire. Mulvey's theory of the **male gaze** claims that male characters are 'bearers of the look' which is aimed – far more often than not – at physically desirable, sexually submissive female characters. Moreover, we the spectators watch cinematic films through the eyes of the dominant male protagonists and are implicitly addressed as though we were men desiring heterosexual pleasures, even if we are – in fact – heterosexual women or homosexuals. To understand this theory of the male gaze, we need to understand two features of the cinematic experience that Mulvey borrows from psychoanalysis, a theoretical tradition that originates in the work of Sigmund Freud who argued that the body and the mind become inextricably linked in the early years of human life and are not – as assumed by Christianity and other, older traditions of thought – separate entities.

First is the notion of scopophilia which means 'pleasure in looking'. Freudian theory suggests that pleasure in looking is a human instinct that develops in the early years of a person's existence when they begin to experience control over their sight and can fix it on various objects, such as toys. Mulvey argues that narrative cinema conventions and contexts of screening (i.e. in darkened auditoriums) foster a sense of 'voyeuristic fantasy' (Mulvey 1989: 17) in the spectator, not unlike the infantile variety. Hollywood cinema is, above all, a provider of visual pleasure, not intellectual stimulation or painful visual representation. However, scopophilic desires accommodate male rather than female voyeurs. While women in Hollywood films connote 'to-be-looked-at-ness', men are doing the looking: 'The determining male gaze projects its fantasy onto the female figure' (Mulvey 1989: 19). Female spectators are excluded from this male-oriented perspective on visual pleasure. Moreover, this visual pleasure is a heterosexual male pleasure that is both narrow-minded and divisive because it constructs a voyeuristic position for the (assumed) male spectator akin to 'playing the Peeping Tom'. The type of visual pleasure constructed by mainstream narrative cinema is therefore gendered and sexist.

This leads to the second feature of narrative cinema that Mulvey explores, which is the notion of identification derived from Jacques Lacan's psychoanalytic theory of the mirror stage (first published in 1966). According to Lacan, when an infant first sees their image in a mirror they consider this image to be more superior – an 'Ideal-I' – than themselves. They do not, at first, identify this image with themselves. Instead, because of their 'motor incapacity and nursling dependence' (Lacan 1993: 34), they view their mirror image as more independent and 'complete' as a human being, and therefore they identify with – and worship – this image as a version of 'self' which they should strive to achieve. Mulvey applies Lacan's ideas to cinema spectatorship. The cinema screen, she suggests, functions in a similar way for spectators as the mirror functions for infants. Spectators are encouraged to identify themselves with on-screen characters – some of whom may already be 'icons'

– and imagine these characters as superior reflections of themselves. Characters in Hollywood films can therefore become 'ego ideals' or 'screen surrogates' (Mulvey 1989: 18, 20) through which we the spectators can live out our fantasies. However, the male protagonists who do the looking become the 'main controlling figure with whom the spectator can identify' (Mulvey 1989: 20). Women spectators – as well as men – are bound to identify with this controlling, dominant male character. This is what Mulvey means by 'the "masculinization" of the spectator position' (Mulvey 1989: 29). Rarely if ever are female protagonists in films framed as bearers of the gaze for the pleasure of female spectators, although an exception would be Sigourney Weaver's strong female roles in films such as *Alien* (1979) and *Copycat* (1995). There are also female characters in films that threaten the male ones, such as the *femme fatales* of the film noir genre. These characters are subject to the male gaze in a different sense because – in Mulvey's Freudian thinking – their lack of a penis (given that they are women) coupled to the fact that they are not fetishized as sexual objects means that they signify for men the threat of castration. These dangerous female characters must therefore be killed or incarcerated in order to protect the phallic power of patriarchal identification.

Mulvey concludes that there are three ways of 'looking' associated with cinema:

1   the look of the camera that records the film;
2   the look of the audience that views the film;
3   the look of the characters in the film.

Narrative conventions of realist filmmaking, however, make the first two ways of looking invisible and instead foreground the third perspective, 'the conscious aim being always to eliminate intrusive camera presence and prevent a distancing awareness in the audience' (Mulvey 1989: 25). All we are consciously left with, therefore, is the look of the characters in the film, and in most Hollywood films the bearers of this look are the male characters, who are usually looking lustfully at the female ones. As a filmmaker herself, Mulvey has worked against the grain of mainstream narrative cinema by making films that self-consciously refer to their own constructiveness. In films such as *Riddles of the Sphinx* (1977), the camera not only *records* but intrudes into the action. A single camera shoots much of the action while slowing moving in a horizontal direction, contrary to the well-made Hollywood movie in which camera shots are edited and spliced together in such a way that they are unobtrusive to the action. While her filmmaking has only harboured modest critical acclaim, Mulvey's theory of the male gaze has been very influential to film and media theory *per se* – not just feminist media theory. A small library of research and theory has been inspired by it (see Kaplan 2000).

Nonetheless, a clear limitation of her theory is that it presumes audience responses rather than asking members of the audience for their own thoughts and feelings. As Annette Kuhn (2000: 442–7) points out, the theoretical analysis of spectatorship is quite different from the empirical analysis of socially situated audiences, and Mulvey's theory of the male gaze can easily be interpreted in such a way that female spectator = passive audience member; male spectator = active audience member. It is surely not the case that female audiences can only gain pleasure in a majority of films by passively subjecting themselves to the male gaze. Of course, Mulvey as a psychoanalyst and structuralist might counter that audience research is doomed to fail because visual pleasure is constructed by unconscious psychological processes and structured by invisible ideologies of patriarchy. Female cinema spectators are therefore repressed without knowing it. For some feminists though, the male gaze is not necessarily omniscient and unavoidable. Mary Ann Doane's (2000) resistant strategy of 'the masquerade' – the notion that a 'flaunting femininity', donning a mask and flamboyant dress, is able to distance itself from the patriarchal ideology of conventional femininity that caters for the male gaze – is an important reworking of Mulvey's theory.

Modleski and Radway: mass-produced fantasies for women

Two feminist theorists influenced by Mulvey's argument that cinema spectators gain pleasure in identification with screen fantasies are Tania Modleski and Janice Radway. Both authors emphasize the importance of women's fantasies – particularly romantic novels and soap operas – as means of temporary escape from the harsh realities of everyday life. First, Modleski argues that soap operas are mass-produced fantasies used by women as a way of fulfilling desires, in an imaginary sense, that are unobtainable in the real world in which they are oppressed. However, this does not mean that soap operas are necessarily pro-women. Rather, they predominantly represent two types of female characters: either the ideal woman/mother or the villainess. These opposite types are deliberately juxtaposed in such a way as to constitute soap opera viewers (mostly women) as good mothers by assuming that they – like the camera – view the villainess as an evil 'other'. As the author states, 'there is one character whom we are allowed to hate unreservedly: the villainess, the negative image of the spectator's ideal self' (Modleski 1990: 94). Modleski laments this state of affairs because the villainess is usually the nearest soap operas come to a feminist figurehead. Of course, this 'villainess–ideal mother' dichotomy functions within moral parameters that are defined by patriarchy. The villainess is evil because she is bad to men; the ideal mother is ideal because she is good to men. Soap operas therefore 'train women to become, like women in the home, "ideal readers" – not of texts but of people' (Modleski 1990: 34). So women can, and do, learn about men and relationships, but the ways in which soap operas represent women and men mean that their educative function serves the interests of a patriarchal society. For instance, while the evil villainess is universally hated, the evil (male) villain is often constructed as a dark but alluring sex object who may be equally cursed and blessed by female viewers.

Modleski's analysis of soap operas is supported by similar work. Christine Geraghty (1991), for example, argues that soap operas do explore 'women's issues' but only within patriarchal norms of the domestic, personal and familial. However, Modleski's and Geraghty's analysis of soap operas (like Mulvey's theory of the male gaze) is textual rather than contextual, with no audience research to prove whether or not these media texts train women to become ideal readers. As a result, 'Modleski's model of the rhythms of reception tends to leave no space for an active female subject who might wish to oppose [two] flows' (Gray 1992: 78) – the repetitious flow of daytime television programmes aimed at women audiences as well as the mundane flow of their daily domestic chores. Ann Gray's ethnographic research into how women use VCR technology to 'time-shift', by recording programmes and watching them during their spare time, is a rejoinder to assumptions about a captivated day-time audience of bored housewives. Women are likely to be 'distracted viewers' who are also able to 'distance themselves from texts' and adopt a 'position of control' (Gray 1992: 125, 162), although the better-educated women interviewed by Gray were able to maintain a greater critical distance from television shows than the lesser-educated women. Media theory informed by research into consumption practices has a clear advantage over Modleski's textual analysis given that it can distinguish between different kinds of women audiences (e.g. in terms of education or socio-economic background) rather than merely an assumed audience of undifferentiated women.

Second, Radway's *Reading the Romance* (1984) does incorporate audience research into its analysis of the practice of 'escape reading'. Women read romantic novels and watch romantic films for pleasure in order 'to diversify the pace and character of their habitual existence' (Radway 1984: 89). Bound to a mundane life of domesticity and in need of more affection and independence, the women readers interviewed by Radway 'escape figuratively into a fairy tale where a heroine's similar needs are adequately met' (Radway 1984: 93). To some extent escape reading is an empowering practice which makes women happy and 'holds out the promise of utopian bliss' (Radway 1984: 100). On the other hand, escape reading amounts to a forlorn hope, perpetuated by patriarchy, that the perfect heterosexual relationship is possible and desirable. According to Radway, women readers of romantic novels seek out utopian bliss in fantasies precisely because it is unobtainable in reality. Escaping into fiction is therefore a reactionary rebuttal of patriarchal power rather than a revolutionary one – escape reading does nothing to change 'real' male domination over women. This distinction between reality and fantasy upheld by Radway – as well as Modleski – has been questioned by postmodern feminists such as Ien Ang (discussed later in this chapter). Ang argues that real pleasures can be fulfilled by women reading romances. Feminists should 'take fantasy seriously as a reality in itself' (Ang 1996: 106) and this is evident in the way modern-day women suspend post-marriage blues by perpetuating pre-marriage freedom to search out romance without commitment. *Sex and the City* (1998–2004) is a television serial symptomatic of the never-ending pur-suit of a feminine – perhaps even feminist – utopia (see Akass and McCabe 2004).

McRobbie: the ideology of teenage femininity

The patriarchal ideologies pervading film and media charted by Mulvey, Modleski and Radway are further examined in Angela McRobbie's analysis of teenage girls' magazines and pop music. McRobbie combines theories of structuralism and feminism – sometimes referred to as 'structural feminism'. Perhaps her best-known work (first published in 1977) is a semiotic analysis of *Jackie*, a magazine popular among adolescent British girls in the 1960s and 1970s (see Figure 6.1). According to McRobbie, *Jackie* constructs a conservative ideology of **femininity** for girls aged 10–14 'predicated upon their future roles as wives and mothers' (McRobbie 2000: 78). McRobbie's theoretical perspective is closely associated with Stuart Hall's (1980) Encoding/Decoding model (see Chapter 4) and associative work at the CCCS where she undertook the *Jackie* study. Another feminist associated with the CCCS, Dorothy Hobson, similarly identifies an ideology of femininity on daytime radio shows that cater for housewives and 'reinforce the sexual division of spheres of interest' (Hobson 1980: 114). Hobson argues that housewives are literally 'put in their place' by light-entertainment radio programming – starkly different to the 'hard' pro-gramming (financial news and documentaries) that constructs the ideology of masculinity. Likewise, McRobbie claims that *Jackie* restricts the capacity of its female readers to act against a patriarchal social order and instead promotes – both implicitly and explicitly – values of gentility and domesticity. It does this by presenting consistent images of home-loving women and implying that these representations constitute the 'natural' progression from girlhood to motherhood. The world outside the home, by contrast, is represented in modernity-like fashion as a 'cloyingly claustrophobic environment where the dominant emotions are fear, insecurity, competitiveness and even panic' (McRobbie 2000: 70). *Jackie* constructs its conformist ideology of femininity through four ideological codes that reflect its dominant themes.

First, the code of romance pervades most aspects of the magazine but

Figure 6.1 *Jackie* front cover

particularly the short stories about (heterosexual) relationships – girl meets boy, boy does wrong, girl sobs, boy makes good – in which 'No attempt is made to fill out social events or backgrounds' (McRobbie 2000: 80). The underlying message being encoded to *Jackie* readers is that they should forge romantic attachments sooner rather than later (but no sex before marriage) because the right man is better than the right job. The same code of romance is repetitively re-articulated along these lines:

1   The girl has to fight to *get* and *keep* her man.
2   She can *never* trust another woman unless she is old and 'hideous' in which case she does not appear in these stories anyway.
3   Despite this, romance, and being a girl, are fun.

(McRobbie 2000: 85)

The romance code encourages teenage girls to be competitive and individualistic. A similar argument is made by Janice Winship in her discussion of the 'aspirational feminism' advocated by women's magazines such as *Cosmopolitan*: 'Whatever its gain for individual women, an aspirational feminism works within, not against the competitive organization of work. It is about "I" rather than "we"' (Winship 1987: 120). Winship refers to the ideology of individual success and competitiveness encoded into women's magazines. For McRobbie and Winship, 'success' means the achievement of romantic attachments rather than career or educational achievements.

Competitive individualism is also a dominant theme in the second code of personal/domestic life that McRobbie identifies. This code is particularly evident in the letters and problem pages in which anonymous editors respond to readers' concerns. Editors deploy the code of personal/domestic life to *individualize* a reader's problems rather than reassure her that these problems are common for teenagers as a whole. Remedies to these problems are always to encourage readers to conform to the norm. As the author notes, 'Girls are reassured about irregular periods, pubic hair, weight and so on, but there is no mention of contraception or abortion' (McRobbie 2000: 94).

Third, we have the code of fashion and beauty – which are deemed to go hand in hand. Emphasis is placed on good looks above personality; appearance above intelligence. The fashion and beauty pages of *Jackie* reinforce this ideology by presenting models that are physically attractive in a conventional sense. These models radiate what McRobbie calls a 'glow' which connotes that 'if you look good, you feel good' and 'looking as good as this you can expect to be treated as something special, even precious ... beauty like this is the girls' passport to happiness and success' (McRobbie 2000: 103–4). Beauty and fashion are constantly changing, however, so *Jackie* keeps its readers 'in the know' about what to wear – and what not to wear. The underlying implication of the fashion/beauty code is that girls should keep up-to-date and not get left behind for fear of losing their boyfriends – or being unable to find any.

Fourth and finally is the code of pop music. Contrary to what we might expect though, this code has little to do with music itself and far more to do with the sweet-looking male pop idols that become 'pin-ups' in girls' bedrooms. Music has the potential to be a subversive force for teenagers – some of whom might identify with subcultures (see Chapter 4) – but McRobbie argues that pop music is marketed to teenage girls via media outlets such as *Jackie* in order to encourage conformity to the 'ideal man' myth. Pin-up posters of the latest pop idol constitute 'an *unequal* relationship between the adoring fan and the star looking down at her' (McRobbie 2000: 110). The pop music industry uses its idols to exploit the romantic individualism that is ideologically encoded into teenage girls' lives through the other three codes that *Jackie* reinforces.

In an article entitled 'Rock and Sexuality' (first published in 1978), McRobbie – with co-author Simon Frith – extends her theory of codes to the construction of conventional gender and sexuality in rock and pop music. A binary construction of pop and rock fandom encourages teenage girls – 'teenyboppers' – to romanticize about boy bands like Take That, while teenage boys are expected to identify with the macho masculinity of 'cock rockers' such as Thin Lizzy and heavy metal front-men. It is this gender split in fan affiliations – perpetuated by music industry marketing ploys – that lead McRobbie and Frith to the following conclusion:

> Cock rock allows for direct physical and psychological expressions of sexuality; pop in contrast is about romance, about female crushes and emotional affairs. Pop songs aimed at the female audience deny or repress sexuality ... few alternative readings are available.
>
> (McRobbie 2000: 148)

Like *Jackie*, teenybop pop presents a conformist ideology of non-sexualized – but always heterosexual – femininity. The sexist divide between pop and cock rock is further evidenced in the music industry itself. How many female rock musicians are there? Answer: far fewer than there are male ones. As the authors state, 'Female musicians have rarely been able to make their own musical versions of the oppositional rebellious hard edges that male rock can embody' (McRobbie 2000: 143). Female performers in the music industry are mostly sweet-sounding solo artists or members of overtly pop-oriented groups.

While McRobbie's codes of romance, beauty, fashion and pop music can still be interpreted as central to the dominant ideologies disseminated by female-oriented media, there is now a greater diversity of choice than was available 20 or 30 years ago. McRobbie's analysis of more contemporary magazine titles such as *More!* and *Marie Claire* continues to insist on the self-regulatory agenda of these magazines 'in defining and producing the norms of cultural intelligibility through which a girl or woman is permitted to understand herself' (McRobbie 1996: 186). And there is 'still the pressure to adhere to the perfect body image as a prerequisite for the success in love which is equated with happiness' (McRobbie 1994: 165). However, McRobbie acknowledges the declining significance of the romance code and more open discussion of new sexualities in these titles – perhaps a new code of sexuality – including advice on masturbation and lesbianism. Female readers of these magazines encounter 'sexual representations which breach the boundaries of what in the past has been considered appropriate for girls and young women' (McRobbie 1996: 185) partly because some of the women journalists employed by these titles are self-proclaimed feminists. As well as new sexualities, McRobbie's ideology of femininity perspective has been questioned by interview research that shows how teenage girls read *Jackie* and similar teen titles lazily, giving little thought to their underlying values and motives (see Frazer 1987).

Ang: pleasure and the ideology of mass culture

Yet another ideological analysis of women's relationship to media texts is Ien Ang's *Watching Dallas* (first published in 1982). Her study of how women watch *Dallas* (1978–91) – a prime-time American television serial that was very popular with audiences in several countries across the world, including the Netherlands (where Ang undertook her research) – combines textual analysis of the programmes themselves with analysis of 42 letters written by female viewers who responded to an advertisement placed by Ang in a Dutch women's magazine called *Viva*. In comparison to behaviourist research on uses and gratifications (see Chapter 2), Ang argues that 'pleasure must be conceived of as not so much the automatic result of some "satisfaction of needs", but rather as the effect of a certain productivity of a cultural artefact' (Ang 1989: 9–10). The success of *Dallas* – which, as Ang states, was watched by 52 per cent of the Dutch population, 69 per cent of whom were women – is seen by its critics to be worrying in two respects: first, it is perceived as a force for American cultural imperialism, spreading American values across the world (see discussion of media and cultural imperialism in Chapter 7); and second, it is perceived as a force for patriarchy, representing men as powerful and women as subordinate. The first point of view is espoused by orthodox Marxist critics; the second by orthodox feminists.

Ang is neither an orthodox Marxist nor an orthodox feminist. Instead, she argues against an orthodox 'ideology of mass culture' that immediately classifies all forms of mass or popular culture – including media productions such as television serials – as 'bad for you'. Ang's theoretical agenda is guided by analysis of the letter-writers, whom she divides into two categories: *Dallas* fans and *Dallas* haters. Those respondents who hated the serial expressed their opinions in terms of the ideology of mass culture. For them, *Dallas* represented all that is unhealthy about American culture – corporate capitalist greed, male chauvinism, disregard for humanity and family values, sexual promiscuity, and so on. On the other hand, those letter-writers who liked (even loved) watching *Dallas* had no such terms to draw on because the ideology they presented – the ideology of populism – did not have the same critical vocabulary associated with the ideology of mass culture. The argument that *Dallas* fans would often adopt, that 'there's no accounting for taste', appeared feeble in opposition to the barrage of arguments at the disposal of *Dallas* haters. In this conflict of ideas we might expect the author's feminist sensibilities to side with *Dallas* haters, but this is exactly what Ang herself resists because she too finds pleasure in *Dallas*. This feeling of pleasure cannot be dismissed as false and futile by Marxists or feminists – it should be analysed on its own terms in order to assess its implications for cultural progressiveness. Taking pleasure seriously now is by no means an entirely antithetical stance in relation to many feminisms – women's talk on soap operas is itself a resistive pleasure according to a later ethnographic study (Brown 1994) – but Ang's study pioneered feminist approaches to the politics of pleasure.

In specific respect to women's pleasure in watching *Dallas*, Ang argues that there is a non-reconcilable conflict between this pleasure and feminist values:

> The project of feminism as a whole is not and never can be based on pleasure alone, because the project itself is impelled by an angry rejection of the existing social order as essentially unpleasurable, and by a projection of pleasure into a (mythical) ideal future.
>
> (Ang 1989: 133)

For feminists, pleasure is the future; for female fans of *Dallas*, pleasure is the 'here and now'. Ang describes how feminist thinkers often refer to 'the tragic structure of feeling' underpinning soap operas and other fictional narratives. This tragic structure excludes the possibility of an ideal future vision in which women become equals to men in success and happiness. Ang agrees that 'feminist fantasies are totally absent in *Dallas*' (Ang 1989: 130) but she contends that non-feminist women's 'pleasure is first and foremost connected with the fictional nature of the positions and solutions which the tragic structure of feeling constructs, not with their ideological content' (Ang 1989: 135). So although female fans of *Dallas* may be prevented from engaging in what orthodox feminists would consider ideal representations of women, they do not seek this kind of 'ideal' pleasure but rather a pleasure that comes from viewing purely fictional representations of reality. This is what Ang means by the melodramatic imagination. To imagine being in the shoes of *Dallas*'s main characters amounts to the pleasure of melodramatic identification – a pleasure that Mulvey's theory of the male gaze, and Modleski's and Radway's accounts, deny female media audiences. Ang argues that the fictional realism of *Dallas* is more pleasurable than – and overrides – any ideological agenda that producers (presumably American men) might encode into the show. The fictional pleasures of the serial do not necessarily amount to passivity in Ang's women viewers either: 'Fiction and fantasy ... function by making life in the present pleasurable, or at least livable, but this does not by any means exclude radical political activity or consciousness' (Ang 1989: 135).

Ang's sympathies with the ideology of populism, and her attack on the '"monstrous alliance" between feminist criticism and the ideology of mass culture' (Ang 1989: 119), would seem to place her within liberal feminism. On the other hand, she has also expounded a postmodern feminism in her concern about matters of everyday media consumption – a pioneering concern that she shares with consumerist perspectives in media theory (see Chapter 9):

> in everyday life gender is not always relevant to what one experiences, how one feels, chooses to act or not to act. Since a subject is always multiply positioned in relation to a whole range of discourses, many of which do not concern gender, women do not always live in the prison house of gender ... media consumption is not always a gendered practice.
>
> (Ang 1996: 124–5)

This perspective clearly differs from more orthodox feminisms that consider all media practices (of production and consumption) as gendered in the interests of men and to the disadvantage of women. It informs two related concepts that Ang considers central to her ideas: radical contextualism (Ang 1996) and cultural contradiction (see Brunsdon 2000: 158–9). A 'subject' (i.e. everyday person) will consume a media text such as *Dallas* in a different cultural context from another, regardless of gender or any other single variable. Consumption cannot be theorized, therefore, without ethnographic insight from within the contradictory and unpredictable contexts in which it is practised. Furthermore, Ang applies theories of postmodernism (see Chapter 8) to a contemporary feminist agenda which questions the 'grand narrative' of feminism – that women as a whole suffer inequalities for the sake of men – by 'eradicating any pregiven guarantee of female unity' (Ang 1996: 128). According to the author, not all women are best served by feminist theory. This is particularly the case in a media age of fluid and ever-changing identities. Ang queries what it means to be a woman and whether these meanings – for there is no single meaning – marry with a universal feminist politics. This theoretical standpoint is shared to some extent by the work of Judith Butler.

Butler: *Gender Trouble*

Like Ang, Butler's work on feminism and the subversion of gender identity presents quite an optimistic view that contradicts more conventional feminist accounts of patriarchal dominance and women's subordination. Butler argues that gender identities are not natural or fixed – rather, they are only given meaning when *acted out* or performed. She shares Simone de Beauvoir's (1989) view that 'one is not born, but, rather, *becomes* a woman' (Butler 1990: 270). Therefore, 'the acts by which gender is constituted bear similarities to performative acts within theatrical contexts' (Butler 1990: 272). Gender is a performance and how it is performed constitutes what it means to any given society or culture in a particular historical moment. For example, many societies today value masculinity (being a man) above femininity (being a woman) but in others we have the reverse scenario – such as the matriarchal Mosuo community in southern China, in which a woman is predominantly the head of the family. Although gender is a process of *acting out* rather than being, it is nevertheless subject to social norms and conditions which restrict the range of gender performances it is feasible for individuals to enact. Gender play, as Butler calls it, is not a free-for-all. However, gender performances can be liberated from social norms if they are played in such a way as to provoke what Butler calls **gender trouble** – which is also the title of her book (Butler 1999, first published in 1990). What she means by this is that traditional lines of division between masculine and feminine identity are capable of being blurred and eroded by gender playing that subverts conventional sex differences; that amounts to troublesome gender performativity in the eyes of traditionalists. Conventional gender identities can be changed through gender play because 'identity is performatively constituted by the very "expressions" that are said to be its results' (Butler 1999: 33). In other words, there is no *natural* gender identity because it is forever enacted both before and after it can become natural or normalized.

Transsexual practices, transvestism and bisexuality are important ways to create gender trouble because they contradict normative femininities (and masculinities) predicated on reproductive heterosexuality. Moreover, media such as popular music provide valuable channels of dissemination for bastions of gender trouble, despite the fact that as discussed earlier in this chapter, mass media stereotyping of radical feminists only reinforces gender norms in line with patriarchal ideologies about what is and is not socially acceptable. Transsexuals and bisexuals – not to mention gay and lesbian sexualities – are rarely the subject of media representations, and on the few occasions when these 'alternative sexualities' are shown and discussed in mainstream media, they are usually misrepresented, in a way that is at best patronizing and, at worst, ridiculing. Mass media in the main are hardly recruiting agents for gender trouble. This absence of mainstream gender trouble has inspired Butler to write a sequel, *Undoing Gender* (2004), which imagines the meanings of sexual and gendered life freed from restrictive social norms. Butler's theory of gender trouble is not directly related to media and she does not deal with mediated performativity in any depth, but her ideas have filtered quite widely through media and cultural theory.

For example, Beverley Skeggs's (1993) interpretation of the early Madonna's music videos, such as 'Like a Virgin', suggests that she embodies gender trouble. In turn, Madonna's shows of lesbianism and autoeroticism hold the promise of radical, empowering implications for feminine identity. As Skeggs notes, 'By playing popular culture so well Madonna is able to use its spaces to make challenges ... and break down the institutional barriers constructed out of women's silence' (Skeggs 1993: 72). Another feminist scholar refers to the liberating impact of Madonna's ambiguous gender and sexuality in her videos and stage shows: 'She forces the spectator to question the boundaries of gender constructs and the cultural constraints on sexual themes and sexual fantasies' (Kaplan 1993: 157). Madonna is one of Butler's best performers of gender trouble, albeit presumably unknowingly. Moreover, Butler's liberating gender politics and gender-bending role models like Madonna proved to be iconic for a new generation of feminist perspectives to which we will now turn.

Postfeminism and the third wave

Since the early 1980s there has evolved a sustained critique of second-wave feminism. 'Postfeminism', as it is commonly known, claims that 'no singular perspective on feminism can speak for women across the multiple differences of class and race' (Ouellette 2002: 318). In a more hostile sense, however, postfeminism 'displays a tendency to blame women because the revolution promised by the second wave has not yet happened' (Whelehan 1995: 220). In stark contrast to the gender equality aims of second-wave feminism, postfeminists assume that equality has been more or less achieved and women are no longer victimized by a patriarchal order. Natasha Walter, for example, confidently claims that 'Everywhere you look, you see individual women who are freer and more powerful than women have ever been before' (Walter 1999: 1). Although postfeminism has become a theoretical endeavour, its origins are to be found in a more popular perception of 'women in power' fuelled by the 1980s media (Faludi 1992; Wolf 1993; Gamble 2001). Postfeminism therefore leads a double life: on the one hand, it is a theory about contemporary women in Western societies; on the other, it is 'the Spice Girls, Madonna . . . women dressing like bimbos, yet claiming male privileges and attitudes' (Gamble 2001: 43). Postfeminism is sometimes referred to as 'popular feminism' because its confident swagger is appealing to public and media interests alike. Moreover, postfeminism is about pandering to mainstream, commercial culture: 'Today, young women can link fashion with power rather than powerlessness. The rhetoric of young female singers like the Spice Girls, who associate their bright clothes with girlpower, has resonated with a new generation of young girls' (Walter 1999: 99). Girl power is also evident in television serials such as *Sex and the City* (1998–2004) and *Buffy the Vampire Slayer* (1997–2003), as well as films like *Clueless* (1995) and *Legally Blonde* (2001). In these media representations, 'Post-feminist woman can try on identities and adopt them' (Brunsdon 1997: 86) – she does not conform to either feminine or feminist stereotypes.

Despite its popular appeal, the postfeminist perspective has undergone a barrage of criticism among feminists who beg to differ from such over-optimism. Germaine Greer, for example, has attacked the 'girl power' phenomenon because although sexuality is no longer oppressed as it had been prior to the second wave, nevertheless representations of the postfeminist woman as 'nothing but a sexual being' are equally oppressive (Greer 2000: 411). The most comprehensive attack on postfeminism is Susan Faludi's *Backlash* (1992). The 'backlash' that Faludi identifies is an anti-feminism backlash that reached its most intense during the 1980s, epitomized in anti-feminist films such as *Fatal Attraction* (1987). Although instigated by a chauvinistic, male-dominated media industry, this backlash was enthusiastically endorsed by postfeminism – not least because postfeminists stood to gain from the demise of their second-wave predecessors. Postfeminists are 'beyond even pretending to care' (Faludi 1992: 95) about continuing gender inequalities and injustices. Likewise for McRobbie, the hypocritical way in which postfeminists acknowledge the gains of second-wave activists – what she calls 'feminism taken into account' (McRobbie 2006: 61) – but then reject these gains as historic relics that are easily forgotten is most concerning. She uses the example of the film *Bridget Jones's Diary* (2001) to show how media representations of the single woman in so-called postfeminist times are hardly full of confidence and optimistic independence. Bridget Jones may be a fictional figure, but the popularity of her character – her fear of weight-gain, ageing and realization that 'there is only the self to blame if the right partner is not found' (McRobbie 2006: 67) – testifies to a version of femininity that is closer to the traditional, patriarchal version than to the postfeminist ideal.

In response to the populist stance of postfeminism, a further theoretical avenue has been paved by 'third-wave feminism'. Unlike postfeminism, the third-wave agenda proposes that 'the second and third waves of feminism are neither incompatible nor opposed' (Heywood and Drake 1997: 3). Whereas postfeminism's focus on powerful individuals separates the personal from the political so that girl power is only really to be found in personal accounts, the third-wave agenda tries to reunite the personal and political for contemporary feminist outcomes. Third-wave feminism continues to engage with second-wave debates about sexual abuse and patriarchal ideologies of femininity, but it also tends to emphasize aspects of genuine female pleasure and desire as well as new dangers to feminine autonomy. The Riot Grrl movement in women's punk music in the early 1990s is associated with a third-wave agenda (see Klein 1997; Whiteley 2000). Unlike the commercial pop of postfeminist heroines, Riot Grrl acts such as Hole aimed at political ends, not least given the historical dominance of male performers in the rock industry (as discussed by McRobbie and Frith, as well as Bayton 1990). Sheila Whiteley points out that the Riot Grrl movement 'attempted to reclaim and politicize the word girl (with its traditional connotations of passivity and immaturity) and to re-present it as a wholly positive term, grrrl' (Whiteley 2000: 208).

Another example of the political and personal in tandem is Kristyn Gorton's (2004) analysis of the television serial *Ally McBeal* (1997–2002). The main character's independence and personal power – she is a high-profile lawyer – are not straightforwardly pro-feminist because, at the same time, Ally McBeal exhibits traditional femininity in dilemmas over what to wear, how to style one's hair, and so on. Regardless of this ostensibly weak representation of the independent woman, the important point is that McBeal can choose to wear one thing or another, and can choose to go out at night (with men or women) or not: 'The power to choose is distinctly political' (Gorton 2004: 160). Third-wave feminism therefore attempts to bridge the gap between second-wave politics and the 'personal choice' rhetoric of postfeminism by arguing that women's personal choice must be politically contextualized.

Masculinity in crisis

The anti-feminism backlash that hailed in postfeminism may have harmed the more progressive women's liberation movement – but the same author who attacked the backlash is nonetheless clear that contemporary men suffer too in a celebrity-driven consumer culture where success is measured in very narrow terms and the achievements of 'the common man' are ignored (see Faludi 2000). Men are expected to be in control of their jobs, their partners, their families, their finances and themselves – and these high social expectations lead some men down the unhealthy path of low self-esteem, stress and depression. This state of affairs is reflected in the death of the patriarchal hero (John Wayne, Clint Eastwood); the 'dominant heterosexual masculine' represented in films and other media whom 'real world variants are encouraged to approximate, but are unlikely ever to match' (McNair 2002: 151). Since the 1990s a theoretical and wider public debate about 'masculinity in crisis' has raged among men (and women). According to one commentator,

> At the beginning of the twenty-first century it is difficult to avoid the conclusion that men are in serious trouble. Throughout the world, developed and developing, antisocial behaviour is essentially male. Violence, sexual abuse of children, illicit drug use, alcohol misuse, gambling all are overwhelmingly male activities. The courts and prisons bulge with men.
>
> (Clare 2001: 3)

In short, men are – in all sorts of ways – a greater social problem than women. However, **masculinity** has only recently been theorized because 'men's lives and experiences have, for social and historical reasons, tended to stand in for general or universal experience' (Benwell 2003: 12). Men's miserable predicament is not helped by an apparent lack of role models other than the 'celebrity heroes' who represent an unattainable aspiration for most men.

Masculinity is now an established theoretical concern, no longer taken for granted as the unproblematic norm. For instance, Bob Connell questions the prevalent idea that masculinity is a coherent category of knowledge able to be analysed through the lens of social science. Instead, Connell (1995) prefers the notion of multiple and dynamic 'masculinities' formed within hegemonic contexts of gender and sexual relations. Similarly, John MacInnes argues that masculinity is not a natural condition but a patriarchal category that divides men (superior) from women (inferior). However, popular perceptions about the 'crisis' debate point to 'evidence of the material and ideological weakening and collapse of patriarchy' (MacInnes 1998: 55) – and the end of masculinity as a distinct category. Second-wave feminism – together with the notion of postfeminism – has weakened the resolve of masculinity. For MacInnes, the sexual division of employment that characterized early modernity has collapsed as women perform better in education, and grow up to compete with men for professional and management roles on a relatively equal footing. Furthermore, the 'advent of postmodernity has resulted in redundancy and downsizing' (Beynon 2002: 77) – a particular problem for older men who also die younger than their female counterparts. Men still tend to dominate the elite of 'Top Earners' but it is now common for women to be the highest wage earners in a typical household. Proof of this colossal social change is obtainable not just from census information, but from how categories used in retrieving census information have altered to reflect the times. The 2001 UK census, for example, asked for details of the highest-earning *parent* in the household, whereas previous censuses had only asked for the *male parent's* earnings because his was assumed to be the higher wage figure.

How is this crisis in masculinity – as well as patriarchy – articulated in media theory and evidenced by contemporary media? John Beynon cites American television shows such as *The X-Files* (1993–2002) and *Friends* (1994–2004) – and we might add, *Two and a Half Men* (2003–) – as examples of the 'preponderance of a "soft and tender" masculinity' (Beynon 2002: 150). This soft and tender masculinity is associated with the 'New Man' figure – emerging in the 1980s – who 'invites the sexual objectification of the male body' and feels comfortable with 'men looking at themselves, and women looking at men' (McNair 2002: 157). New Man is subject to the female gaze in much the same way that Mulvey theorizes women as subjects of the male gaze in narrative cinema. According to Brian McNair, New Man 'is not just a feminized, but a *homo*sexualized vision of masculinity' that embraces 'the mainstreaming of gayness' in contemporary societies (McNair 2002: 157). Representations of New Man – typified in the 'look' exhibited by male models in magazine fashion images – convey an ambivalent blend of boyish softness and assertive masculinity (Nixon 1997). Evidence of the New Man ideal is to be found in modern-day male sports stars – such as soccer star David Beckham – who are family men and no longer subscribe to the 'hard man' stereotype associated with sports stars of a bygone age. Beckham's effeminate image has received hostility from male soccer fans, which can be seen as symptomatic of a widely felt fear of emasculation troubling contemporary masculinity (Whannel 2002: 203–6). Despite this hostility, Beckham has contributed to a changing definition of masculinity that is far more narcissistic and image-conscious than ever before, and he has tapped into 'a whole new generation of young people tired of sex-typing' (Cashmore 2004: 142).

While the evolution of New Man lifestyle magazines such as *Men's Health* and *FHM* appear to have been a step in the right direction, they have performed similar ideological functions to women's magazines by representing fantasy versions of masculinity that are impossible for the everyday male reader to live up to: 'Modern men, according to the magazines, can work really long hours, develop new and satisfying relations with women and children, while preserving their bodies against ageing and decay more generally' (Jackson et al. 2001: 93). Jackson et al.'s study of men's magazines included focus-group interviews with readers, though, who expressed scepticism about the idealized images of men that they represent. Perhaps in response to such idealized images, the New Man represented in *Men's Health* was challenged in the 1990s by the 'New Lad' figure, personified by 'rock 'n' roll stars' such as Liam Gallagher from Oasis and articulated in new titles such as *loaded*, and more recently *Nuts* and *Zoo*. The appeal of this figure for many men was his naturalness:

> the image of the 'lad' was a more natural form of masculinity than the contrived image of the 'new man' ... more authentic (true to men's real selves) and less contrived (unlike images of the 'new man'). The idea that the 'new man' was a media fiction was widely shared.
>
> (Stevenson et al. 2003: 124)

Moreover, the New Lad was 'a backlash against the feminism that gave birth to him' (Gill 2003) – he was both anti-feminist and rather partial to post-feminism. So who won the fight: New Man or New Lad? In more recent years the New Lad figure appears to have faded in comparison to the steady, durable character of New Man. Less oppressive forms of masculinity are now the norm, and the man who cares equally for his career, his family and his own body tolls the bell for the old patriarchal order. Nevertheless, masculinity is still in something of a crisis as women outperform men at school, work and in the home. Whatever quarrels feminists may have with each other about the merits of postfeminism versus the second wave, feminism as a whole would certainly seem to have contributed to a situation in which patriarchal power is rendered increasingly impotent.

Summary

This chapter has considered:

- Historical and theoretical developments in feminisms and feminist media theory, as well as media and gender.
- Radical feminism and especially Dworkin's anti-pornography campaign.
- Mulvey's theory of the male gaze, including concepts of scopophilia and identification as well as the three ways of looking associated with Hollywood.
- Mass-produced fantasies in the form of soap operas (Modleski) and romance fiction (Radway) that enable women's fulfilment of imaginary desires.
- McRobbie's structural feminist analysis of the ideology of femininity in magazines and other media, as identified through codes of romance, personal/domestic life, fashion/beauty, pop music and new sexualities.
- Ang's ethnographic analysis of the ideology of mass culture versus the ideology of populism, the latter of which cites pleasure in melodramatic identifications with the characters and narratives in *Dallas*.
- Butler's theory of gender trouble, including concepts of performativity and play that position gender as a social – not a natural – category.
- Postfeminism that separates the personal from the political (e.g. girl power) in comparison to third-wave feminism that explores political factors that shape personal manifestations of contemporary women.
- The 'masculinity in crisis' debate reflected in media representations of the New Man and New Lad.

Further reading

Carter, C. et al. (eds) (1998) *News, Gender and Power*. London: Routledge.

An accessible edited collection of articles that deal with the gender politics of journalism and the gendered realities of news. Articles included on the sexualization of the press and newsroom accounts of power at work. Suitable for all media students.

Connell, R. W. (1995) *Masculinities*. Cambridge: Polity.

An influential analysis of contemporary masculinity informed by a broad historical perspective on changing representations of men. Chapters included on men's bodies, the social organization of masculinity, and masculinity politics. Recommended for advanced undergraduates and postgraduates.

Hollows, J. and Moseley, R. (eds) (2005) *Feminism in Popular Culture*. Oxford: Berg.

An edited collection of articles that critically analyse how different meanings of feminism have informed and been represented by popular media and cultural texts. Articles included on postfeminism, feminism in the news, and the beauty industry. Recommended for advanced undergraduates and postgraduates.

Thornham, S. (2000) *Feminist Theory and Cultural Studies: Stories of Unsettled Relations*. London: Arnold.

An accessible overview of feminism, media and cultural studies, including chapters on psychoanalysis, feminist ethnography, women and consumer culture, and technologies of the body. Suitable for all media students.

7   Political economy and postcolonial theory

Introduction

This chapter will consider two distinct but related themes in media theory, commonly referred to as **political economy** and **postcolonialism**. Both fields of inquiry are concerned with media power and issues of media ownership and control. Theories of political economy, as the term suggests, focus on the politics and economics of media institutions and the texts they produce. Some traditions of political economy – such as Adorno's theory of standardization that we will discuss first – also consider how capitalist politics and economics exert themselves on media audiences. Political economy is associated with classical Marxist theory and Marx's statement (back in 1859) that social consciousness is determined not by the collective will of individuals but by the ruling classes who own the means of capitalist production (see Easthope and McGowan 1992: 45–6). However, it should now be clear from discussion of structuralism (Chapter 4) that political economy is not the only tradition of media theory influenced by Marxism. Theories of political economy tend to differ from structuralist approaches to Marxism, though, by analysing the economic structures that characterize media institutions rather than considering how these structures are articulated in the language and ideology of media texts. For the sake of brevity and without wishing to generalize, political economy perspectives place emphasis on *economic* and *political* processes of media ownership and control, while structuralist perspectives – aligned to cultural studies – emphasize *social* and *cultural* processes of ideological and hegemonic power in media texts, both produced and consumed. In the case of a critical tradition of political economy, we shall see that there is a distinct turn towards media economics and not the same concern with politics.

Postcolonial theory is a field of inquiry that considers a shift from military and political occupation of foreign lands (colonialism) to cultural and media dominance of international markets (postcolonialism). The power of media representations to determine our conceptions of the world is an underlying assumption of the postcolonial approach. Like political economy theory, postcolonialism cites white, Western capitalism as the dominant framework for global media power. Western (particularly Anglo-American) media become dominant in two senses: first, their own media productions – and ways of producing, say, Hollywood films – are exported around the world and set the standard for local media production; and second, Western media productions that represent non-white, non-Western cultures have the power to generate stereotypical conceptions of 'the Other' that become accepted as true representations by the Western world. This first sense of domination is explored by theorists of media and cultural imperialism, including Herman and Chomsky (to be discussed). Media and cultural imperialism can be placed neatly between political economy and postcolonial theory. The second sense, on the other hand, is more distinctive to postcolonial theory and will be explored in discussion of Said's Orientalism as well as media representations of race.

Adorno: culture industry or cultural industries?

Theodor Adorno's theory of mass media and culture is frequently dismissed for its 'cultural pessimism' (along with the modernist criticism of the Leavises and others, as discussed in Chapter 3) but such dismissals have not prevented him from becoming one of the most renowned and discussed thinkers of our times. Adorno's pessimism emerges most noticeably in his work on the 'culture industry' and, in particular, the manufacture of popular music. The culture industry – as Adorno and his colleague Max Horkheimer use the term – is synonymous with the capitalist-driven entertainment industry and its mass production of commodities such as films (Hollywood) and music (Tin Pan Alley). The problem is that what the culture industry produces is 'rubbish' or – for want of a more intellectual expression – 'mere twaddle' (Adorno and Horkheimer 1973: 121, 144). There is method in the culture industry's madness, however. Adorno argues that consumers are forced to accept what the culture industry provides. The products of the culture industry, moreover, possess ulterior motives to repress imagination and render 'the masses' socially and politically inactive. Furthermore, the culture industry is omnipotent: 'The consumers are the workers and the employees, the farmers and lower middle class. Capitalist production so confines them, body and soul, that they fall helpless victims to what is offered them' (Adorno and Horkheimer 1973: 133).

The culture industry is owned and controlled by the capitalist classes who enjoy the prerequisite economic and technological power that enables them to spread their ideas and values – their advertising-driven ideology – through the popular consciousness. According to the authors, 'men in top posts maintain the economy in which a highly-developed technology has in principle made the masses redundant as producers' (Adorno and Horkheimer 1973: 150). They cite the dependence of the culture industry on the 'most powerful sectors of industry – steel, petroleum, electricity, and chemicals' (Adorno and Horkheimer 1973: 122) as evidence of the divisive, deep-seated concentration of capital within the political economy of media.

The main defining feature of the culture industry for Adorno is **stan-dardization**. It is important to understand, though, that Adorno's theory of standardization refers not only to the products of the culture industry but to its consumers too. Standardization is about political economy only in so far as it accounts for both 'almighty production' and consumer demand for such production. Standardization results in the liquidation of individuals – like commodities – to mere statistics and classificatory labels: 'There is nothing left for the consumer to classify. Producers have done it for him [*sic*]' (Adorno and Horkheimer 1973: 125). This pursuit of consumer demand generates superficial differences between mass-produced commodities based on stylistic quirks, as opposed to substantial variations in quality. Standardization ensues:

> Marked differentiations such as those of A and B films, or of stories in magazines in different price ranges, depend not so much on subject matter as on classifying, organizing, and labelling consumers. Something is provided for all so that none may escape.
>
> (Adorno and Horkheimer 1973: 123)

In the classical Marxist sense of commodity fetishism, Adorno argues that during consumption the masses become characterized by the commodities which they use and exchange among themselves. In the case of easy-listening American popular music that emerged out of Tin Pan Alley, 'As one particular song scored a great success, hundreds of others sprang up imitating the suc-cessful one' (Adorno 1990: 306). Concurrently, those who initially made these products popular – that is, listeners to the first hit songs – spurned subsequent generations of listeners who insured that imitations of the first hit songs received new audiences and Tin Pan Alley remained profitable.

So why do consumers keep on coming back for more if the culture industry's products – sweet-sounding melodies, and so on – are so standar-dized and predicated on the same old formula for bland success? To explain this paradoxical situation it is argued that the mundane, workaday routines of the masses dull their sense of creativity and enthusiasm so severely that, during those brief intervals of leisure afforded to them, if a song or film or any other medium of entertainment is 'to remain a pleasure, it must not demand any effort ... No independent thinking must be expected from the audience: the product prescribes every reaction' (Adorno and Horkheimer 1973: 137). Industrial work leads to industrial leisure. Consumers' needs are therefore produced and controlled by the absolute power of capitalism, both at and outside of work. The culture industry serves the ideological interests of eco-nomic and political powers by producing music, films and other sentimental novelties designed to make people cathartic, amused, satisfied with their lot, sleepy and – after a good night's sleep – re-charged for tomorrow's chores at the office, farm or factory. For Adorno, commercial popular music is the ultimate medium of social control. Indeed, the social and psychological functions of popular music act like a social cement (Adorno 1990) to keep people obedient and subservient to the status quo of existing power structures. The overthrow of capitalism predicted by Marx cannot be realized precisely because mass culture – music in particular – appeals to people's instinctive emotions and obstructs their reasoning. If the masses were able to escape the culture industry's manipulative power and for one moment think independently and collectively, they would see the mass of misery which they endure every day and would activate their energies to rise up against the ruling capitalist elite.

Unfortunately, the masses have become conditioned by the culture industry in such a way that – like infants – they are deaf and dumb to rational thinking: 'If nobody can any longer speak, then certainly nobody can any longer listen' (Adorno 1991: 27). Popular music not only destroys the trained musical ear; it also 'commands its own listening habits' (Adorno 1990: 309). Adorno's theory of standardization is applied to both the production and consumption of popular music, which is compared entirely unfavourably to 'serious music'. Serious music achieves excellence when its whole is greater than the sum of its part. For instance, 'Beethoven's greatness shows itself in the complete subordination of the accidentally private melodic elements to the form as a whole' (Adorno 1991: 32). In popular music, by contrast, 'The detail has no bearing on a whole' (Adorno 1990: 304) – the whole is merely a standard song structure common to all 'well-made' commercial hits. The individual parts of a popular song are interchangeable with endless other parts of other songs because each part has no bearing on the music as a whole. In any given hit song, 'The beginning of the chorus is replaceable by the beginning of innumerable other choruses' (Adorno 1990: 303). On the other hand, anything composed by Beethoven is a unique musical experience and its complete structure would be irrecoverably damaged if, say, any particular note were to be replaced by another. The popular music industry conceals the standardized structure of its products, according to Adorno, by emphasizing the individual creativity of its 'artists' and marketing these pop stars in an attempt to appeal to the individuality of consumers, who are readily identified as 'fans'. This is what Adorno calls 'pseudo-individualization' – the pretence that music is made by individual genius for individual pleasure when, in fact, it is made by a few highly-trained, profit-seeking producers and packaged for mass consumption.

Two types of music consumers emerge from the culture industry: the 'emotional' and the 'rhythmically obedient' type. The emotional type is best represented by the shy young male who 'has no luck with girls' and whose bedroom-bound show of technical capability – mixing on decks or uploading online music would be contemporary examples – is ironically symptomatic of his regressive subjugation to the products of mass culture: 'he becomes the discoverer of just those industrial products which are interested in being discovered by him' (Adorno 1991: 47). Interestingly, 'Over forty years after Adorno wrote this, such an image was often used to caricature the male fans of The Smiths and the other melancholic guitar rock bands that followed them' (Negus 1996: 11). The Smiths' fans, on the contrary, might point to the lyrics of a rock anthem like 'Panic', and its incessant call to hang DJs, as a starkly non-melancholic incitement to active cultural resistance. But as Adorno's second type of listener illustrates, the problem with Morrissey from The Smiths telling listeners to burn down discos is that young people should not be on dance floors to begin with. The jitterbug dance directly alludes to its participants' 'neurotic stupidity' (Adorno 1991: 41). This rhythmically obedient type – typified by jitterbug and jive dancers – engages in an 'ecstatic ritual [which] betrays itself as pseudo-activity by the moment of mimicry' (Adorno 1991: 46) and their 'adaptation to machine music necessarily implies a renunciation of one's own human feelings' (Adorno 1990: 313). Adorno's simplistic categorization of music consumers' practices into two opposing types has been criticized because it 'reduces a complex social process into a simple psychological effect' (Frith 1983: 57). Rather, Simon Frith favours Benjamin's theory about the increasing accessibility of mechanically-reproducible art intensifying a political struggle between production and consumption (see Chapter 3) rather than – as Adorno would have it – a psychological warfare in which producers call the shots. It is also convenient for Adorno not to have considered any psychological types of *serious* music consumers.

As well as these limitations to his bleak theory of standardized consumption, Adorno's conception of a monolithic culture industry – note the singularity of this term – churning out standardized production has been confronted in more recent times by a 'cultural industries approach' (see Miege 1989; Garnham 1990). The cultural industries approach rejects the top-down model of economic determinism that underpins Adorno's theory of standardization and instead prefers to emphasize the contested ground upon which different kinds of cultural texts are produced. David Hesmondhalgh uses the term 'symbol creators' to refer to 'the personnel responsible for the creative input in texts, such as writers, directors, producers, performers' (Hesmondhalgh 2002: 34). Remarkably, symbol creators and the organizations in which they work have been largely ignored not only by Adorno – who is concerned with issues of ownership and consumption rather than creative personnel, whom he sees as victims of the culture industry – but by political economists in general. Hesmondhalgh's approach to the cultural industries foregrounds the experiences of symbol creators that reveal

> the extreme inequalities and injustices (along class, gender, ethnic and other lines) apparent in contemporary capitalist societies. There

are vast inequalities in access to the cultural industries ... and many
people who want to create texts struggle to earn a living.

(Hesmondhalgh 2002: 5–6)

Nonetheless and without succumbing to Adorno's pessimism, Hesmondhalgh
argues that owners in the cultural industries are not in complete control of
what gets produced. Symbol creators are given a voice in decisions about
which texts are produced and this measure of artistic licence is comparably
greater than the freedom afforded to workers in other industries. Contrary to
Adorno's conception of the culture industry versus the creative artist, within
the cultural industries approach 'Attention is redirected from how capitalism
impacts upon creative work to how capitalism manages, organizes and provides the conditions within which creativity can be realised' (Negus and
Pickering 2004: 50). Capitalist economics certainly threaten but do not
entirely stifle the creativity of workers in the cultural industries.

Media and cultural imperialism

Theories of **media and cultural imperialism** argue that one nation can
dominate and control the economic and cultural values of another in the
same way that one nation can invade and colonize another through political
and military power. Such theories have borrowed from and overlap with
political economy and postcolonial perspectives (the latter of which will be
discussed later), but they nonetheless amount to a distinct tradition of their
own in theorizing media power. Before the First World War, the two major
imperialist powers were Britain and France. These two countries colonized the
bodies and minds of nations throughout the world, particularly on the Afri-
can and Asian continents. In more recent times, the United States has
replaced Britain and France as the great imperialist power. The 'War on Terror'
is arguably a thinly veiled guise concealing colonialist intentions of the historic kind. We should be clear that 'media imperialism' and 'cultural
imperialism' are similar but not synonymous concepts. French cultural
imperialism, for example, has been historically challenged by localized media
production within its colonies. As 'ex-French territories start to develop their
own media, the ties with France are very considerably weakened' (Tunstall
1977: 260). Media imperialism is therefore not an inevitable outcome of
cultural imperialism. The reverse scenario is also true. One nation cannot
impose its media upon another until it has spread its broader cultural values –
its language, customs, religion, history, and so on – across the colonized land.
Media imperialism cannot succeed without cultural imperialism. Moreover,
cultural resistance – always brewing underground among the colonized

peoples (and discussed later) – is likely to threaten and eventually topple imperialist powers, as the French example testifies.

Of course, cultural imperialism aimed at overcoming resistance does not usually necessitate military occupation of other nations given today's global communications systems, although the American-led invasion of Iraq in 2003 is an example of a more traditional imperialist route. The state-controlled Iraqi television network once awash with state propaganda – the former Information Minister, Mohammed Saeed al-Sahaf (Comical Ali), is the most famous perpetrator of such propaganda – soon fell on deaf ears and has been replaced by a much more Western-inflected network. Rather than consider Iraq as a subject of media and cultural imperialism, though, it is perhaps more appropriate to theorize Iraq using the concept of 'cultural dependency' (Boyd-Barrett 1988). In this case, post-Saddam Hussein, Iraq's aim to rapidly develop its media systems has meant that it has become dependent on certain models and formulas operating in other countries, such as commercial radio and tabloid-style newspapers. Iraq is also dependent on other countries – particularly the USA – for its supply of foreign and national news, as well as a ready supply of entertainment content such as comedies and popular music. Cultural dependency implies a more willing acceptance to follow the example of dominant media and cultural powers, while media and cultural imperialism implies a greater degree of force that is exerted by powerful upon weaker regimes. However, the two concepts are closely linked: 'the media imperialism approach ... developed as a corollary to the dependency model' (Fejes 1981: 285). Imperialist thinkers such as Herbert Schiller, to whom we now turn, though, would claim that 'dependency' is less common than 'imperialism' in the modern age.

Schiller's attack on the corporate capitalist economics of American mass media is perhaps the most comprehensive theoretical and historical account of media and cultural imperialism. In *Mass Communications and American Empire* (first published in 1969), the author claims 'a staggering global invasion by American electronic communications' (Schiller 1992: 124). Moreover, this global invasion by American media has led to the global commercialization of television and other broadcast media, since successive federal American governments have allowed media to be predominantly owned by commercial operators rather than public ones. Before the global television age, American media's commercialism was the exception rather than the rule, with most European countries operating state-owned public service broadcasting. However, the Second World War had left much of Europe 'fascist-occupied and war-ravaged' but 'the United States would emerge from the conflict physically unscathed and economically overpowering' (Schiller 1977: 105) which meant that many countries would yield to the US model of commercial broadcasting. According to Schiller (1992: 139), one example of this yielding to US media commercialism was the establishment of

Independent Television (ITV) in Britain in 1954. On the surface, the global commercialization of media may appear not particularly sinister. Schiller's theoretical point probes below this surface perception, though, to argue that American-led media commercialism reflects the advertising-driven character of the rampant US capitalist economy. By extension, US economic values are propagated around the world via media-cultural exports such as television programmes that other countries readily schedule on their broadcasting networks because US exports are cheaper than locally produced television. US-exported media fit well into the scheduling of overseas commercial broadcasters influenced, in turn, by US broadcasting values. Moreover, American television shows and films exported around the world help to sell goods produced by US-owned multinational companies, some of whom may manufacture their goods in overseas markets where media are also distributed.

What are the consequences of American media invasion on a global scale? Not dissimilar to Adorno's theory of standardization, Schiller fears that the 'cultural homogenization that has been underway for years in the United States now threatens to overtake the globe' (Schiller 1992: 156). A combination of consumer demand and pressures to secure advertising revenue means that overseas broadcasters tend to cave in to the temptation of buying more US-exported media productions. There is a need to fill air-time with cheap programming that also contains high-quality production values, and American exports fulfil this need better than other alternatives. Some countries, such as Japan and Britain, have placed quotas on the amount of American media products permitted to be shown by broadcasters, but – so they say – quantity is not as important as quality when US television shows start to look like Hollywood movies. American media and cultural imperialism is also evident when non-American products are nonetheless made in almost identical ways to American ones. Brazilian soap operas about wealthy business-people, for instance, are locally produced by Brazilian media firms but appear like the clones of existing US soap operas both in terms of content and commercial intent (Schiller 1997). Surely the most significant impact of American media and cultural imperialism, though, has been global recognition of English as the 'international language' given that it is the second language in most non-English-speaking countries (Tunstall 1977: 126–7). Media institutions such as the BBC World Service (radio) and BBC World (television) play a vital imperialist role in helping non-English speakers to learn the English language, which implicitly requires them to learn about Anglo-American cultural and political values.

While the global power of Anglo-American culture cannot be denied, there is always a danger of accepting theories of media and cultural imperialism at face value. A necessary counterweight to this danger is the **cultural resistance** thesis. Tamar Liebes and Elihu Katz (1990) examined cross-cultural reception of *Dallas* (as discussed in Chapter 6 in relation to Ang's work) by audiences whom they interviewed in several countries in which the American television serial had been exported. Israeli Russian focus groups, far from embracing the American cultural values represented in *Dallas*, felt that they served 'the hegemonic interests of the producers or of American society' (Liebes and Katz 1990: 75). Oppositional readings of this kind were the norm, and suggest the ease with which audiences identify and resist imperialistic media texts. The authors also tried to explain the failure of *Dallas* in Japan, concluding that Japanese focus groups dismissed the image of America which the serial portrayed because it was unrepresentative of the contemporary West (Liebes and Katz 1990: 113). These focus-group findings provide evidence to support a theory of cultural resistance and to dismiss a cultural imperialist one, which in any case would be much harder to prove:

> To prove that *Dallas* is an imperialistic imposition, one would have to show (1) that there is a message incorporated in the programme that is designed to profit American interests overseas, (2) that the message is decoded by the reader in the way it is encoded by the sender, and (3) that it is accepted uncritically by the viewers and allowed to seep into their culture.
>
> (Liebes and Katz 1990: 4)

Theories of media and cultural imperialism cannot be entirely convincing without audience research to support their case. Moreover, the success of American media productions overseas does not necessarily follow from a capitalist invasion on uncritical audiences. It could be argued that the diverse, 'melting pot' population of the United States provides media producers with the best possible 'testing ground' for multinational success.

Herman and Chomsky: *Manufacturing Consent*

Another version of the media and cultural imperialism approach is Edward S. Herman and Noam Chomsky's *Manufacturing Consent* (first published in 1988). In this book the authors outline a **propaganda model** which describes 'a very important aspect' (Herman and Chomsky 1994: xi) of the function of mass media – that is, to serve the dominant hegemonic interests of powerful groups such as governments and global corporations. Of course, media do not overtly disseminate propaganda unless they are state-controlled or controlled by powerful economic interests. On the contrary, Herman and Chomsky endorse Gramsci's theory of hegemony (see discussion of Hall in Chapter 4) by claiming that mass media are usually sympathetic to government policies and corporate decisions, and tend to marginalize dissenting voices. Their central argument is that media produce consent among 'the public' by reporting government concerns at face value but neglecting to examine wider economic, social and historical factors that shape international affairs. Indeed, this mode of 'self-censorship' (Herman and Chomsky 1994: xii) is considered by the authors to be more effective in granting consent to the words and actions of governments and other power elites than more traditional models of state censorship. Unlike the state-produced, top-down model of propaganda discussed by Lasswell (see Chapter 2), this propaganda model is altogether more sophisticated and subliminal because it hides behind claims to 'neutrality' that media institutions insist upon. Media may appear to be free in democratic societies but – as Hall has demonstrated (see Chapter 4) – they are by no means neutral or unbiased in the way they represent real events and people.

The propaganda model proposed by Herman and Chomsky is made up of five 'news filters' that mass media deploy – consciously or unconsciously – when they report on current affairs. The first filter they refer to is the size, ownership and profit orientation of mass media institutions. In a bygone age it was possible for a newspaper, say, to be produced and distributed across quite a significant geographical expanse at a manageable cost by a relatively small business (Curran and Seaton 2003). Nowadays, however, the huge costs involved in establishing any mass media enterprise capable of achieving long-lasting success mean that smaller companies cannot compete within existing ownership structures. This means that there is little scope for new, alternative media institutions to challenge the giant corporate networks such as Disney and Viacom. On the rare occasions when a challenge surfaces, large corporations are likely to buy out smaller firms for an attractive return. The power of media corporations is decisive because they tend to have far wider economic interests in sectors such as pharmaceuticals, oil and IT, while at the same time 'non-media companies have established a strong presence in the mass media' (Herman and Chomsky 1994: 12). All these big businesses depend upon governments and existing large corporations for consent to go about their business, so it is not difficult to understand why they are keen for media outlets (some of which they might own or have shareholdings in) to report on political and international affairs in a way that sympathizes with their government's point of view.

A second news filter is the advertising licence to do business. Again, we might look back nostalgically to an era when media institutions did not depend on advertising for their revenue. Early newspapers solely obtained revenue from sales and had no commercial intentions other than to 'sell their news', but the Northcliffe Revolution in Britain (as discussed in Chapter 3) together with the widespread growth of US media commercialism saw that advertising would become by far the most effective source of revenue for all kinds of media. Herman and Chomsky note that this dependency on advertising has the effect of forcing mass media institutions to tailor their material to an affluent audience – that is, the ideal audience for advertisers. As such, they argue: 'The idea that the drive for large audiences makes the mass media "democratic" thus suffers from the initial weakness that its political analogue is a voting system weighted by income!' (Herman and Chomsky 1994: 16). The 'mass audience' as defined by advertising-led mass media is therefore a distinctly middle-class or even upper middle-class one. By contrast, media that aim to cater for working-class or more radical, anti-consumerist audiences are discriminated against because, in this ad-fuelled climate, companies will not invest in advertising space for audiences who lack spending power – or lack the will to spend. Moreover, even mainstream media that cater for affluent audiences can easily lose advertisers unless they 'avoid programmes with serious complexities and disturbing controversies that interfere with the "buying mood"' (Herman and Chomsky 1994: 17). Serious programming such as documentaries and critical debate shows that challenge the consensus of government and corporate economics will not only impede the 'flow' of media-generated consumerism but could also upset advertisers whose interests are to maintain consensus. Media credibility – like media revenue – depends more on advertising than cutting-edge, ground-breaking content.

The third filter Herman and Chomsky refer to is the sourcing of mass media news. Most of the news we receive is derived from 'official' news sources such as the White House or Downing Street. These sources are given special status by media institutions because they are traditional, reliable and accessible providers of news. Of course, these are government sources designed to communicate public information (or propaganda) via mass media to the public at large, and mass media give a privileged voice to government sources in return for a ready supply of news streaming. Furthermore, 'taking information from sources that may be presumed credible reduces investigative expense, whereas material from sources that are not prima facie credible, or that will elicit criticism and threats, requires careful checking and costly research' (Herman and Chomsky 1994: 19). What appear at first to be suspicious news sources can nonetheless become valuable counter-perspectives on particular events and issues if only mass media would pay greater attention to them. Unfortunately, according to Herman and Chomsky, journalists prefer to rely on regular, familiar sources with which they have good working relationships. However, these relationships are prone to abuse from the news source: 'The media may feel obligated to carry extremely dubious stories and mute criticism in order not to offend their sources and disturb a close relationship' (Herman and Chomsky 1994: 22). Sources can also circumvent challenges to their authority from dissident media experts – such as scientists who fear about climate change – by 'putting them on the payroll as consultants' (Herman and Chomsky 1994: 23). In these ways, official government and corporate sources can manipulate and manage news media for their own ends by privileging their own messages over those of oppositional sources.

The fourth news filter is 'flak', meaning negative responses to a media statement or programme. According to the authors, 'Serious flak has increased in close parallel with business's growing resentment of media criticism and the corporate offensive of the 1970s and 1980s' (Herman and Chomsky 1994: 26). Flak is not just instigated by businesses though: 'The government is a major producer of flak, regularly assailing, threatening, and "correcting" the media, trying to contain any deviations from the established line' (Herman and Chomsky 1994: 28). Flak was most certainly produced by the Blair Government in 2003, faced with BBC reports alleging that public relations personnel – particularly Tony Blair's Head of Communications, Alistair Campbell – had made last-minute changes to the dossier on Iraq's so-called 'weapons of mass destruction' in order to sensationalize the threat and make the dossier more convincing as a justification for war. The BBC was bombarded with criticism from the British Government, which then led to a legal inquiry – known as the Hutton Report, written by a close ally of Blair and New Labour – that found no malpractice on the part of Government and biased journalism on the part of the BBC. Greg Dyke, then Director-General of the BBC and someone who staked his authority on the principle of journalistic independence in this case, subsequently resigned.

The fifth and final filter is the ideology of anticommunism that is widespread across American and Western media more generally. Western ideologies of free-market capitalism are implicitly and explicitly regarded by mass media as superior to communist ones. As such, 'issues tend to be framed in terms of a dichotomized world of Communist and anti-Communist powers' (Herman and Chomsky 1994: 30). The politics of Western mass media are therefore very much in keeping with the politics of the countries in which they operate. The United States, in particular, has spent much of its military and political energies over the course of the twentieth century fighting communist enemies – the Cold War with the Soviet Union being the most prolonged but further wars with Vietnam and Laos among others – that threaten the 'American way'. Moreover, anticommunism functions as a control mechanism by which governments and corporate powers can justify quite divisive capitalist policies within their home countries that widen inequalities in socio-economic class stratifications. The underlying message is: 'at least we're not living under an oppressive communist regime'. The communist model of absolute equality is not the answer, but neither is a rampant capitalist model of absolute inequality that – due to media propaganda – goes unnoticed.

These five filters constitute the main ways in which media follow a propaganda model. Although quite convincing and applied substantially to historic examples, we can identify two main criticisms of this model. First,

Herman and Chomsky do not sufficiently consider the complexities of the powerful elites that they believe can manage and manipulate media. There is an oversimplified assumption that all governments and large corporations have common interests and homogeneous intentions in their dissemination of propaganda. The kind of consent that they try to manufacture on their publics is not necessarily uniform and universal. Powerful elites have differences of political opinion and outlook in similar ways that society in general is marked by such differences. Second, there is no sustained acknowledgement that audiences may resist and reject mass-mediated propaganda. In a later book, Chomsky refers to the 'bewildered herd' (Chomsky 2002: 21) who cannot figure out the propaganda imposed upon them. Although he recognizes dissident cultures such as the feminist movement, he tends to share a behaviourist conception of 'the passive masses' by suggesting that media disinformation can control people and has not yet been overcome. It might also be argued that mass media institutions do not always share instrumental ties with ulterior government or corporate motives, and that media who can demonstrate some genuine independence from powerful interests – such as the non-commercialized BBC during the Iraq conflict – gain credibility among audiences. Criticisms aside, Herman and Chomsky's propaganda model has become a very influential media theory of political economy.

Critical political economy

The term 'political economy' would seem to indicate a shared concern with the politics and economics of any given institution, including mass media. In the case of critical political economy, however, the primary interest is in economic factors. According to one author associated with this field, 'a political economy, as I understand it, rests upon ultimate determination by the economic' (Garnham 1995: 219). This concern with economics can be contrasted with structuralist theories of media such as Hall's work on ideology and hegemony. Whereas ideology and hegemony are associated mostly with how the ideas and values of dominant cultures (the ruling elites) are encoded into media texts such as news bulletins, critical political economy argues that 'this process of ideological reproduction cannot be fully understood without an analysis of the economic context within which it takes place and of the pressures and determinations which this context exerts' (Murdock and Golding 1977: 19).

This contrast between cultural conceptions of ideology and economic conceptions of power is partly based on Karl Marx's distinction between the superstructure and the economic base. Marx argued that the economic base – the relations between those who own the material means of capitalist production and the labour force – was distinct from but related to the superstructure, by which he meant the various social, political and cultural frameworks (such as the legal system or state education) that helped to maintain order among people despite class inequalities (see Williams 1980). In its primary concern with the economic base, critical political economy is 'associated with macro-questions of media ownership and control, interlocking directorships and other factors that bring together media industries with other media and with other industries' (Boyd-Barrett 1995: 186). Nonetheless, political and social factors both shape and are shaped by economics, so political economy in a broader sense is also 'the study of the social relations, particularly the power relations, that mutually constitute the production, distribution, and consumption of resources' (Mosco 1996: 25).

The theoretical approach of Graham Murdock and Peter Golding has been the most sustained case for a political economy of media. Central to their thesis is the issue of concentration, whereby ownership becomes centralized into the hands of a few major companies in any given industrial sector of a capitalist economy. Closely associated with the notion of concentration is that of conglomeration, in which major companies (known as conglomerates) operate in several different sectors, such as banking, property construction and telecommunications. According to Murdock and Golding in their seminal article, 'For a political economy of mass communications' (first published in 1973), concentration and conglomeration result from three processes: integration, diversification and internationalization. First, integration is the process by which companies operating in a capitalist economy engage in mergers and takeovers. There are two types of integration – horizontal and vertical:

> Horizontal integration enables companies to consolidate and extend their control within a particular sector of media production and to maximize the economies of scale and shared resources ... Vertical integration occurs when a company with interests in one stage of the production process extends its operations to other stages such as the supply of raw materials, the provision of capital equipment, and the organization of distribution and retailing.
>
> (Murdock and Golding 1995: 206)

Figures 7.1 and 7.2 illustrate these two forms of integration. Figure 7.1 shows how COMPANY A is able to horizontally integrate three smaller companies (B, C and D) into its ownership or control by buying out or merging with them. Figure 7.2, on the other hand, sees COMPANY A vertically integrating by expanding its operations beyond one level of production to several other levels, again through takeovers and mergers. Large media corporations in any

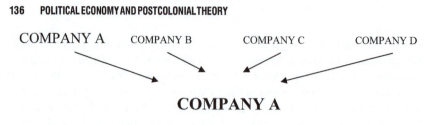

COMPANY A

Figure 7.1   Horizontal integration

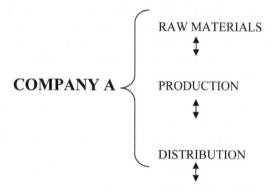

RETAIL/EXHIBITION

Figure 7.2   Vertical integration

given sector of the communications industry are active in both horizontal and vertical integration.

A second process of concentration is diversification, which 'occurs whenever a company with interests in one particular sector branches out and acquires interests in another sector' (Murdock and Golding 1977: 25). Diversification is an archetypal practice of media conglomerates such as the Walt Disney Company, which has interests in film studios, television and radio networks, internet operations, music publishing, theme parks and holiday resorts, and toys and merchandise among other things. Diversification, like integration, is associated with takeovers and mergers, although more commonly it is associated with institutional investment in share-holdings. As such, conglomerates may not own all the companies in which they have interests but they will usually have a significant degree of control over those companies by investing the largest stakes in their share value. Diversification also enables conglomerates 'to cushion the effects of recession in a particular sector' (Murdock and Golding 1995: 211) – for example, radio or newspaper production – safe in the knowledge that the other sectors in which they do business (perhaps non-media ones such as tourism) are generating substantial profits. The authors note that 'as concentration and diversification advance, so less and less voices survive in each media sector' (Murdock and Golding 1977: 37). Newspaper ownership is indicative of this state of affairs. The majority of newspapers make no or very little profit for their owners, or in some cases operate at a routine financial loss. Nonetheless, they survive because diversified media conglomerates such as Rupert Murdoch's News Corporation would rather cope with these losses than close down newspaper presses and run the risk of leaving a gap in the market for competitors to exploit by developing new press titles, which subsequently express hostility towards global corporations and offer challenging alternatives.

A third and final process of concentration is internationalization, which returns us to the central concerns associated with theories of media and cultural imperialism. Processes of internationalization and diversification are closely tied because media conglomerates often diversify into different sectors in different international markets. News Corporation, for example, has television networks in several different regions of the world (FOX in the USA, Sky in Britain, FOXTEL in Australia, STAR in Asia) as well as film, newspaper and internet operations in these regions. Also linked with processes of internationalization and diversification is the notion of corporate synergy. Media and cultural production is 'strongly influenced by commercial strategies built around "synergies" that exploit the overlaps between the company's different media interests' (Golding and Murdock 2000: 79). Corporate synergy enables News Corporation, for example, to advertise its televised sports coverage across its newspapers and other media outlets. After securing television rights to show live English Premiership football matches in the early 1990s, News Corporation used its popular British press titles such as *The Sun* to promote its Sky Sports subscription channel. It also exploited synergies with its various business interests across Asia to enable its Premiership football coverage to gain international exposure. In countries such as Japan and Thailand this has led to the widespread popularity of English football, and has helped to expand the global business operations of football clubs such as Liverpool and Manchester United (both now owned by American businessmen). Although internationalization through corporate synergy may appear a positive development, the 'effect is to reduce the diversity of cultural goods in circulation' (Golding and Murdock 2000: 79). It could be argued that Premiership football is such an expensive sport to televise and promote that it effectively silences other kinds of alternative sports excluded from media coverage because they fail to attract the same commercial support and advertising revenue.

These on-going economic processes of media concentration are considered by political economists not only to threaten cultural diversity but also to reproduce existing class inequalities. Debates about the 'digital divide' and technological exclusion tend to support this claim: 'The disposable income required for communication and information goods and services is tilted radically and increasingly towards more affluent groups' (Golding and Murdock 2000: 86). The authors also argue that media representations of a nation's social structure constitute the major source of information and imagery about social class divisions (Murdock and Golding 1977). Unfortunately, given that media production is controlled by those at the top end of the class structure, media representations of class inequalities tend to paper over the cracks and neglect to highlight major social problems such as child poverty and homelessness. However, we can point to a flaw in critical political economy theory – akin to criticisms of Adorno – in assuming that audiences passively accept and reproduce the dominant images and ideas that they glean from media representations. We might therefore sympathize with one critic who cites 'the relative absence of research to show that audiences did indeed respond to media content in the way that [political economy] theory suggested they would and research, when it came, was less supportive of the thesis than had been assumed' (Boyd-Barrett 1995: 189). Ralph Negrine (1994) also questions the idea that patterns of ownership stamp their ideological control over all media institutions and texts. Some media are tighter controlled than others: 'it is highly unlikely that the same pattern of control will be in evidence across diverse organizations and forms of ownership ... newspaper editors sometimes do not even exercise control over large sections of their newspapers' (Negrine 1994: 63–4). Media barons like Murdoch, likewise, are not necessarily control freaks in the instrumentalist sense of critical political economy.

Said: *Orientalism*

Edward Said's theory of **Orientalism** presented in a book of the same name (first published in 1978) has resonances with theories of political economy, and media and cultural imperialism. However, while media and cultural imperialists identify flows of information and propaganda that mainly travel from Western to non-Western countries, and while political economists tend to focus on Western economies, Said demonstrates how representations of non-Western cultures have mainly been conceived and authorized by Westerners. As such, Orientalism is closer associated with postcolonial theory (to be discussed later in this chapter) than political economy. Said argues that the Orient – by which he means 'the East' and especially the Middle East – has been conceived by the West (Europe and North America) as 'one of its deepest and recurring images of the Other' (Said 1995: 1). According to the author, from 'the comparatively greater strength of the Occident (British, French, or American) comes the large body of texts I call Orientalist' (Said 1995: 4). Orientalist texts such as exotic poems about Egyptian camels or

POLITICAL ECONOMY AND POSTCOLONIAL THEORY   139

anthropological studies of Indian tribes generate a Western discourse (language/knowledge) about the Orient that is biased, condescending, misrepresentative and interpreted solely through the eyes, words and media of non-native onlookers. This discourse is by no means harmless either. Like Foucault (see Chapter 4), Said considers discourse to be a linguistic form of knowledge and power. Historically, Westerners have wielded the power to develop their own representations of the Orient as seen from their perspectives, which have become sources of wider knowledge. Over time, these representations of the Orient become inseparable from a more universal sense of the 'real Orient'. The 'real Orient' becomes discursively constructed as the Other according to accepted opinion in the West.

Figure 7.3 provides some examples of how binary differences between the West and the Orient are constructed by representations in Western discourse.

WEST (us)	ORIENT (the Other)
Modern/Developed	Primitive
Rational	Emotional
Cultivated	Natural
Masculine/Powerful	Feminine/Vulnerable
White/Pure	Coloured/Stained
Civilized	Barbaric

Figure 7.3   The West versus the Orient

These binary differences are 'man-made' (Said 1995: 5) and have no natural foundation in truth. Indeed, Said refers to Orientalism as a science in which 'certain things, certain types of statements, certain types of work have seemed for the Orientalist correct' (Said 1995: 202). A well-known figure of authority who upheld these differences and perceived them to be correct was Rudyard Kipling in Orientalist texts such as *Kim* and *The Jungle Books*. Kipling, like other Western writers, did not so much represent as maliciously misrepresent and distort the reality of the Orient:

> every European, in what he could say about the Orient, was consequently a racist, an imperialist, and almost totally ethnocentric ... Orientalism aided and was aided by general cultural pressures that tended to make more rigid the sense of difference between the European and Asiatic parts of the world.
>
> (Said 1995: 204)

Although racist and imperialist, Said suggests that Orientalist texts became instilled into Western learning and consciousness through hegemonic filters in such a way that their ideological biases materialized into objective truths about a great gulf dividing the Occident (i.e. the West) from the Orient.

Said has since developed his theory of Orientalism and applied it to more contemporary instances of media and cultural imperialism. For instance, he argues that two current terms prevalent in Western discourse about non-Western cultures – 'terrorism' and 'fundamentalism' – emerged in the 1980s from Western systems of power including news agencies. These two terms 'signify moral power and approval for whoever uses them, moral defensiveness and criminalization for whomever they designate' (Said 1994: 375). Moreover, global media systems such as Hollywood perform 'a very efficient *mode of articulation* knitting the world together' (Said 1994: 374) but this mode of articulation is an Americanized discourse that represents non-Western cultures in often inaccurate, misleading ways. We might consider, for example, the stereotypical depiction of a shady Arab salesman in Disney's *Aladdin* (1992):

> Disney's version of *Aladdin* attracted immediate attention from Arab-American groups, who denounced some of the images and musical lyrics. The protests led to a change in the lyrics of one of the songs for the video version, but the offensive images of certain Arab characters remained.
>
> (Wasko 2001: 140)

Janet Wasko's (1994; 2001; 2003) political economy perspective on the global power of Hollywood film production, distribution and exhibition/retail is inextricably linked to postcolonial themes, as this instance of public reaction to unfair representations of race in *Aladdin* testifies.

Numerous studies have sought to apply Said's theory to further media representations of the Other. 'Islamophobia' has become a much discussed phenomenon since al-Qaeda attacks on New York, Washington, London and Madrid. A study of British news reporting on Islam and Muslims by Elizabeth Poole identifies 'The creation of a dichotomy between Islam and the West ... presented in the press along a series of binary oppositions in which the West stands for rational, humane, developed and superior, and Islam for aberrant, undeveloped and inferior' (Poole 2002: 43) (Figure 7.4). Moral panics about young Muslim men, fuelled by the tabloid press in particular, only serve to widen the perceived gulf in difference between Islam and the West. Islam becomes distorted as an extremist, fundamentalist religion and at the same time is labelled as if it were a homogeneous faith, in which all Muslims share the same opinions about non-Muslims (i.e. 'us'). But as Poole states, when Christianity is mentioned by Western media it is considered more complex, moderate and tolerant of competing views in comparison to the Other (i.e. Islamic fundamentalism).

Figure 7.4   Abu Hamza (aka Captain Hook), Islamic extremist

Clearly, Said's theory of Orientalism has a great deal of relevance to contemporary media theory if we acknowledge the power of media to inform and shape our views about other cultures and religions. The Alliance of Civilizations, a cross-cultural group of 20 prominent world figures such as Anglican Archbishop Desmond Tutu and former Iranian President Moham-med Khatami, has recently reported to the United Nations about the pressing need to bridge the West–Muslim divide (BBC Online 2006). Several criticisms of Said's theory should be noted, however. First, we might ask: what is Said's own mode of discourse? His work is written in the English language – not in any Arabic form of discourse – and presents its evidence within an academic, rational mode of discourse that Said has clearly derived from the West, even if his upbringing might be considered non-Western (he was born in Israel and spent some of his childhood in Egypt). Is Said an Orientalist? Given the evidence it would be plausible to answer 'yes' to this question, in which case he is a hypocrite! Second, we might ask: who can claim to offer a genuinely true, 'real' representation of any given culture? Kipling may have distorted the Orient but would a native's representation have been fairer and more genuine? Third, and finally, we might question the lack of cultural resistance accounted for in Said's theory of an all-powerful Orientalism – a criticism he has subsequently acknowledged in declaring that 'in the overwhelming majority of cases, the resistance finally won out' (Said 1994: xii). Blasphemous cartoon images of the prophet Muhammad published in Danish newspapers in 2005 were not permitted to penetrate into Western consciousness because they were met with forceful – in some cases, violent – resistance from Muslims and people of other faiths.

'The postcolonial' and race

What does 'postcolonial' mean in relation to media theory? Postcolonialism is a complex theoretical field that is more associated with literary and historical studies than media studies. 'The postcolonial' as a concept enables us to 'describe or characterize the shift in global relations which marks the (necessarily uneven) transition from the age of Empires to the post-independence or post-decolonization moment' (Hall 1996b: 246). In this sense, it has resonances with the older notion of 'colonialism' but points to newer, more recent relations between colonizing and colonized peoples that are no longer straightforwardly oppositional. Stuart Hall's theoretical accounts of ideology and particularly hegemony (see Chapter 4) point to power relations that are not top-down (as in 'the elite versus the masses') but are maintained through a degree of dialogue with, consent from and concession to the people. Said's postcolonial theory of Orientalism as well as some approaches to political economy (see discussion of Herman and Chomsky in this chapter) are conceived of as hegemonic struggles rather than wholesale oppressive encounters. Whereas colonialism refers to political and military occupation of another nation, postcolonialism can be understood as a more covert form of occupation that does not require physical invasion but is instead linked to processes of media and cultural imperialism. The two Gulf Wars in Iraq (1990–91 and 2003) were fought through information warfare and psychological operations – supported by sophisticated technologies to enable mediated propaganda, including global news channels such as CNN – as much as through colonial-style, military warfare (see Taylor 1997). The US-led 'War on Terror' is not primarily a war against particular nation-states – like colonial wars of the past – but is predominantly a cultural war between 'Western democracy' and extremist religious and political organizations such as al-Qaeda, that could be construed as remnants of the postcolonial turn in international relations.

The postcolonial turn has also influenced contemporary theories of **race** and (media) representation. Hall's discussion of 'the postcolonial' is sceptical about the idea of decolonization and his 'grammar of race' argument (Hall 1995) suggests that minority ethnic groups in white, Western cultures continue to be misrepresented by racist tendencies. Here he distinguishes between overt racism and less intentional forms of inferential racism which rely on unquestioned assumptions that 'blacks' or other ethnic minorities are the 'natural' cause of problems in race relations (Hall 1995: 20). The 'grammar of race', typically articulated by media texts such as documentaries about race relations or films about black people in white communities, reproduces persistent images of ethnic minorities as 'the Other'. Hall cites three examples. First, there is the 'slave figure' who appears to be devoted to his white Master but is seen as a threat to civilized white manners and decorum, as represented by films like *Gone with the Wind* (1939). Then there is the 'native figure' who is dignified but ultimately connotes barbarism and savagery. This native figure is not unlike the black ghetto gangsters in films like *New Jack City* (1991). And third there is the 'clown or entertainer' figure who jokes about their ethnic peculiarities: 'It is never quite clear whether we are laughing with or at this figure' (Hall 1995: 22). Charlie Williams, the first successful black comedian on British television, told white hecklers: 'If you don't shut up, I'll come and move in next door to you.' To some extent this phrase only served to draw attention to racial inequalities in Britain, not unlike Will Smith's character in the American sitcom, *The Fresh Prince of Bel-Air* (1990–96). As well as fictional representations of race, Hall et al.'s (1978) analysis of news reports on 'mugging' show how emotive language is used to construct criminals – particularly impoverished black men – as 'evil thugs' and 'animals' which, the authors argue, justifies more punitive sentencing of petty crimes and disregards the socio-economic problems experienced by ethnic minorities. Elsewhere (Alvarado et al. 1987), four themes in media representations of race from a white perspective have been identified: (1) the exotic (e.g. Aladdin and his magic lamp); (2) the dangerous (e.g. Osama bin Laden); (3) the humorous (e.g. minstrel performers); and (4) the pitied (e.g. starving refugees in Sudan).

Media and cultural representations of race are not always so stereotypical, however, and not least when they are generated from within minority ethnic groups. The politics of race in relation to music is discussed by Paul Gilroy (1987; 1993) in his concerns about the exclusionary effects of racist British policies since the 1950s. Gilroy deploys the notion of 'diaspora' to understand how black cultures experience dislocation from their homelands (such as Jamaica) and relocation in new 'homes' such as Britain. Hebdige's (1979) study of subcultures (see Chapter 4) considered the complex relations between working-class white and black youth in the post-war period, with both groups influencing each other's ethnic identities despite frequent confrontations. Gilroy (1987) argues that black culture – and black music in particular – articulated diasporic experiences of resistance to white capitalist culture. This is evidenced in three anti-capitalist themes. First, black music and expressive culture are critical of capitalist productivism and divisions of labour that were typically experienced by first-generation black immigrants who worked in heavy manufacturing industries. The lyrics of reggae musicians such as Bob Marley 'connect with the active rejection of certain kinds of work by young blacks' (Gilroy 1987: 200). Second, black music is critical of the state and its ties with other forms of domination such as the legal system and the military. And third, black music cultures have 'a passionate belief in the importance of history' (Gilroy 1987: 199) – including the painful but sacred history of black slavery – which critiques the emphasis on temporal trends under late capitalism. Also important to Gilroy's argument is the doubt he expresses as to whether there is, in essence, a unified – and not white-inflected – definition of 'black music' (Gilroy 1993; see also Tagg 1989).

Resistance to white capitalist policies and white representations of black cultures are also expressed in rap music, which originated in the mid-1970s in New York's South Bronx and which 'prioritizes black voices from the margins of urban America' (Rose 1994: 2). Tricia Rose's analysis identifies how rap culture and lyrics 'articulate the chasm between black urban lived experience and dominant, "legitimate" (e.g. neoliberal) ideologies regarding equal opportunity and racial inequality' (Rose 1994: 102). So while there are plenty of media representations of race that serve dominant, white capitalist inter-ests, there are some arenas of mediated resistance to these dominant ideol-ogies too. However, it is without doubt the case that white musicians exploit the images and symbols of black cultural resistance as a means of constructing their own authenticity. Madonna – in her various reinvented personas – 'appropriates and commodifies aspects of black culture' for 'her own oppor-tunistic ends' (hooks 1992: 157, 159). bell hooks (1992) compares the for-tunes of black female musicians such as Tina Turner – who was sexually and materially abused on her road to fame – unfavourably with white stars such as Madonna. hooks argues that white women such as the young Madonna can be represented as 'pure' and 'sexually innocent' in a way that black women cannot because they are tarnished with the myth that they are 'sexually aggressive' and 'fallen'. This evidence supports hooks's theory of race and representation which asserts that black women are constructed as 'the Other' – much like Said's Orient – by the dual oppressive forces of white supremacist culture and patriarchy.

Summary

This chapter has considered:

- Definitions of political economy and postcolonial theory.
- Adorno's theory of standardization and his conception of a mono-lithic 'culture industry' churning out rubbish (especially popular music) for the deceived masses, as well as challenges to this con-ception of cultural production that adopt a more dynamic model of the 'cultural industries'.
- Theories of media and cultural imperialism (e.g. Schiller) –

particularly American-led media commercialism – and opposing theories of cultural resistance.

- The propaganda model of political economy (Herman and Chomsky) in which mass media serve the hegemonic interests of governments and big businesses.
- Processes of concentration and conglomeration – integration, diversification and internationalization – as analysed by critical political economy theory (e.g. the work of Murdock and Golding).
- Orientalism (Said) and the postcolonial argument that Western representations of the Other (e.g. Islam) are misconceived, imperialist and racist.
- Postcolonial theories of representations of race, particularly in relation to black music and expressive culture.

Further reading

Curran, J. and Park, M-J. (eds) (2000) *De-Westernizing Media Studies*. London: Routledge.

Debates and issues to do with media power and globalization in authoritarian, democratic and transitional societies are explored in depth. Recommended for advanced undergraduates and postgraduates.

Dyer, R. (1997) *White*. London: Routledge.

This book considers representations of whiteness in relation to Christianity, race and colonialism – a surprisingly unexplored subject area. Recommended for advanced undergraduates and postgraduates.

Hartley, J. (ed.) (2005) *Creative Industries*. Oxford: Blackwell.

An edited collection of articles on creative and cultural industries in several countries. Sections included on creative cities, creative enterprises and creative economy. Suitable for all media students.

Tunstall, J. and Machin, D. (1999) *The Anglo-American Media Connection*. Oxford: Oxford University Press.

The economic and political power of British and American media – familiar ground for Tunstall – is reinforced and updated with respect to Hollywood genres, the US-UK world news duopoly, sports media, and advertising agencies among other case studies. Suitable for all media students.

Wasko, J. (2003) *How Hollywood Works*. London: Sage.

This is a political economy perspective on the global dominance of the US film industry. Chapters included on Hollywood production, distribution, exhibition and retail, as well as useful statistical data on the power of media conglomerates. Suitable for all media students.

8   Postmodernity and the information society

Introduction

Postmodernity and **postmodernism** are difficult theoretical themes to define succinctly. The two terms are closely related, although – like the distinction between modernity and modernism – there are fundamental differences. Postmodernity refers to social, economic, political and technological developments that have characterized the transition from modern to newly-organized, postmodern ways of life. Two aspects of postmodernity are often marked out: first, the emergence and proliferation of new media, information and communications technologies that trigger social change and are particularly indicative of globalization; and, second, the rise of consumer culture and simultaneous demise of certain forms of production (Lyon 1999: 10). Some other important developments related to postmodernity are listed in Figure 8.1. Essentially we see a transition from the elitist values of modernity – espoused by a capitalist ruling elite and manifested in 'high culture' – to a postmodern 'flattening of hierachies' (Bauman 1992: 34). At first, this seems like social progress, but postmodern critics such as Zygmunt Bauman consider postmodern relationships to be fragmentary, shallow, driven by consumerism, and lacking moral responsibility to others – especially disadvantaged groups unable to reap the rewards of this so-called progress (see Bauman 1996). In contrast to postmodernity, the term 'postmodernism' refers to art, literature and cultural criticism that have supplanted the modernist tradition. Postmodernism is seen as a reaction to the elitism of high modernism (evident in, for example, the Leavisite tradition as discussed in Chapter 3) and a rejection of realism – the artistic endeavour to represent an objective reality (e.g. Dickens's realist novels about everyday poverty).

This chapter deals with *postmodernity* in relation to media theory, but by definition there are significant overlaps with theories of postmodernism. Dominic Strinati (1995) refers to five key features of postmodernism:

1   *Breakdown of the distinction between culture and society*: as he states, 'the importance and power of the mass media and popular culture mean that they govern and shape all other forms of social relationships' (Strinati 1995: 224). Our perceptions of the social environment in which we live are largely informed by mediated cultural representations such as news images.

2   *An emphasis on style over substance*: we consume images and

Women gain the right to vote (1920 in the United States, 1928 in Britain).

Education and literacy levels increase throughout the social strata.

Increased affluence – also experienced by the working-class population – means greater social mobility.

Rise in demand for service industries to serve the masses (mass retail, mass consumerism, mass media).

Technological innovation propels globalization – a combination of cultural homogenization and diversity.

Figure 8.1 Postmodernity and the empowered masses: some reasons for the decline of modernism and elitist 'high culture'

spectacles, as opposed to forms of communication such as the written word that encourage us to ponder and reflect.

3 *Breakdown of the distinction between high art and popular culture*: this is a modernist distinction that is now threatened by postmodern media culture that embraces both 'art' and 'the popular' (pop music, Hollywood, and so on).

4 *Confusions over time and space*: the globalizing tendencies of communications technologies, economics and politics are distorting traditional conceptions of time and space dimensions.

5 *Decline of metanarratives*: grand theories such as Marxism, Christianity and, of course, modernism have lost their currency for modern societies.

All these five features – in their original conceptions – will be applied to media and postmodernity in the course of this chapter. Somewhat challenging the fifth feature, however, will be our discussion of the **information society** thesis that could be construed, paradoxically, as a postmodern metanarrative.

Baudrillard: hyperreality and simulation

Jean Baudrillard is the best known and arguably the most elusive theorist of postmodernity. His elusiveness is partly due to the cryptic style in which he writes but is also due to the controversial – and apparently absurd – character of his theories. 'The Gulf War did not take place' and 'Disneyland is the *real* America' appear to be ridiculous claims but, as we shall see, Baudrillard presents a complex argument that offers a specific interpretation of these theoretical statements. He argues that postmodern societies – saturated by media and information technologies – have entered an age of **simulation**, and more particularly an age of third-order simulation. Third-order simulation differs from two earlier forms of simulation, as detailed in Table 8.1.

Table 8.1 Baudrillard's three orders of simulation

Order of simulation	Type	Description
First-order	Signification (signs which imitate real things)	Reality is constructed through representation (e.g. maps, paintings)
Second-order	Reproduction (signs refer to signs which imitate real things)	Representations of reality (first-order) are reproduced by mechanical technologies (e.g. photography, film)
Third-order	Simulation (signs no longer represent real things but serve to mask this absence of reality)	No connection exists between reality and representation – instead we have hyperreality (e.g. Disneyland)

First-order and second-order simulation maintain a relationship between reality and representations (signs) of reality – indeed, second-order simulation is the type celebrated by Benjamin (as discussed in Chapter 3). By contrast, third-order simulation amounts to a system of signs that bear no relation to reality or its representations, but function to conceal this absence of genuinely real things. Disneyland, according to Baudrillard, is a third-order simulation. Disneyland is pure fantasy, of course, but it simultaneously functions 'to make us believe that the rest is real, when in fact all of Los Angeles and the America surrounding it are no longer real, but of the order of the hyperreal and of simulation' (Baudrillard 1983: 25). This is what Baudrillard means when he states that Disneyland is the *real* America, because the *real* America is actually a hyperreal phenomenon divorced from the once genuinely real place called America that has now vanished from human experience. **Hyperreality**, therefore, is the outcome of simulated imagery – what Baudrillard calls **simulacra**: 'The simulacrum denies not reality, but the difference between the image and the real ... there is no difference between the image and other orders of experience' (Fiske 1991b: 57–8). Los Angeles *is* its media images and cultural myths more so than it is a real, material, geographical location. We have nothing real to believe in except hyperreal (more *real* than genuinely real) simulation and simulacra.

What has brought about this postmodern age of simulation and hyperreality? For Baudrillard, the transformation of signs no longer referring to real things as they are channelled through media and communications technologies – especially television – has collapsed the separation between the real (the physical, terrestrial habitat) and the metaphysical (knowledge beyond this habitat). Like 'an astronaut in his capsule' each human being is 'at the controls of a micro-satellite, in orbit, living no longer as an actor or dramaturge but as a terminal of multiple networks. Television is still the most direct prefiguration of this … regulating everything from a distance' (Baudrillard 1985: 128). Just as prisons conceal the fact that society as a whole is imprisoned in the sense of being unable to access genuine reality, so television and other electronic media conceal processes of simulation which effectively regulate and restrict our versions of the 'reality' (hyperreality actually) we sense around us. As Bauman states, 'For Baudrillard, society itself is now made to the measure of television … One can no longer speak of the distortion of reality: there is nothing left to measure the image against' (Bauman 1992: 33). Similarly, the omnipresence of mediated advertising 'invades everything, as public space (the street, monument, market, scene) disappears … Not a public scene or true public space but gigantic spaces of circulation, ventilation and ephemeral connections' (Baudrillard 1985: 129–30). This media power to saturate public and private spaces or *scenes* by harassing us with *obscene* simulations – what he refers to as 'a whole pornography of information and communication' – is what Baudrillard calls 'the ecstasy of communication. All secrets, spaces and scenes abolished in a single dimension of information' (Baudrillard 1985: 130–1). Television, telephone and radio are just three media technologies that partake in this ecstasy of communication – they invade our lives and confuse our sense of knowing what we want. This, in turn, creates a new form of schizophrenia caused by 'too great a proximity to everything' (Baudrillard 1985: 132).

Baudrillard's theory of media-saturated simulation owes much to McLuhan's statement that 'the medium is the message' (as discussed in Chapter 3). His suggestion that information devours its own content and that 'Only the medium can make an event – whatever the contents' (Baudrillard 1994: 82) is clearly McLuhan-esque, and Baudrillard draws on McLuhan's ideas in several of his works. However, Baudrillard's hyperreality theory goes a step further than McLuhan's medium theory:

> there is not only an implosion of the message in the medium, there is, in the same movement, the implosion of the medium itself in the real, the implosion *of the medium and of the real* in a sort of hyperreal nebula, in which even the definition and distinct action of the medium can no longer be determined
>
> (Baudrillard 1994: 82).

The medium is the real message in McLuhan's theory of modernity but, having undergone postmodern transformation, the medium and the message collapse into a third-order simulation of *the real* (i.e. the hyperreal). For Baudrillard, medium (technology) and message (content) are no longer real because they saturate any genuine sense of reality that distinguishes between them. There are some other fundamental differences between the two theorists that are often understated. One commentator argues that McLuhan's emphasis on the power of technological form over content is counteracted by Baudrillard's theory of simulation which emphasizes 'the sign-form, not technology per se' (Merrin 2005: 50). The semiotic transformation of signs and symbols (that no longer refer to real things) is not determined by technology but by human perception of – and participation in – the ecstasy of communication. Technology is therefore secondary to the implosion of the message (and the medium) into simulation. Another difference cited by William Merrin is McLuhan's 'global village' perspective that electronic media foster retribalization compared to Baudrillard's vision of 'an indistinct mass created by, refusing and imploding with the circuit of communication' (Merrin 2005: 53). Baudrillard's claim that media power abolishes social relations and transforms individuals into networked terminals is far less optimistic than McLuhan's version, the latter of which is closer to theories of progressive information society (as discussed later in this chapter).

We cannot leave our discussion of Baudrillard, however, without considering how his theory of simulation casts doubt on the 'reality' of the first Gulf War (Baudrillard 1995) as well as the 9/11 terrorist atrocities (Baudrillard 2002). The Gulf War did not take place, according to Baudrillard, because it was won by the mighty US Air Force before it had begun. The lasting memories of this war for most people were screened images – transmitted via military operations to CNN and other Western media – showing how US pilots pinpointed and then bombed Iraqi targets (bridges, hospitals, military camps) from thousands of miles above land. As such, 'This war is conducted according to the media model: war as a technological relationship . . . founded on the abolition of symbolic exchange and the simulation of real communication' (Merrin 2005: 84). This is not a war in the sense of prolonged combat and conflict (the first two world wars, by contrast, *really* did take place); instead, we experience a virtual war, much like a video game simulates real warfare, and therefore this real-time, media-saturated spectacle is nothing other than what Baudrillard calls a 'non-event'. Subsequent wars in Afghanistan and Iraq amount to 'a rehash of the past, with the same deluge of military forces, bogus information, senseless bombardment, emotive and deceitful language, technological deployment and brainwashing. Like the Gulf War: a non-event, an event that does not take place' (Baudrillard 2002: 34).

What happened to the weapons of mass destruction that Iraq was supposed to possess? They did not exist. Baudrillard might use this evidence of 'bogus information' and the emotive language it engendered to argue that the subsequent conflict is a mere simulation to those who fight and witness it. Then again, one obvious criticism of this 'non-event' thesis is that no simulated, virtual war that 'did not take place' has ever resulted in so many casualties and fatalities, not to mention changes to world order. It is easy to sympathize with one critic who refers to Baudrillard's 'stupid and irresponsible position' and 'his rampant relativism which refuses to discriminate between degrees of authenticity' (Webster 2002: 256–7).

9/11, on the other hand, did take place and was 'the absolute event': 'The whole play of history and power is disrupted by this event' (Baudrillard 2002: 4). Terrorist violence – unlike the violence of the Gulf War – amounts to an exchange of symbolic violence in which 'the media are part of the event, they are part of the terror' (Baudrillard 2002: 31). Although the destruction of the World Trade Center was a real event, however, its symbolic collapse was more significant and came before its physical collapse. According to Baudrillard, 'The architectural object was destroyed, but it was the symbolic object which was targeted and which it was intended to demolish ... no one, not even the terrorists, had reckoned on the total destruction of the towers' (Baudrillard 2002: 48). The objective of the terrorists was to demonstrate 'the terrorism of spectacle' as opposed to the spectacle of terrorism (Baudrillard 2002: 30). Even though the twin towers did collapse and thousands of people died, Baudrillard insists that this Manhattan disaster movie was not a real event for those who witnessed it on television because 'the fascination of the attack is primarily a fascination with the image', and 'The image consumes the event, in the sense that it absorbs it and offers it for consumption' (Baudrillard 2002: 27–9). The event and the image present entirely different experiences. In the case of real-time media coverage, 'the image is there first, and the *frisson* of the real is added' to create 'a fiction surpassing fiction' (Baudrillard 2002: 29). While Baudrillard makes a convincing point about the power of imagery over unmediated experience in contemporary culture, he neglects to pursue his initial claim in *The Spirit of Terrorism* (2002) that the events of 9/11 – far from mere simulation – had a very *real* consequence for history and the events that were to follow.

Boorstin and Debord: the image and the spectacle

Two important influences on Baudrillard's theory of simulation are Daniel J. Boorstin's *The Image* (first published in 1961) and Guy Debord's *The Society of the Spectacle* (first published in 1967). Boorstin explores the concept of 'pseudo-events', especially rife in news media and not dissimilar to Baudrillard's media-simulated 'non-events'. Boorstin argues that the omnipresence of images, which are so easy to produce and distribute via multi-media channels in the late twentieth century, are indicative of a Graphic Revolution

(Boorstin 1992: 13) – a wholesale change in the way we view the reality of our world. Instead of increasing our awareness of the world, however, Boorstin suggests that news media do not usually report 'real', truthful events but instead deal in a currency of false, pseudo-events. A pseudo-event is 'not spontaneous, but comes about because someone has planned, planted, or incited it. Typically, it is not a train wreck or an earthquake, but an interview' (Boorstin 1992: 11). Boorstin lays the blame for this state of affairs at the feet of public relations and journalistic practices. The press conference, for example, is a contrived pseudo-event carefully planned by newsworthy individuals or institutions in order to satisfy journalists' insatiable appetite for fresh 'news'. It is a self-fulfilling pseudo-event that offers little genuine news value at all. The British Prime Minister's weekly press briefing, for example, is staged and usually reported in news bulletins even if the Prime Minster has nothing really *new* to say. An up-to-date image of the Prime Minster along with his latest spin doctoring message is enough to hit the headlines. Boorstin even suggests that pseudo-events have diminished what it means to be a famous public figure. Real heroes of the past who undertook great feats have been replaced by manufactured, image-conscious celebrities who have no genuine talent. The technological progress that would lead to intellectual and political enlightenment – as promised by Benjamin and McLuhan – is not shared by the impotence of this postmodern Graphic Revolution.

Guy Debord offers a similarly cynical perspective on what he terms 'the spectacle' which 'is both the outcome and the goal of the dominant mode of production' (Debord 1994: 13). He notes: 'the world we see is the world of the commodity' (Debord 1994: 29). By extension, Debord's theory of the spectacle is not limited to mass media images, but is more centrally to do with modern capitalist economies that produce a form of spectacle which isolates and alienates those who are forced to consume it. It is only when 'the spectacle is *capital* accumulated to the point where it becomes image' (Debord 1994: 24) that it fulfils this function of alienation, and the spectacle only becomes image when mediated through technologies such as television which 'serve as weapons for that [spectacular] system as it strives to reinforce the isolation of the "lonely crowd"' (Debord 1994: 22). The spectacle is therefore not primarily a collection of images but 'a social relationship between people that is mediated by images' (Debord 1994: 12). Nonetheless, this relationship is entirely based on appearances and images – a false reality – that conceals a real world of capitalist exploitation and class division. Echoing Baudrillard, Debord states that 'the spectacle's job is to cause a world that is no longer directly perceptible to be *seen* via different specialized mediations' (Debord 1994: 17). The word *seen* is italicized by Debord because sight is the human sense most vulnerable to deception and false belief. After all, *seeing is believing* – but we do not always *see through* artifice and manipulation.

Although originally intended as Marxist rather than postmodern theory,

Debord's work has since been closely associated with the postmodernist emphasis on style over substance; image over reality. This is particularly evident in one of the two forms of the spectacle he outlines (Debord 1994: 41–3). First, we have the concentrated form of spectacle, which is associated with bureaucratic ownership and restriction of choice in the capitalist realms of production and labour. More significant, though, is a second form that Debord calls the diffuse form of spectacle, which is associated with the abundance of commodities in the capitalist mode of consumption. He identifies 'the pseudo-need imposed by the reign of modern consumerism ... Waves of enthusiasm for particular products, fuelled by the communications media, are propagated with lightning speed' (Debord 1994: 44). The triumph of the spectacular economy, therefore, springs from its 'ceaseless manufacture of pseudo-needs' (Debord 1994: 33) that strike a familiar chord with Boorstin's pseudo-events. One such 'specialized mediation' of these false needs is the media celebrity. While Boorstin ridicules the emptiness of the image-conscious media celebrity, Debord conceives them as spectacular representations of ordinary people who turn their spectacle into 'images of possible roles' for us to identify with so as 'to compensate for the crumbling of directly experienced diversifications of productive activity' (Debord 1994: 38). Celebrities provide us with false representations of life, which reinforces Debord's argument that the spectacle they produce – via media – is not perceptible to direct experience and is predominantly experienced as a series of appearances. However, this spectacle *becomes* the reality of our everyday lives to the extent that social life becomes an alienating scenario grounded entirely in appearances (first impressions). On the other hand, real class inequalities, poverty and social exclusion – created by the capitalist mode of production and its uneven distribution of wealth – are concealed by the spectacle in order to protect the dominant order of power from the proletariat uprising predicted by Marx.

Jameson: pastiche and intertextuality

Although principally a postmodernist, Fredric Jameson's theories of contemporary media and culture, like Debord's theory of spectacle, owe much to Marxism. Jameson argues that we have entered a stage of late capitalism associated with post-industrial, consumer societies and globalization in the shape of multinational economics. Postmodern culture 'replicates or reproduces – reinforces – the logic of consumer capitalism' (Jameson 1998: 20) by embracing all things 'popular' and rejecting the modernist values of non-commercial, 'high art'. While modernism sought to clearly distinguish high culture from mass or popular culture, the onset of postmodernism – from the post-war boom of the 1950s onwards – has meant that 'the line between high art and commercial forms seems increasingly difficult to draw' (Jameson 1998: 2). This cultural turn from modernism to postmodernism is centred on 'The disappearance of the individual subject, along with its formal consequence, the increasingly unavailability of the personal style' (Jameson 1991: 16). Modernist art and literature cherish the value of individuality and the 'first-person' voice in stark contrast to the hostility of an outside world marked by rampant modernity – industrialization, scientific and technological advance, rationalization, and so on (see theories of modernity in Chapter 3). James Joyce's 'stream of consciousness' technique – in which an author's thoughts and feelings are directly translated into a rambling written style – typifies the individual style of modernism. Postmodernist culture, from Jameson's point of view, dismisses the possibility that an individual style can still exist in a late capitalist era where all new styles are immediately incorporated to serve the intentions of global, consumer capitalism.

Jameson's notion of **pastiche** – and the way pastiche differs from the practice of 'parody' – is central to his postmodernist perspective on the disappearance of individuality and originality. Parody is a general technique of mimicry, not peculiar to postmodernism, which has the comic intention to 'produce an imitation which mocks the original' (Jameson 1998: 4). Impersonators deploy parody to mimic the actions and behaviour of others, especially famous people. Importantly, parody acknowledges what it imitates and does not ignore the sanctity of the original form. As such, 'there is a linguistic norm' (Jameson 1998: 4) behind parody. Parody mocks but does not threaten the existence of original meanings (language). By contrast, pastiche is a technique peculiar to postmodernism because it denies the existence of – refuses to acknowledge – the original form it *appears* to be imitating. Pastiche is less about comedy and more about plagiarism. Pastiche does not accept that 'some healthy linguistic normality still exists' (Jameson 1991: 17) because, unlike parody, it has no satirical purpose and does not distinguish its own mimic from an original form. As such, 'Pastiche is blank parody, parody that has lost its sense of humour' (Jameson 1998: 5). Pastiche is the outcome of wider trends in postmodernity that have arisen from the compartmentalization of the professions since the earlier developments of modernity. For Jameson, the fragmentation and privatization of language into different styles associated with these professional practices – medicine, law, literature, and so on – have meant these styles are now impossible to ridicule because there is no longer a universal 'linguistic norm' through which to parody such styles. Postmodernist, pastiche styles therefore arise from both the disappearance of originality (linguistic norms) and the disappearance of parody, which relies on an original form with which to mock.

Pastiche is closely linked with Jameson's theory of **intertextuality** that he defines 'as a deliberate, built-in feature of the aesthetic effect, and as the operator of a new connotation of "pastness" and pseudo-historical depth, in which the history of aesthetic styles displaces "real" history' (Jameson 1991: 20). As well as the disappearance of individuality and originality, postmodern culture has lost its sense of the past because the past has become romanticized by artistic representations of history that are clouded by nostalgia. As the author states, 'we seem condemned to seek the historical past through our own pop images and stereotypes about the past, which itself remains forever out of reach' (Jameson 1998: 10). Mike Featherstone makes a similar point about the aestheticization of the present day as evidenced by 'the rapid flow of signs and images which saturate the fabric of everyday life in contemporary society' (Featherstone 1991: 66), of which MTV and its 'three-minute concentration span' philosophy is a prime example. For Jameson, intertextuality is a practice typically found in postmodern films and other media texts that borrow features from other texts. Like pastiche, intertextuality is not about an overt acknowledgement of the original text (or texts) from which it is borrowing certain features but rather about an insistence on the disappearing sense of anything original or historical that has gone before. Intertextuality operates in a perpetual present because postmodernity has effectively obliterated any genuine sense of the past. Jameson identifies the 'nostalgia film' as an example of pastiche and intertextuality in practice. *American Graffiti* (1973), for example, aims to 'recapture all the atmosphere and stylistic peculiarities of the 1950s United States' (Jameson 1998: 7–8) by imitating – in pastiche form – both the content and the formal filmic techniques associated with earlier representations of the rock and roll generation. *Chinatown* (1974) likewise is a pastiche of 1930s America and aesthetic styles of American filmmaking familiar to this period.

Pastiche as it operates in a nostalgic mode differs from imitation as practised in the more generic category of 'historical film', however, because it colonizes 'even those movies today which have contemporary settings, as though, for some reason, we were unable today to focus our own present' (Jameson 1998: 9). Films more or less about the present day – such as *Star Wars* (1977) and *The Day After Tomorrow* (2004) – are incapable of creating new, original representations of contemporary life, and are therefore forced to pastiche aesthetic (filmic) styles of a previous age, such as science-fiction literature and the 'disaster movie' genre, as evidenced by covert, intertextual references. Usually these references to previous films or generic conventions operate on an unconscious level and are not easily identifiable. In these cases, film directors may well refuse to acknowledge their indebtedness to a particular filmic style or scene – in keeping with the practice of pastiche – but instances of intertextuality are always able to be drawn because so-called 'new' styles have 'already been invented; only a limited number of combinations are possible; the unique ones have been thought of already' (Jameson 1998: 7). There are occasions, though, when intertextual references are self-consciously constructed for purposes of parody, in 'spoofs' like the *Naked Gun* films (1988; 1991). In these films or other media texts, intertextuality is not a specifically postmodern facet.

Jameson's postmodernist theories of pastiche and intertextuality can certainly be applied to various media and cultural examples, and not just films. Certain forms of popular music, for example, 'sample' or draw from previous sounds and tracks (pastiche), and these forms can be distinguished from overt 'covers' that – like parody – acknowledge an original version. We should be keen to critically evaluate these theories, though. Is originality really impossible today? This partly depends on what we mean by originality. Jameson appears to define the individual style as unique and entirely new, according to high modernism, but that famous modernist T. S. Eliot understood the 'individual talent' as emerging from a concern with both tradition and novelty; with an historical sense 'not only of the pastness of the past, but of its presence' (Eliot 1951: 14). Eliot's definition of originality, therefore, is not about uniqueness but about adding a distinctive contribution to an existing 'ideal order' of canonical art and literature. What Jameson defines as unoriginal intertextuality, then, amounts to a more conservative interpretation of tradition-minded individual talent in Eliotian terms. Another criticism we might level at Jameson is that by referring to the disappearance of our sense of history, he also appears conveniently to neglect a long history of pastiche-like intertextuality. Shakespeare's plays, for instance *Anthony and Cleopatra*, are full of intertextual references to earlier chronicles without overtly acknowledging the historical origins of their narratives. Jameson does make it clear that aesthetic practices of pastiche have existed longer than postmodernism but that 'we have something new when they become the central features of cultural production' (Jameson 1998: 18). Is pastiche so central to contemporary media and cultural texts? Films and music – associated with genre traditions – are perhaps often pastiche-like, but what about less predictable media texts such as live (television) coverage of news or sports events? Are not live, 'real-time' media texts, by definition, original? Jameson might argue that while the content of live media may be original, the formal ways in which media represent live action always draw on pre-existing aesthetic styles.

Lyotard: the decline of metanarratives

For Jean-François Lyotard, the forces of multinational capitalism have not so much brought about the death of modernist 'high art' as the delegitimation of assumed scientific knowledge. The sacred truth of science, like art, so coveted in the age of modernity, is threatened by the onset of postmodernity. Lyotard's postmodern theory of knowledge is grounded in the decline of two types of **metanarrative** (or **grand narrative**): the narrative of emancipation and the narrative of speculation. Both of these narratives sought to legitimize – justify as true – their claims about the virtues of science and knowledge against the sins of ignorance, religion and superstition characteristic of pre-modern societies (see Figure 3.1 in Chapter 3). The narrative of emancipation or freedom is a political narrative, often utilized by the state in their provision of school education, which tells of science as a great, liberating force against the shackles of an older, feudal, medieval order (also known as the 'Dark Ages' given that the medieval period had not yet been enlightened by the truth of scientific knowledge). Likewise, the narrative of speculation sought to legitimize scientific knowledge, but in the form of a philosophical narrative associated with the rise of university education that was not so bound to state politics. Narratives of speculation differed from those of emancipation by not accepting statements of knowledge at face value and emphasizing a holistic approach to unified learning – combining the arts and sciences – rather than, in the unification of the narrative of emancipation, separating knowledge into distinct but related disciplines (e.g. physics, mathematics and economics). Regardless of their political and philosophical differences, both types of metanarrative are in decline. Lyotard's perspective is clearly contrary to Foucault's (1989) theory of discourse as exclusionary power and knowledge (see Chapter 4).

According to Lyotard, postmodern culture has led to a situation in which 'The grand narrative has lost its credibility, regardless of what mode of unification it uses, regardless of whether it is a speculative narrative or a narrative of emancipation' (Lyotard 1984: 37). Reasons for this loss of credibility in metanarratives are not fully accounted for by Lyotard, but he tentatively suggests that several outcomes of advanced liberal capitalism have affected such a decline in belief about grand ideas and ways of knowing the world. Like Jameson, he suggests that consumerism and 'the individual enjoyment of goods and services' are indicative of postmodernity in its denial of the 'communist alternative' (Lyotard 1984: 38) or any other grand theory about society other than a liberal capitalist one. As well as the capitalist prosperity enjoyed by advanced societies in the latter half of the twentieth century, Lyotard argues that it is understandable that 'the disorienting upsurge of technology would have an impact on the status of knowledge' (Lyotard 1984: 38). The proliferation of communications technologies including transportation, media and information systems have meant that 'knowledge has become the principal force of production over the last few decades' (Lyotard 1984: 5). Technological advances of this kind have also threatened the narrative of emancipation produced by nation-states because knowledge is able to flow freely across different nations regardless of attempts at state intervention. The computerization of society has meant that information and intellectual property rights, now 'even more mobile and subject to piracy' (Lyotard 1984: 6), have become the new battleground for knowledge and power, not between nation-states but between multinational corporations in pursuit of lucrative consumer markets.

As well as the decline of grand narratives such as communism, Marxism, Christianity and Einstein's theory of relativity as a result of this commodity production of knowledge by way of information-processing technologies, we might also point to the decline of media metanarratives such as public service broadcasting and 'freedom of the press' as the Fourth Estate. On the one hand, public service broadcasters such as the BBC have lost much of their belief in Reithian values of high culture, educative and informative programming. Competition from commercial media systems founded on consumer capitalist values has forced public service broadcasters to produce television and radio shows that appeal to popular tastes more so than the Arnoldian principle of 'the best of what has been thought' (see discussion of Schiller in Chapter 7). For example, the appeal of the 'reality TV' genre is equally embraced by public service and commercial broadcasters in Britain, given the widely held assumption that such programmes are popular among audiences. The 'high culture' metanarrative espoused by Lord Reith – appointed in 1927 as the BBC's first Director-General – has declined immeasurably in the present-day, ratings-obsessed BBC. The close association between popular aesthetics and postmodernity is no better manifested than in the case of twenty-first-century public service broadcasting, which in highly competitive television markets – such as the USA – is diminishing fast.

On the other hand, the grand narrative of emancipation associated with the Fourth Estate loses its credibility when we consider that access to knowledge production is mostly in the hands of a few multinational news conglomerates (see Chapter 7). Prior to postmodernity, access to mediated knowledge production was in the hands of either the state or a multitude of private enterprises, but concentration of (economic and knowledge) capital alongside a decline in metanarratives of emancipation have effectively delegitimized such knowledge and replaced it with the logic of mass media and mass consumption. A counter-argument in this case, though, is that public service broadcasters and the free press are still alive even if their narratives of emancipation are no longer so convincing. Another criticism we might level at Lyotard's account is that he appears to be implicitly condoning a *new* grand narrative of postmodernity despite his claim that grand narratives are no longer credible. If metanarratives really are in decline, nothing theoretically universal like 'the postmodern condition' would surely explain what is replacing them. Moreover, Lyotard's claims about the power of technology and computerized societies resonates with another paradoxical metanarrative of postmodernity, known as the information society thesis.

The information society

Theories of the information society are extensive and diverse in their arguments, and by no means exclusively postmodern in their approach. In the wider scheme of media theory, though, the idea of an information society is closer associated with postmodernity than modernity or any other theoretical theme. One of the most influential theorists in this regard is Daniel Bell, whose work entitled *The Coming of Post-industrial Society* (first published in 1973) inspired new ways of thinking about a post-industrial, postmodern, information age. Bell's perspective on technological innovations in the information sector is largely optimistic. He argues that 'technology has transformed social relationships and our ways of looking at the world' (Bell 1999: 188), increasing human control over nature and transforming economic productivity. Five positive outcomes in this technological transformation of the social world are that:

1   Living standards have risen throughout the world, wages have increased in real terms (taking into account inflation) and social class inequalities in Western societies have been reduced.
2   A 'new class' of engineers, technicians and other planning occupations has been created.
3   A new definition of rationality in the sense of efficiency and optimization – using resources with the least cost and effort – has introduced 'quantitative techniques of engineering and economics [that] now jostle the older modes of speculation, tradition, and reason' (Bell 1999: 189) by enabling more accurate forecasting of social and economic trends.
4   'New networks of social relationships have been formed' (Bell 1999: 189) which mark a shift from kinship to occupational ties.
5   Perceptions of time and space have been altered, as evidenced in modern art's portrayal of new standards of 'speed' and 'height' compared to an earlier age.

For Bell, these five areas of progress indicate a wider social change from an industrial to a post-industrial society, evident particularly in the United States. Table 8.2 indicates some of the radical differences between the two types of society.

Bell's conception of a post-industrial society is also one in which information and knowledge have replaced material forms of production in a post-Marxist, Baudrillardian sense. No longer is there a division between those who own the means of goods production and the proletarian masses – as some political economists would still suggest – but instead there is a

Table 8.2   Radical differences between the industrial and post-industrial societies

	Industrial society	Post-industrial society
Regions	Western Europe, Japan	United States
Technology	Energy	Information
Economic sector	Secondary (goods manufacturing and processing)	Tertiary (services), Quaternary (finance, insurance), Quinary (health, education, research)
Occupations	Semi-skilled worker Engineer	Professional and technical Scientist
Time perspective	Projections (ad hoc)	Forecasting (future orientation)

Source: Adapted from Bell's (1999: 117) 'General Schema of Social Change'.

bureaucratic division between 'those who have powers of decision and those who have not, in all kinds of organizations, political, economic and social' (Bell 1999: 119). Although post-industrial society is seen by Bell as expanding scientific and technical knowledge to all levels of the social strata, the central problem remains how to adapt public policies to these scientific and technological advances so that the full potential of free-market, post-industrial economics can be realized. In a 1999 Foreword to a new edition of his post-industrial society thesis, Bell discusses the internet as an example of technological empowerment: 'It provides enormous access to the cultural resources of humankind in a way never known of before. It multiplies the number of affinity groups – people with like-minded interests and common professions – across national boundaries' (Bell 1999: lvii). The internet could certainly be theorized in the optimistic terms of Bell's post-industrial, information age. Social relationships, economic productivity (i.e. e-commerce) and the means of forecasting consumer trends are – at least to some extent – transformed by new media infrastructures like the worldwide web.

Other theorists share Bell's optimism – for example, see Negroponte (1995) on the revolutionary promise of the digital age. Alvin Toffler's (1981) account of a third wave that follows the first wave (agricultural) and second wave (industrial) in the historical development of modern societies is not dissimilar to Bell's distinction between the pre-industrial, industrial and post-industrial. For Toffler, the third wave 'info-sphere' wrought by technological change is resulting in a de-massified media. Instead of mass media production that prevailed in the second wave, the third-wave emphasis on small-batch, localized production tailored to consumer trends has led to an expansion of choice and competition within media sectors. For example, mass-circulation newspapers that flourished in the second wave have declined in response to third-wave news and magazine publications 'that serve not the metropolitan mass market but specific neighbourhoods and communities within it' (Toffler 1981: 170). Radio and television programming geared towards particular regions or common interests likewise mark this shift to a de-massified media in the third wave. The third wave also means – unlike Jameson's idea of postmodern pastiche – more diversity:

> Today, instead of masses of people all receiving the same messages, smaller de-massified groups receive and send large amounts of their own imagery to one another … This, in part, explains why opinions of everything from pop music to politics are becoming less uniform. Consensus shatters.
>
> (Toffler 1981: 176)

The de-massification of media signals an enormous change in the range and quantity of information we exchange with each other. As we become more individualized and less uniform in our outlooks, we need more information to forecast how others will behave and respond to our behaviour (Toffler 1981: 178). This is why Toffler situates the third wave, above all, within the context of an information society (see also Toffler and Toffler 1995).

Reading Bell and Toffler, we might gain the impression that all is well with an information society. However, there are as many critics as there are exponents of the information society thesis. Philip Elliott (1995) outlines two criticisms: first, he questions the suggestion that information can be equally accessed by all by pointing out that it is in the interests of commercial corporations to keep secret certain kinds of information; and, second, he argues that what appears to be information is very often merely *infotainment* – a mixture of tabloidized information and entertainment – that has little educative substance. David Lyon's (1988) counter-perspective outlines three further problems with this so-called progressiveness in information societies. First, he argues that vested interests mean access to information technologies favours those who can afford to invest in them. For example, 'the collusion of military with microelectronic interests in the modern world' does not harness mutual communication among different social groups – quite the opposite, these vested interests are 'dedicated to hostile, destructive and lethal ends' (Lyon 1988: 18). Second and related to this first point, capitalist economic interests mean that 'private gain is constantly set against efforts to "socialize" production' (Lyon 1988: 18). Public information providers such as public libraries and public service broadcasters find it increasingly difficult to afford access to certain forms of information in competition with multinational corporations, and the privatization of previously public services such as the telephone network further pushes up prices. And third, the assumption that information society marks a 'natural' progression – following the agricultural and industrial revolutions – forecloses alternative ways of thinking about contemporary societies, including the starkly alternative Luddite argument that technologies restrict choice and should be (indeed, often are) resisted by individuals. Lyon's theory of information society is situated between optimistic and pessimistic (Luddite) accounts, although he is closer to pessimism than optimism in his later account of a Foucauldian surveillance society (see Lyon 2001).

Manuel Castells's theory of the network society (outlined in three large volumes first published in 1996 and 1997) is closely associated with the concept of the information society but is, in part, a sustained critique of the liberal, optimistic approach. Unlike Toffler, he considers the informational economy of the network society to be overlapping with and penetrating agricultural and industrial economies (informational agriculture, informational manufacturing) rather than replacing them. Castells also differs from Bell in arguing that while information flows within a global economy, 'This is not the same as a world economy' (Castells 1997: 7). While the global economy reaches out to the whole world, it only incorporates the wealthier nations who benefit one another through the technological systems of 'interconnected' global financial markets (Castells 2000: 102). International trade between powerful economies, however, is contrasted with un-networked societies in parts of Africa, South America and rural Asia that remain regionalized and untouched by global economics. The network society is also characterized by a transformation in employment that amounts to the individualization of work (Castells 1997: 9). In contrast to traditional full-time, salaried work closely tied to trade unions, more contemporary developments point to an increase in self-employment, temporary work and the practice of 'subcontracting' labour to specialist consultancies. Rather than create a new class of worker, information-led network societies create new types of employment that fragment or individualize 'labour's bargaining power' (Castells 1997: 10). Small and medium-sized enterprises engage in inter-firm networking – often with much larger businesses – and the interdependence between big and small firms largely maintains existing economic and social structures. Individualization of the workforce and the breakdown of the welfare state as a result of weakening trade unions also lead to what Castells identifies as widening social polarization and exclusion.

Castells is not a postmodern theorist *per se*, although what he calls 'the culture of real virtuality' serves to implicate electronic media in a theory of network society resembling the postmodern. As opposed to virtual reality, real virtuality implies that media texts are not substitutes for real experiences but have 'become the experience' (Castells 2000: 404) in a network society driven by mediated communications. Unlike the mass media age theorized by McLuhan in terms of a 'global village' where 'the medium is the message' (see Chapter 3), Castells argues that by the 1990s multi-media systems and their power to target diverse audiences mean that 'the message is the medium' (Castells 2000: 368). This change is evident in multinational corporations that take certain messages (content), such as teenage music, and shape them into a niche medium (technological format), such as MTV. Furthermore, the mass media age is obsolete, given the rise of computer-mediated communications – not least the internet – that herald 'increased interaction by and among individuals that break up the uniformity of a mass audience' (Castells 1997: 11). Similar to Toffler's ideas about de-massified media, new media technologies enable the inclusion of different cultural expressions that, in turn, weaken mass media organizations that promote traditional cultural values (Castells 2000: 406). So despite social exclusion and maintenance of the economic status quo, the network society offers sophistication in catering for the diverse cultural traits and identities of those who experience it (see Castells 2004).

This culture of real virtuality carved out by interactive media also radically transforms time and space. Castells refers to 'timeless time' as an outcome of new media and information technologies that aim to annihilate time by compressing years into seconds and breaking 'natural' sequences (i.e. past, present and future). However, timeless time is only available to powerful groups that can, for example, fight and win 'instant wars' with enemies (Castells 2000: 484–91). Elsewhere, societies without new technologies rely on biological or clock time, and the wars they fight last for years. As well as timeless time, what Castells terms 'the space of flows' enable powerful groups – major financial markets, global media, and so on – to engage in distant interactions involving the movement of people and goods. The 'global city', such as New York or London, arises from this space of flows that link up production, management and information. By contrast, un-networked societies 'perceive their space as place-based' (Castells 2000: 453), fixed in a particular locale, and unaffected by the global space of flows in a network society. The notions of timeless time and the space of flows – as Castells acknowledges – are reminiscent of David Harvey's (1989) concept of time–space compression. Contrary to the work of Jameson which marks off postmodernity as a new era in reaction to modernity, Harvey sees continuities between the two. Indeed, 'the changing experience of sense and time had much to do with the birth of modernism' (Harvey 1989: 283). Nevertheless, 'the rapidity of time–space compression in recent years' caused by the pressures of capital accumulation – akin to Castells's interconnected global market economy – is distinctly postmodern and 'exacts its toll on our capacity to grapple with the realities unfolding around us' (Harvey 1989: 305–6). The technological endeavour to tighten time-spans and space-distances for economic gain has catastrophic implications when it hastens the need for quick, unconsidered decision-making in political, military and financial realms.

Ritzer: McDonaldization

It seems appropriate to end this chapter with what is, partly at least, a counter-perspective on postmodernity. George Ritzer suggests that there are more continuities than differences between modernity and a so-called post-modern age. According to Ritzer (1993), we live in a McDonaldized society reminiscent of advanced modernity. This is not to say that McDonald's is a typical feature of social life but that the corporate structure and practices associated with the fast-food chain are symptomatic of wider global production trends – a similar perspective, known as 'Coca-colonization', has a longer tradition (see Nederveen Pieterse 2004: 49). Based on Max Weber's theory of bureaucracy and rationalization, Ritzer's **McDonaldization** thesis states that the rules, regulations and structures characteristic of a McDonald's-style global corporation are put in place so as to maximize four profit-making concerns:

1   *Efficiency*: this is about being cost-effective and preventing waste. For example, 'The Egg McMuffin is basically an entire breakfast … combined into one handy sandwich that can be eaten quickly, easily, and without utensils' (Ritzer 1993: 40).
2   *Calculability*: this is about uniformity of size, quantity and production time. So 'great care is taken to be sure that each raw McDonald's hamburger weighs 1.6 ounces, no more, no less … The precooked hamburger measures precisely 3.875 inches across' (Ritzer 1993: 66).
3   *Predictability*: we expect the same tastes, packaging and people employed to serve us. Predictable ingredients and predictable forms of storage (i.e. freezing) aid this rationalizing process of McDonaldization.
4   *Control*: this is to be found in rigid management structures and huge wholesale purchasing of supplies. Not even the 'chefs' have much control over how the food is delivered to the customer: 'Much of the food prepared at McDonald's arrives at the restaurant preformed, precut, presliced, and preprepared, often by nonhuman technologies' (Ritzer 1993: 105).

These four features of McDonaldization are not only evident within fast-food industries. Ritzer refers to the media and information industries in terms of similar structures and practices of production as McDonald's. Efficiency, for instance, is identifiable in what the author terms 'News McNuggets' (Ritzer 1993: 57–8) – very short stories presented in tabloid newspapers such as *USA TODAY* and *The Sun* – in contrast to the more substantial and intellectually challenging reports found in inefficient broadsheets. Calculability is evident in televised sports such as basketball and football with their uniform time periods which allow for easy programme scheduling and commercial breaks. By contrast, competitive pursuits less constrained by time and calculability – such as chess and mountaineering – are less media-friendly and therefore receive little media coverage. Predictability is an important technique by which the Hollywood film industry constantly searches for remakes, sequels and films based on 'tried and tested' formulas. Ritzer (1993: 89) uses the example of *Psycho* (1960), a box-office hit film which spurned predictable offshoots such as *Halloween* (1978) and *A Nightmare on Elm Street* (1984). Control is evident when politicians and other public figures utilize media training and spin-doctors in their media appearances: 'Most of [President Ronald] Regan's TV appearances were carefully managed to be sure that the right message was communicated' (Ritzer 1993: 117). Like Adorno's theory of standardization and Boorstin's concept of pseudo-events, Ritzer's McDonaldization thesis proposes that media and popular culture are starved of originality, creativity and diversity due to the rationalized structures of global capitalist corporations. The main challenge to the McDonaldization thesis is the concept of 'glocalization' or global localization, which is based on the premise that 'corporations only succeed if and to the extent that they adapt themselves to local cultures and markets' (Nederveen Pieterse 2004: 50; see also Sreberny 2000). The recent Bond film, *Casino Royale* (2006), may have all the hallmarks of a predictable Hollywood espionage thriller but it had to adapt to the lucrative Chinese market, for example, by renaming the main character 'Ling ling qi' – Chinese for 007 (Yahoo! News UK 2007). The importance of localizing global media productions further suggests the persistence of traditional, local ways of life in many aspects of contemporary culture – far from the breakdown of history and tradition associated with postmodernity.

In his original conception of a McDonaldized society, Ritzer argues that global capitalism today is an outcome of modernity rather than postmodernity – an argument clearly at odds with Jameson among other postmodernists. In a sequel to his first book on McDonaldization, however, Ritzer is less hostile to theories of postmodernity and instead refers to 'the utility of *both* modern and postmodern theory' (Ritzer 1998: 132) in our understanding of new means of production and consumption. Ritzer accords with Baudrillard's view of postmodern society as a consumer society saturated by simulations. Moreover, 'As a result of the necessity for ever-increasing consumption, the focus of capitalism has shifted from exploiting workers to exploiting consumers' (Ritzer 1998: 121). This, in part, explains why 'instead of "real" interactions with servers in fast-food restaurants ... we can think of these as simulated interactions' (Ritzer 1998: 121), determined by point-of-sale technologies including the electronic checkouts increasingly 'employed' by supermarket chains. These simulated interactions, which we might also apply to technologies such as video on-demand and internet banking, are now such a routine feature of postmodern life that any sense of real interaction between individuals is lost – indeed, consumed by simulations. Simulated interaction is more real than real, face-to-face interaction. Likewise, the fast food we are encouraged to eat in a consumer capitalist society – McDonald's hamburgers, pizzas, chicken nuggets – is akin to a simulation of 'real', homemade, freshly cooked food that we were once encouraged to consume, before the days of hyperreality. Notwithstanding plasticity, the McDonald's burger has become the 'real' American burger, concealing the *really* real origins of any authentic, original burger (Ritzer 1998: 122). Mediated advertising and promotional campaigns serve to reinforce this deception. Moreover, the simulated McUniversity – literally realized by CNN Ted Turner's idea of an electronic university (Ritzer 1998: 159) and supported more recently by Google's digitalization of millions of academic books and journals – is a postmodern manifestation of McDonaldization in practice.

Summary

This chapter has considered:

- Definitions of postmodernity and postmodernism, including the main features that characterize postmodernity.
- Baudrillard's theory of simulation, including concepts of hyperreality and media saturation as they apply to televised coverage of warfare and other global 'non-events'.
- Postmodern theories of image in relation to 'pseudo-events' (Boorstin) and spectacle in relation to the pseudo-needs of consumerism (Debord).
- Lyotard's theory of the decline of metanarratives – narratives of emancipation and of speculation – and how this theory applies to media metanarratives.
- Information society debates, including competing theories of the post-industrial society (Bell) and the network society (Castells), and ideas about media de-massification and time–space compression.
- The McDonaldization thesis, which both challenges and – in Ritzer's revised version – reaffirms the distinction between modernity and postmodernity.

Further reading

Genosko, G. (1999) *McLuhan and Baudrillard: The Masters of Implosion*. London: Routledge.

An interesting and amusing account that traces parallels between Baudrillard's postmodern theories of media and the renaissance enjoyed by McLuhan's medium theory since the boom in postmodernist perspectives. Recommended for advanced undergraduates and postgraduates.

McGuigan, J. (2006) *Modernity and Postmodern Culture*, 2nd edn. Maidenhead: Open University Press.

An innovative approach to theories of postmodernity that questions postmodern accounts and reaffirms the place of modernity in contemporary media culture. Chapters on 'declaring the postmodern' and the information age. Recommended for advanced undergraduates and postgraduates.

Slevin, J. (2000) *The Internet and Society*. Cambridge: Polity.

This book presents a social theory of the internet as an interactional community for the transmission of cultural values and information (note that this book is also useful in relation to interactionist perspectives discussed in Chapter 5). Chapters on globalization, regulation and 'the self'. Suitable for all media students.

Winston, B. (1998) *Media Technology and Society – A History: From the Telegraph to the Internet*. London: Routledge.

A cautious approach to the notion of an 'information society' revolution. Media technologies throughout history are seen to have suffered from problems of suppression (particularly economic constraints) and competence. Useful for all media students.

9 Consumerism and everyday life

Introduction

The final strand of media theory that we will consider are theories of media consumerism and media audiences that heralded the move away from reception theory – emphasized by the uses and gratifications approach (see Chapter 2) but typical in many strands of media theory – towards theories of **consumption**. Since the 1980s, partly as a consequence of feminist theory along with the cultural turn in postmodern theory, media studies of **consumerism** have emerged as a major and distinct theoretical tradition of their own. Theories of consumerism have responded to an orthodox behaviourist, modernist, structuralist, patriarchal and Marxist emphasis on the power of material production. Ethnographic accounts of active, creative audiences take precedence over the idea that mass culture is bad for you. Moreover, media texts and products are considered to empower as well as, if not more so than, exert power over consumers. With media products as with capitalist production more generally, 'goods are both the creations and the creators of the culturally constituted world' (McCracken 1990: 77). As such, texts and products may contain meanings, such as profit motives, but we also create meanings from what we consume. Consumerist media theory is also – more straightforwardly – a response to the rise of consumerism in a 'consumer society' from circa the 1950s in Western countries (Corrigan 1997: 2).

Like all the traditions of media theory considered in this book, consumerism is theorized within a contested arena of competing perspectives and arguments. For example, it is a matter of debate merely to define who and what media audiences are, given that they are – unlike, say, theatre audiences – geographically dispersed and therefore invisible. As Shaun Moores (2000) suggests, it 'becomes harder to specify exactly where broadcasting's audiences begin and end. The boundaries of "audiencehood" are inherently unstable' (Moores 2000: 17). A further contestation is the relationship between media consumption and production. As we shall discuss, Fiske and de Certeau position consumers either in resistance to or untainted by the media and cultural industries. By contrast, Jenkins, Silverstone, Abercrombie and Longhurst consider consumers to be producers themselves. As such, the clear-cut distinction between media consumption and production no longer holds firm, and this is facilitated by new communications technologies like the internet that provide media-literate individuals with the tools to encode – not only decode – their own mediated messages by creating websites, online music hubs, and so on. The pervasiveness of media consumption and, increasingly, production in **everyday life** is a theoretical concern explored throughout this chapter. We will end our discussion of consumerism on a cautious note, however, with the work of Bourdieu that returns us to the question addressed by Giddens's structuration theory (see Chapter 5) about how structure – particularly capitalist structures of media and cultural pro- duction – determines agency (i.e. everyday consumerism).

Fiske: consumer resistance

John Fiske is the archetypal exponent of consumer power. Contrary to Adorno and orthodox political economy theories, he asserts that 'Popular culture is made by the people, not produced by the culture industry' (Fiske 1989: 24). 'Power to the people', as John Lennon sang, is actualized in Fiske's theory of **consumer resistance**. By 'the people', he does not mean a homogeneous 'mass' of passive individuals but a fluid, heterogeneous for- mation of productive consumers who embody 'a shifting set of allegiances that cross all social categories' (Fiske 1989: 24). This explains why advertisers waste so much money trying to target particular demographic groups. Fiske would argue that men aged 18–35, for instance, do not exhibit similar interests and patterns of consumption, so external sociological factors (age and gender in this case) are inadequate in classifying such a diverse group. Commercial breaks during televised football matches will always carry advertising aimed at young men – razors, cars, video games – but not all young men need to shave regularly, and not all young men drive or can afford to buy a car, and not all young men play video games. Fiske compares the desperate pursuit of the people by advertisers to 'a conflict between an occupying army and guerrilla fighters ... the hegemonic forces of homo- geneity are always met by the resistances of heterogeneity' (Fiske 1991a: 8). Media and cultural industries speak of *serving* consumers with high-quality products, entertainment and information – 'that's what they want, that's what they'll get' says the wise newspaper editor – but the two sides are actually engaged in prolonged warfare.

Of course, the people cannot entirely decide what is advertised to them or what products are offered to them by industries under the dominant influ- ence of white, patriarchal capitalism. We can choose *not* to watch a television programme or *not* to see a film, but we cannot choose what we want to watch on television or at the cinema. Fiske acknowledges this situation but still insists that consumers make popular culture because they determine what becomes popular. Cultural and media products are rejected by consumers – they become expensive flops, such as *Waterworld* (1995) and *Thunderbirds* (2004) – if they only serve dominant ideological interests that provide no scope for alternative meanings or pleasures. By contrast, cultural products become popular when they 'carry contradictory lines of force' (Fiske 1991a: 2) that provide scope for alternative, resistant readings, which in turn allow the people to make meaning and pleasure from them. Whereas Hall's Encoding/ Decoding model (see Chapter 4) emphasizes the power of dominant ideologies to impose preferred readings of media texts (the *dominant code*) upon audiences, Fiske suggests that Hall's *oppositional code* is not the exception but the rule. He argues that audiences routinely resist and reinterpret the preferred meanings of media texts such as celebrities and pop songs. This resistance is located not only in the texts themselves – although, as previously discussed, a celebrity such as Madonna is only popular because she provides scope for alternative readings of her persona – but in the contexts of everyday life in which these texts are used by consumers. Fiske identifies two kinds of resistance that are interrelated: semiotic and evasive resistance. Semiotic resistance succeeds in constructing oppositional meanings from texts, whereas evasive resistance escapes any constraints of meaning within texts by producing pleasures that override such meanings.

Although resistance is commonplace, it only exists in surrogate form against the dominant ideology of profit-driven capitalist production. Resistance and dominance are like twins, constantly quarrelling but dependent on each other for their meanings. Fiske refers to two economies of television: the financial economy and the cultural economy (Fiske 1987; 1989: 26–32), differences of which are compared in Figure 9.1. The financial economy of commercial television is focused on the production of popular programming that will attract high audience ratings and, subsequently, substantial advertising revenue. The audience is nothing more than a commodity in this financial economy – a statistical category (say, ten million people mostly aged 18–35) – that can be sold to advertisers in return for profitable revenues. In stark contrast, the cultural economy of television is centred on the consumption of programming that essentially determines which programmes become popular and which become short-lived flops. In the cultural economy the audience is no longer a mere commodity but, rather, a producer of

Financial economy	Cultural economy
Production	Consumption
Audience as mass commodity	Audience as active consumers
Products as commodities	*Texts* as meaningful and pleasurable
Advertising-driven	Audience-driven
Dominant code (ideology) encoded	Oppositional code (resistance) decoded
Media/culture industry	Popular culture

Figure 9.1   Fiske's two economies of television

meanings and pleasures through semiotic and evasive forms of resistance. Media texts are produced by both media industries and audiences, depending on which of the two economies we locate the texts in, but the cultural economy is the ultimate producer of popular culture. The cultural economy is the key point at which the discursive relationship between media industries and audiences transforms a text into either a success or a flop. The financial economy cannot determine outcomes in the cultural economy. Producers in the financial economy can decide to withdraw an unsuccessful television drama if ratings – governed by audiences in the cultural economy – are low, or they can commission a new series if ratings are high, but they cannot predict the ever-changing moods and preferences of the cultural economy.

Several case studies provide Fiske with evidence for his theory of consumer resistance. For example, he identifies semiotic resistance in young female fans of Madonna. Madonna as a media text (pop star) in the cultural economy enables her fans to identify with a rebellious, subversive, feminist representation that they can transpose into their everyday relations with others. As the author states:

> The teenage girl fan of Madonna who fantasizes her own empowerment can translate this fantasy into behaviour, and can act in an empowered way socially, thus winning more social territory for herself. When she meets others who share her fantasies and freedom there is the beginning of a sense of solidarity, of a shared resistance, that can support and encourage progressive action on the microsocial level.
>
> (Fiske 1989: 172)

Madonna's fans are guerilla fighters who use the meanings that they produce from the star's persona to activate a 'felt collectivity' (Fiske 1989: 24) against existing patriarchal structures. These fans draw on the fantasy of the Madonna persona to empower their status in 'real' social contexts, such as their relations with boyfriends and 'their refusal to give up the street to men as their territory' (Fiske 1991a: 11). Over time, this guerilla fighting is likely to affect social change and gradually erode the patriarchal structures that disempower young women. Another example of consumer resistance – here closer to what Fiske defines as evasive resistance – is video gaming. Video gamers are less interested in searching out resistant meanings against dominant ideologies, but instead experience resistant pleasures in intense bodily action and concentration. Gamers become authors of their consumption, performing their bodies in sophisticated enactments that produce intense displays of emotional, orgasmic release – losing themselves in the game – which constitute 'moments of evasion of ideological control' (Fiske 1991a: 93). Such intense pleasure threatens the financial economy of popular culture, not least, by internalizing desire in bodily practices rather than external, cosmetic products.

Fiske has extended his theory of consumer resistance to a multicultural perspective on the United States as an embattled society moving closer towards a heterogeneous social order in which a wide range of forms of consent are given to its people (see Fiske 1993). However, he has since acknowledged deficiencies in a universal view of everyday consumption as radically resistant to corporate intentions (see Fiske 1996). He has certainly had his fair share of criticism, most notably in accusations of cultural populism (McGuigan 1992). Jim McGuigan attacks Fiske's celebratory perspective on consumer resistance, 'never countenancing the possibility that a popular reading could be anything other than "progressive"' (McGuigan 1992: 72). McGuigan argues that Fiske's theory of consumer resistance panders to the populist jargon of free-market cultural industries that also insist on *empowering* consumers, but only – implicitly – those obedient consumers who purchase the products that are supposed to empower them. He also criticizes Fiske for neglecting to discuss issues of corporate ownership, regulation and technological innovation that have characterized the increasingly concentrated financial economy of television and other media industries in the contemporary era. Nonetheless, recent widespread warfare between the occupying army of major record companies and guerilla fighters – in the shape of illegal uploaders and downloaders of pirated internet music (MP3 file-sharing) – does resonate with Fiske's theory. If we turn to Michel de Certeau's ideas about everyday tactics which inspired Fiske's theory of consumer resistance, however, some key differences between the two theorists can be revealed.

De Certeau: everyday tactics

The practices of everyday life detailed by de Certeau (1984) consist of a range of **tactics** deployed by consumers within the formal 'strategies' of powerful – i.e. corporate capitalist, scientific, and so on – institutions. Both tactics (consumer practices) and strategies (corporate ones) are types of action that seek to occupy space and time. Strategies operate so that space is successfully won over time, through property acquisition and ownership for instance. These spaces become isolated as places of power (like scientific laboratories) and acquire a panoptic function in tandem with Foucault's theory of discourse in disciplinary societies (see Chapter 4). Tactics, in comparison, win time rather than space, for 'a tactic depends on time' (de Certeau 1984: xix) as it is an action performed within the complex ebbs and flows of everyday schedules. A tactic 'must vigilantly make use of the cracks that particular conjunctions open in the surveillance of the propriety powers. It poaches in them' (de Certeau 1984: 37). An example of everyday tactics is the act of reading as poaching. While authors write books with the intention that their every word is read and preferably remembered, in everyday poaching tactics such as speed reading there is a freedom of movement and 'an autonomy in relation to the determinations of the text' (de Certeau 1984: 176). This is partly an historical outcome of the transition from oral to silent reading (most of us now read books in silence). Oral reading once served as a strategy for powerful institutions such as the medieval Church to control the places where it exercised its religious doctrine – as Innis's and McLuhan's medium theories testify (see Chapter 3) – but with the expansion of near-universal literacy the silent reader is 'Emancipated from places, the reading body is freer in its movements' (de Certeau 1984: 176). Readers, free to make their own meanings from texts, are 'nomads' or travellers, not constrained by place (property) in the strategic sense.

It should be noted that de Certeau's theory of everyday tactics is similar to a strand of literary theory that suggests a text (novel, poem, play, and so on) only begins to have meaning when it is read. Moreover, if we the readers cannot afford the time to sit down and read a whole book or watch a whole film, we might speed read or speed watch by skipping pages or fast-forwarding the DVD to *find out what happens at the end*. The case of speed reading points to a fundamental difference between de Certeau and Fiske. Whereas Fiske emphasizes resistance in the discursive relations between the production and consumption of media texts, de Certeau offers a more radical theoretical perspective. He states that 'the operation of encoding, which is articulated on signifiers, produces the meaning, which is thus not defined by something that is deposited in the text, by an "intention", or by an activity on the part of the author' (de Certeau 1984: 171). In short, an author's intended meanings are at the mercy of the textual meanings produced by readers. Hall's Encoding/Decoding model is turned on its head by de Certeau, who argues that consumer tactics amount to practices of encoding – not decoding – that determine how texts are made to mean things. Authors and producers also encode texts (strategies) but the encoding of consumers (tactics) transcends this moment of original encoding. These two processes of encoding exist in arbitrary relation to one another due to the temporal quirks of everyday life. The strategies of producers are superior to tactics in their occupation of space – evidenced by their places of production, such as state-of-the-art record studios or huge manufacturing plants – but they cannot control how everyday people play with time and *make* time for their own tactical practices. So 'the two ways of acting can be distinguished according to whether they bet on place or on time' (de Certeau 1984: 39). Strategies bet on – and win – places; tactics bet on – and win – time.

As well as the poaching tactics of speed reading, de Certeau cites tactics in another everyday practice which in France is called *la perrugue*: 'the worker's own work disguised as work for his employer' (de Certeau 1984: 25). Those who indulge in *la perruque* are usurping their contracted work time for a different sort of time that might be spent writing love letters or playing online games. Moreover, *la perruque* is 'infiltrating itself everywhere and becoming more and more common' (de Certeau 1984: 29), not just in work contexts but also in contexts of consumption and use. Everyday consumer tactics in winning time escape the knowledge of researchers (whether academic or market researchers), however, because of their elusiveness: 'The practices of consumption are the ghosts of the society that carries their name' (de Certeau 1984: 35). Evidence based on analysis of texts or statistics about audience numbers reveals nothing about such practices. For example, 'once the images broadcast by television and the time spent in front of the TV set have been analysed, it remains to be asked what the consumer makes of these images and during these hours' (de Certeau 1984: 31). Television, like the medieval Church, aims to isolate texts (programmes) from readers (viewers) in order to control their meanings in line with powerful strategic interests, but it is helpless in the face of 'the silent, transgressive, ironic or poetic activity of readers (or television viewers) who maintain their reserve in private and without the knowledge of the "masters"' (de Certeau 1984: 172). This utilization of private time by ordinary consumers is the practice of 'making do' with the cultural resources offered by strategic powers, and they make do with these resources – TV programmes, popular music, and so on – in their own ways, outside any constraints on their time that profit-driven producers aim to impose. The transgressive tactic of switching channels during commercial breaks is one way that television viewers make do with what is offered to them.

De Certeau's idea that media texts have no determining influence on consumers (i.e. media audiences) has been widely criticized (see Brunsdon 1989; McGuigan 1992; Buckingham 1993). An alternative approach is offered by studies of **media literacy** that aim to explore to what extent media texts are used by consumers – like readers of books – to gain knowledge and learn skills. Although a very different theoretical approach to consumer tactics, media literacy research tends to uphold de Certeau's – and Fiske's – argument that media audiences are sophisticated *users* of texts rather than passive consumers. David Buckingham's (1987) research with young viewers of British soap opera *EastEnders* (1985–), for instance, found that they were highly critical of its implausible storylines and 'did not confuse its representation of the world with reality' (Buckingham 1987: 200). Likewise, Buckingham's (1993) later research with children found that they were sceptical about the intentions of television advertisements, showed awareness of how audiences – including themselves – were targeted, and understood how celebrities were used in advertisements to promote a brand image. These high media literacy levels among Buckingham's interviewees demonstrate their 'metalinguistic competencies' (Buckingham 1993: 257) and contradict Postman's medium theory perspective on the 'disappearance of childhood' (as discussed in Chapter 3): 'In regarding children as passive victims of television, [Postman] ignores the diverse competencies that are involved in making sense of the medium' (Buckingham 1993: 127; see also Buckingham 2000). Buckingham argues that children should be encouraged to use television as a means of developing critical perspectives – not, as Postman would have it, kept away from television and handed a pile of books.

In a similar vein, Marie Messenger Davies's (1989) research with children found that they take pleasure in recounting the music and narratives of ads on television, but rarely feel the desire to purchase the products being advertised, which often are forgotten about. Furthermore, David Gauntlett's (1996) creative video project in which children filmed their local environment concludes that 'the children demonstrated a high level of media literacy ... Making a video came naturally to them' (Gauntlett 1996: 143). More recently, Sonia Livingstone's (2002) research on young people's new media use advocates a 'learning by doing' approach evident, for instance, in the empowering experience of computer game-playing: 'the skills that young people have developed within their leisure time are only now being recognised as, potentially, crucial for ICT literacy (or literacies) more generally' (Livingstone 2002: 232). Children and young people, indeed, are often more media and computer literate than adults, precisely because they have learnt how to watch television or play computer games – just like they have learnt to speak, read and write – from a young age. However, the young continue to be treated as vulnerable victims of media texts and technologies, not least the dangers of the internet. Livingstone (2002: 242) agrees that regulation is needed but that existing forms – instead of regulating commercial contents – tend to regulate the 'learning through fun' practices that hone young people's media literacy skills. Ofcom, the regulatory body for the British media and communications industry, recently (2006) banned junk food ads from television and other media that target young consumers. Even the most adept practitioner of de Certeau's consumer tactics, it could be argued, is only offered a *restricted* freedom in relation to media regulation.

Textual poachers and fandom

Henry Jenkins's ethnographic study of fan practices is heavily influenced by the theories of Fiske and particularly de Certeau. He rejects the negative stereotype of a fan as a 'fanatic' (from which the word 'fan' derives) who is too emotionally obsessed by a particular 'fad' or 'craze' that is usually considered by others to be trivial or even infantile. Fan as 'fanatic' resonates in at least three theoretical traditions we have encountered: Adorno's political economy theory of the culture industry (Chapter 7), the ideological construction of popular music fandom (Chapter 6 under discussion of McRobbie's work), as well as theories of media effects (Chapter 2). Frenzied teenage girl fans, otherwise known as teenyboppers, queuing to see their pop idols at a concert are cited as evidence of mindless consumption. However, in *Textual Poachers* (1992) Jenkins strongly defends fan practices as meaningful pursuits that are both creative and productive. Echoing de Certeau, he argues that 'fans actively assert their mastery over the mass-produced texts which provide the raw materials for their own cultural productions and the basis for their social interactions' (Jenkins 1992: 23–4). He also agrees with de Certeau's claim that readers are nomadic and freely move from one text to another without permanently becoming immersed in any particular text. Fans, like nomadic readers, are not led – like a dog on a lead – to decode dominant, negotiated or oppositional codes in media productions. On the contrary, a fan is 'continuously re-evaluating his or her relationship to the fiction and reconstructing its meanings according to more immediate interests' (Jenkins 1992: 34–5). Fans, like other consumers, wander away from any preferred meanings in a singular text because they consume texts intertextually – as Jameson theorized (see Chapter 8) – and experience pleasure in these fleeting intertextual connections.

Despite the obvious similarities with de Certeau's theory, Jenkins suggests two differences between his perspective on fans and de Certeau's perspective on everyday consumers. First, fans interact with each other on a reasonably regular basis – de Certeau's consumers, by contrast, appear isolated from each other, not least because they are *imagined* consumers in the sense that de Certeau neglects to consider audience research into real consumption practices. Jenkins, on the other hand, is a participant observer in the network of real fan practices that he researches and subsequently theorizes. Fans interact with each other through, for example, fanzines, social events and even – in the case of Trekkers (fans of *Star Trek* (1966–69)) – annual conferences. Second, Jenkins shows that fans are not split apart from relations with producers – in the way that Fiske's resistant consumers and de Certeau's speed readers are – but actively become involved in their own forms of production that might also affect producer decision-making within media institutions. Jenkins refers to fan artists (as opposed to fan consumers) who engage in entrepreneurial activities such as producing fanzines and art work dedicated to their favourite television dramas, rock bands, and so on (see Figure 9.2). Media fandom is 'founded less upon the consumption of pre-existing texts than on the production of fan texts' (Jenkins 1992: 47). Moreover, fans often try to interact not just with themselves but with media producers in order to express their own views, for example, on what should happen next in a relationship between two characters in a television serial, or what the sleeve design should be for a rock band's latest album. Fans are therefore readers and

Figure 9.2 *Star Trek* fan art

writers – not just travellers – who encode their own fan texts and may, in some cases, affect encoding in the institutional production of their favourite text.

Fans of media productions interact with each other and with institutional producers in what Jenkins describes as a 'participatory culture'. This concept derives from Howard Becker's (1982) concept of 'art worlds'. Consistent with Becker's interactionist perspective (see Chapter 5) but more often discussed as a concept that brings together production and consumption practices, art worlds consist of disparate groups – artists, distributors, publicists and audiences, for example – that nonetheless collude in collective activities that together give meaning and substance to the end products. These collective activities dispel the myth that works of art are created by some intrinsic talent or genius on the part of an individual producer. On the contrary, all who participate in art worlds breathe life into the activities of that world and perhaps bring it to the attention of interested outsiders. Like art worlds, participatory cultures of fandom 'transform the experience of media consumption into the production of new texts, indeed of a new culture and a new community' (Jenkins 1992: 46). The outcome is an autonomous, 'self-sufficient fan culture' (Jenkins 1992: 47) that can exist outside the frames of reference determined by media texts and actively seeks – and often succeeds –

to exist as a counterweight to decisions made in the determination (i.e. institutional production) of media texts. A recent example of a cult media text that has attracted a significant fan following and been the topic of discussion on endless online message boards is the television drama *Lost* (2004–). Jenkins's conception of fandom as participatory culture has inspired a growing body of ethnographic research and theory into fan cultures (see, for example, Bacon-Smith 1992; Hills 2002; Sandvoss 2005).

Silverstone: the cycle of consumption and mediated experience

Roger Silverstone's (1994; see also Silverstone et al. 1992) consumption cycle usefully attempts to understand how everyday consumer practices feed back to producer practices, which are in turn fed back to consumers. His model of mutually dependent consumption and production is not dissimilar to Jenkins's concept of participatory culture, and similarly rejects structuralist theories that cite production (or the encoding of texts) as determining consumption (how texts are decoded). Silverstone notes six phases in the cycle of consumption. The first phase of *commodification* (institutional production) in material and mediated products both influences and is influenced by five other 'dependent moments of consumption' termed imagination, appropriation, objectification, incorporation and conversion (Silverstone 1994: 123–4). Second, the phase of consumer *imagination* usually occurs before – but sometimes after – the purchasing of a product. Imagination and anticipation of the pleasure that might arise from a prospective purchase as well as the work of attaching pleasurable meanings on to the purchased product 'either as a compensation for disappointed desire or as a celebration of its fulfillment' (Silverstone 1994: 126) are compared by Silverstone to those productive, imaginative tactics outlined by de Certeau and typified by speed readers. Following imagination, the third phase of *appropriation* occurs when consumers transform the mediated and public meanings of products – that are initially consumed via advertisements or supermarket shelves – into their personal and private meanings in post-purchase contexts such as living rooms. *Objectification* – the fourth phase – then occurs through the embedment of new products alongside existing ones in everyday domestic consumer lives. Television, for instance, becomes objectified in everyday household interactions: 'accounts of television programmes, the characters in soap operas, or events in the news, provide a basis for identification and self-representation' (Silverstone 1994: 128–9).

Following objectification, a fifth phase of *incorporation* occurs when household products become 'a part of the furniture' and float freely within the ebbs and flows of everyday life, such as 'the use of radio as a companion for the tea-break' (Silverstone 1994: 129). The sixth and final phase within the consumption cycle involves the *conversion* of products with everyday personal and domestic meanings into products that are capable of conveying meanings outside the home, in public contexts such as offices and cafés. Television programmes form topics of conversation beyond close-knit family members and friends, and become talked about with classmates, colleagues and even strangers. Consumption has now turned full circle to inform the phase of production or *commodification* that began the cycle:

> The consumption cycle, perhaps more of a spiral in its dialectical movement, acknowledges that objects not only move in and out of commodification as such ... but that their status as commodities (and their meaning as a commodity) is constantly in flux.
>
> (Silverstone 1994: 124)

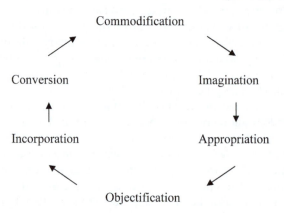

Figure 9.3   Silverstone's cycle of consumption

Figure 9.3 shows the cyclical process involved in these six phases of consumption. Significantly, this cyclical model questions the emphasis on the commodity values of media and cultural products associated with theories of commodity fetishism (Adorno 1991) and ideology. If consumers routinely feed back their thoughts and feelings to producers at the phase of commodification, this would banish the theory that commodities have purely ideological functions, given that they must be – to some extent – inflected with consumer values. However, Silverstone's cycle only rotates in one direction from public to private (through appropriation) and later from private to public (through conversion) contexts of consumption. Although the purchasing of mediated products such as television programmes or music on the radio never physically occurs – and Silverstone acknowledges this point about non-material products – it is still implied that both mediated and material products go through some sense of personal embodiment or private ownership within this consumer cycle. The many media consumer practices that do not involve private, personal purchase or commitment – watching televised sports coverage in public places, for example – would appear to break the cycle somewhere between appropriation and conversion, and would therefore never feed back to the phase of commodification, leaving media institutions oblivious to such elusive, impersonal consumer trends.

Elsewhere, Silverstone (1999) has outlined three dimensions of mediated experience that overlap but are nonetheless distinctive:

1 *Play*: this is not a dimension regularly associated with media experience but we *play* with media routinely as a source of pleasure, and media play is not only applicable to computer and video gamers: 'Watching television, surfing the net, doing the crossword, guessing the answers in a quiz, taking part in a lottery, all involves play' (Silverstone 1999: 60–1). Play is an act of participation in a make-believe situation which temporarily lifts us out of the ordinariness of everyday life: 'players can safely leave real life and engage in an activity that is meaningful in its rule-governed excess' (Silverstone 1999: 60).

2 *Performance*: unlike play, performance is a very real activity: 'performances are not just games ... Our lives and identities depend upon them. They become real, the real thing' (Silverstone 1999: 70). This is performance in the Goffmanian sense of believing in the 'fronts' that we present to others – even when they are an *act* – but Silverstone also suggests that media consumers move 'across the boundary between performer and audience, with increasing ease, as a matter of course' (Silverstone 1999: 71). The internet – MySpace and YouTube in particular – provides us with scope to be performers and producers as well as audiences, albeit not *mass* performers for a captive audience: 'Technology has given me a stage. I can perform on it. I can claim a space. If someone would only listen' (Silverstone 1999: 77).

3 *Consumption*: like play and performance, consumption is an *acting out* of meanings and pleasures, but it is an act of everyday ordinariness in contrast to the slightly more extraordinary experiences of media play and performance. Like de Certeau, Silverstone argues that consumption is about the dynamic, creative use of time, which means different things to different people. For many of us our time is scarce and precious, but we succeed nonetheless in *making* time our own and contradicting mediated attempts (e.g. advertising) to determine our time within the parameters of obedient consumption.

These three dimensions of mediated experience are consistent with Silverstone's cycle of consumption because they do not consider consumption as a separate process following production, but instead consider the two processes as dynamically intertwined in the everyday. The interaction between mediated experiences and our everyday lives is a theme that Silverstone continues to explore in his last book, *Media and Morality* (2007), which introduces the notion of 'the mediapolis': 'The mediapolis is, I intend, the mediated space of appearance in which the world appears and in which the world is constituted in its worldliness, and through which we learn about those who are and who are not like us' (Silverstone 2007: 31). Moreover, media technologies intrude into and affect how we manage our everyday lives. The mediapolis with its mediated appearance of the world 'provides a framework for the definition and conduct of our relationships to the other, and especially the distant other' – but the immediacy of mediated experience via internet and mobile phones, for example, tends to obscure differences between people and cultures in social reality to the point that mediated appearances are 'easily mistaken for life itself' (Silverstone 2007: 110, 114). So while a new kind of 'publicness' is facilitated by mediated technologies, Silverstone also fears that the mediapolis disguises the difference between peoples located in it: 'Such difference is what constitutes the basis for what we have in common. *What we have in common is our difference*' (Silverstone 2007: 118). Use of the internet by terrorists to mediate their message, for example, is a dark side of the mediapolis that threatens the creative and performative potential of mediated experience.

The diffused audience and consumer authority

A new paradigm – or theoretical framework – for understanding media consumption is proposed by Nicholas Abercrombie and Brian Longhurst in *Audiences* (1998). The two authors argue that what they call the Incorporation/Resistance Paradigm (IRP) should be replaced by a Spectacle/Performance Paradigm (SPP). The IRP emerged from structuralism and the work of Hall in particular (see Chapter 4), but its influence can also be traced to Fiske's theory of consumer resistance. Although Fiske argues that consumer practices such as gaming routinely resist or evade incorporation by dominant ideological and commercial interests, his theory is still located within this paradigmatic tension between dominance and opposition; incorporation and resistance. Abercrombie and Longhurst show how the IRP has become the orthodox paradigm for theorizing media but they argue that 'the *ordered* structure given by the IRP is being undermined by the *disorder* of actual audience response – a disorder of *unpredictability* not of *resistance*' (Abercrombie and Longhurst 1998: 32). Instead of a receptive, captivated audience assumed by Hall's Encoding/Decoding model, we see the emergence of a more recent generation of skilled media audiences. According to the authors, audiences today use media texts and technologies in more sophisticated ways than older generations who grew up with the intense visual media experience offered by cinema and theatre. Today's media audiences tend to consume and communicate through multi-media technologies that dispel the myth of the disciplined audience member who pays close attention to – and decodes a position in relation to – a single media text. Indeed, media today are better understood as *resources* rather than *texts* given the symbolic creativity with which they are put to use by young consumers in particular, often for productive ends (see Willis 1990). Hegemony theory and its assumption of a dominant power bloc no longer make sense in contemporary culture where power is far more diffused (Abercrombie and Longhurst 1998: 36).

Three types of audience are distinguished:

1   *Simple audiences*: examples would be theatre audiences or spectators at a football match, as well as studio audiences for a television show. Simple audiences are co-present at and participate intensely in the performances they witness: 'the performance conventions for simple audiences demand high attention' (Abercrombie and Longhurst 1998: 54).

2   *Mass audiences*: while simple audiences exist in co-present contexts, mass audiences exist in mediated ones (e.g. watching television, listening to music online). Mass audiences are not tied to the ceremonial rituals of simple audiences – such as attending a theatre performance, which requires an *immediate aesthetic* – but instead they require a mediated or *constructed aesthetic* in order to appreciate what they consume. However, both mass and simple audiences can only be understood in relation to distinctive performances and 'involve a communication between producers and consumers who are kept physically and socially separate from one another' (Abercrombie and Longhurst 1998: 58).

3   *Diffused audiences*: unlike simple and mass audiences, the **diffused audience** is not party to any singular performance but consumes several via 'a fusion of different forms of the media' (Abercrombie and Longhurst 1998: 76). For example, someone who watches the news on TV at the same time as sending a text message via mobile phone and listening to music via MP3 player is exhibiting the skills of a diffused, multitask consumer. Being a diffused audience member in modern societies is 'constitutive of everyday life' and a performative experience because media 'provide an important resource for everyday performance' (Abercrombie and Longhurst 1998: 68, 74; see also Longhurst 2007, who discusses ordinary life experiences of belonging to and distinguishing from others in diffused audience and performance contexts). Diffused audiences are also less clearly demarcated in their relation to producers, and like Jenkins's textual

poachers and Silverstone's concept of performance, the boundary between diffused audiences/consumers and performances/producers becomes increasingly blurred.

Although simple and mass audiences are still commonplace in contemporary media and culture, diffused audience contexts are a more pervasive and mundane feature of everyday life. Furthermore, diffused audiences can be situated within the SPP – they engage in interactive processes of spectacle and performance, including narcissism, because 'the aim of modern life is to see and be seen' (Abercrombie and Longhurst 1998: 81). The SPP foregrounds the fluidity of identity formation. Diffused audiences are like Anderson's (1991) imagined communities (as discussed in Chapter 3) – participants perform identities to imagined audiences and their relations with others are 'a reflection, as in a mirror, of the self' (Abercrombie and Longhurst 1998: 92). These processes of narcissism and identity formation so central to the SPP are also evident in the notion of 'mediascapes' (Appadurai 1993). Mediascapes (media landscapes) emphasize the omnipresence of media images and narratives in our own, self-narratives (i.e. biographies). Media constitute our principal resources for learning about the world beyond our habitual spheres, and these resources are utilized skilfully and imaginatively by diffused audiences, particularly fans, enthusiasts and even petty producers such as Jenkins's fan artists (see Abercrombie and Longhurst 1998: 140–50). Further evidence of the skilful, diffused audience is provided by Joke Hermes's (1995) study of everyday media use in which she found that 'People read women's magazines because it suits their everyday routines' (Hermes 1995: 20). Women's magazines do not, on the whole, function as mass-produced fantasies as suggested by Modelski's analysis of soap operas and Radway's analysis of romance readers (see Chapter 6). If magazines seek to break everyday routines and lull their readers into a fantasy world, they are 'easily put down' according to Hermes. She also argues that 'Meaningful study of media use has to take the "media ensemble" into consideration' (Hermes 1995: 24). Hermes's media users, like diffused audiences, refer to an array of media – rarely does a single medium or media text 'consume them' with its meaningfulness – in everyday talk with others.

The idea of a skilled, diffused audience is also evident in Abercrombie's theory of **consumer authority**. According to the author, sociological accounts 'make it difficult to get at the idea of resistance to *authority* because they are more usually concerned with resistance to *power*' (Abercrombie 1994: 48). The problem with thinking in terms of power with respect to contexts of consumption and production is the assumption that power is either something that an individual or group possesses, or does not possess. Power is not easily theorized by degrees. Typical measures of power – social class, wealth, property ownership and rights – are grounded in assumptions about exclusion and (lack of) inclusion. Resistance to power is therefore typically associated with large-scale changes in the social and political order, such as the de-stratification of social class structures or the de-privatization of property ownership. Resistance, to this extent, is hardly a routine event and is only ever likely to occur during a revolution. Although 'power' is clearly an important concept in understanding media consumer-producer relations, Abercrombie argues that it is a restrictive concept because it neglects to consider everyday consumer activities that can erode powerful institutions such as media corporations. If power and resistance are two sides of the same coin, operating in the currency of the IRP, Abercrombie's concept of authority – consistent with diffused audiences – allows for subtler and more dynamic shifts in relations between consumers and producers. If power is about ownership of products (the means and meanings of production), consumer authority is about the right to *claim* ownership of a product and its meanings.

Authority contexts, according to Abercrombie, are pervasive in contemporary life and subject to frequent changes in character. A traditional example of an authority context would be the teacher–student relationship, where the authority of the teacher (both in terms of knowledge and discipline) is expected to – but does not always – hold sway. In the realm of late capitalist economies, the relationship between consumers and producers – unlike the orthodox teacher–student relationship – has become ever more intimate to the extent that most production is now consumer-led: 'The shift from producer to consumer means that the capacity to determine the form, nature and quality of goods and services has moved from the former to the latter' (Abercrombie 1991: 172). By extension, authority contexts involving consumer and producer groups are dynamic, collusive and insecure. Two components of authority contexts as discussed by Abercrombie are expertise and meaning. These two components serve to legitimate the voices of authority. In the case of expertise, consumers will only accept the legitimacy of producer authority if producers are shown to 'deploy their expertise successfully in the ways recognized by both superordinates and subordinates. Clearly, this recognition breaks down from time to time, undermining the basis of authority' (Abercrombie 1994: 47). In the case of meaning, 'the authority of the producer is sustained by the capacity to define the meaning of the transactions involved and is lost as consumers acquire that power' (Abercrombie 1994: 53). Authority contexts, like art worlds, involve collective interaction between producers and consumers, but are more prone to changes of direction in flows of expertise and meaning between participants.

Authority within diffused media consumer-producer contexts rests, therefore, on how expertly claims can be made about owning the meanings of products. For every legally purchased U2 album, there are plenty of bootlegged versions that can be downloaded free of charge. The music industry has felt the full force of consumer authority in recent years due to the proliferation of internet piracy, facilitated by peer-to-peer software (see McCourt and Burkart 2003; Woodworth 2004; Leyshon et al. 2005). While download sites such as Napster have 'gone legal' and become incorporated into the mainstream music industry, there are many more examples of unlicensed sites that continue to freely supply music, regardless of ongoing investigations by music industry bodies. As my own research has found, illegal MP3 music file-sharing continues to be a widespread, everyday practice among young people in particular (Laughey 2006). Indeed, the music industry as a whole can only conjure up a 'fantasy consumer' model for its own marketing purposes – predicated on highly unreliable evidence and forecasting – which explains why 'record companies spend a considerable amount of their time producing "failures" ... the "public verdict" is allowed a retrospective authority' (Frith 1996: 60). Only about one in ten albums suc-ceed in making a substantial profit – many more suffer heavy losses.

eBay is another breeding ground for authorial battles over expertise and meaning. eBay sellers may lack expertise in several aspects of their work, thus threatening their producer authority. Inaccurate or misleading information on auction listings, amateurish images of products, and neglecting to reply to customer emails are just some of the discrepancies that can affect consumer perceptions about levels of expertise, and in some cases afford opportunity for consumer authority in the form of negative feedback comments. Meanings of eBay products are prone to consumer authority too. It is quite possible – given internet access and basic computer literacy skills – for eBay users to acquire quite sophisticated levels of knowledge and skills in evaluating certain pro-ducts, to the extent that enables them to buy comparable products (at car boot sales, trade fairs, and so on) in order to sell them on eBay or elsewhere. Of course, eBay demonstrates consumer authority over large retailers and manufacturers in a wider sense, given that its consumer-to-consumer site is a facilitator of global consumerism (see Hillis et al. 2006), and that it has a tendency to attract counterfeit goods (e.g. 'Burberry-like caps') which directly confront the 'brand power' of big producers. Consumer authority is also deemed by one commentator to be an empowering outcome of web-logging: 'Blogs can, and do, provide and link information that equips audiences with the knowledge to question media conglomerates and other powerful inter-ests' (Bird 2003: 184). Blogging and other online discussion forums enable individuals to exchange advice and opinions on an unprecedented scale, often to the detriment of commercial interests.

Bourdieu: the habitus and field theory

The notion of autonomous consumer power or authority – together with the populist perspective that taste cannot be accounted for (see discussion of Ang in Chapter 6) – is critiqued in the work of Pierre Bourdieu, especially *Distinction* (1984). His theory of 'the habitus' (Bourdieu 1977) aims to show how consumer taste – in clothes, music, television shows, and so on – is not a purely personal choice but, rather, is structured according to social circumstances. **Habitus theory** is based on the conviction that 'although diverse and varied, consumption practices are socially structured' (MacKay 1997: 5). Any individual's habitus, therefore, simultaneously produces and reproduces 'a stable and group-specific way of seeing or making sense of the social world; in other words, a *distinctive mode of cultural consumption*' (Lee 1993: 34). Operating below the level of individual consciousness, the habitus is at work in taken-for-granted consumer tastes for food, films, and so on, as well as in one's bodily expressions and dress (Lury 1996: 85). In short, the habitus is an invisible classificatory system that shapes consumer tastes. However, this is only half the story. The habitus is not – like ideology – a fixed set of values that filters down from the ruling classes. On the contrary, the habitus is both a structured and a structuring principle – we make our habituses while at the same time being made by them. As Bourdieu states, the habitus is a 'strategy-generating principle enabling agents to cope with unforeseen and ever-changing situations' which is 'laid down in each agent by his [*sic*] earliest upbringing' (Bourdieu 1977: 72, 81). Note the term 'agent' here. Like Giddens's theory of structuration (see Chapter 5), habitus theory tries to understand the correspondence between social structures (i.e. institutional power) and individual agency. The phrase 'we are what we eat' gives agency to us – we decide whether to be healthy or not – but, at the same time, the habitus determines that what we eat is not entirely of our own choosing. To use Bourdieu's words: 'Through taste, an agent has what he likes because he likes what he has' (Bourdieu 1984: 175).

For Bourdieu, taste is manifested in one's habitus by a set of predispositions that each individual learns to adopt from an early age in relation to their levels of economic and cultural capital. In terms of economic capital, we are *predisposed* to act (and consume things) in certain ways depending on whether we are born into wealth or poverty. Economic capital, of course, is an important structuring marker of consumer taste. However, money is not the only marker of taste. What Bourdieu calls 'cultural capital' also influences an individual agent's predispositions. Cultural capital consists of resources that one is able to draw on in order to demonstrate competence in social practices (such as speaking a language, eating a meal, reading a book, dancing to music, and so on). Bourdieu refers to 'The very close relationship linking cultural practices ... to educational capital (measured by qualifications) and, secondarily, to social origin (measured by father's occupation)' (Bourdieu 1984: 13). In other words, levels of cultural capital are closely linked to education and occupation (social class). Those individuals with high cultural capital are likely to be well educated as well as wealthy, while those with low cultural capital are less well educated and less affluent consumers. Central to Bourdieu's ideas about the habitus and its social structuring of taste, however, is his claim that despite the close relationship between economic and cultural capital, the two forms of capital are nevertheless distinct and not inextricably linked. For example, a university student has high cultural capital (especially once they have graduated) but is likely to be low in economic capital (unless they have wealthy parents). See Figure 9.4 for other examples of occupational types that are low in economic but high in cultural capital, and vice versa.

Economic capital

	LOW EC, LOW CC	HIGH EC, LOW CC
Cultural capital	Unskilled labourers	Lottery winners
	Long-term unemployed	Drug dealers
	LOW EC, HIGH CC	HIGH EC, HIGH CC
	Students	Leading scientists
	Freelance writers/artists	Head teachers

Figure 9.4   Some occupational classifications based on levels of economic capital (EC) and cultural capital (CC)

Bourdieu (1984) argues that economic and cultural capital are the key social markers through which the habitus works to classify consumer tastes. In practice, this means that the habitus structures the relationships we are *voluntarily* predisposed to form with others. We include and exclude others in our social networks based on a sharing of cultural tastes (liking the same music, sport, and so on) and economic circumstances (being of similar social class), while at the same time being included and excluded by others according to the same classifications. Bourdieu's concept of 'social capital' – propensity for individuals of similar economic background to bond with each other through friendships, business dealings, and so on – is associated with this process but is a different form of capital again (see Bourdieu 1986). These practices of inclusion and exclusion – what Bourdieu means by 'distinction' – explain why, generally, it is possible to classify (i.e. predict) an individual's predisposed tastes based purely on information about their economic status and educational history. For example, Bourdieu (1984) argues that consumers with high economic and high cultural capital are far more likely to enjoy classical music than consumers in the lower classes who are less well educated, the latter being more prone to like pop music. This distinction is not just a coincidence or a personal matter, but an outcome of the structurally marked classifications (i.e. habituses) that consumers are predisposed to practise in relations with each other. In short, we associate with similar others according to social expectations that we are predisposed to fulfil. Despite endless opportunities, we do not – on the whole – associate with individuals of a different social class and educational background.

Bourdieu's theory of the habitus is informed by survey data on consumer tastes in his native France. While his theoretical discussion of this data is exceptionally sophisticated and has become canonical in sociology and other disciplines, including media studies, the data analysis itself is questionable. The habitus is premised on the idea that consumer tastes are closely related to occupational status. While occupations may well affect tastes, they do not necessarily determine economic status. Home ownership and the value of one's property, for example, are other determining factors in economic status, as well as inherited wealth. This problem of 'measurement' is widely regarded as a major weakness of the survey method *per se*. Furthermore, Bourdieu's avid search for cultural distinctions often distorts a situation in which such distinctions are slight between different social classes or barely exist at all. In the case of music consumers:

> 41 per cent of classical music albums are purchased by those in social classes AB, pointing in the direction of a Bourdieu distinction paradigm. However, only 17 per cent of the albums purchased by AB social classes are of this type. They are far outnumbered by the purchase of rock and pop albums which constitute 52 per cent of purchases.
>
> (Longhurst and Savage 1996: 288)

This example of how Bourdieu's data analysis can be interpreted with different outcomes underscores how his survey research lacks a complementary ethnographic component to understand broader, more meaningful practices in the contexts generated by everyday consumer tastes. Perhaps not surprisingly, de Certeau doubts the claims made by Bourdieu about the structuring structures of the habitus: 'In order to assume that the basis has such a stability, it must be unverifiable, invisible' (de Certeau 1984: 58). Invisible structures are clearly acrimonious in relation to de Certeau's notion of consumer tactics that are non-formalized practices 'neither as deterministic nor as rooted in social class as Bourdieu tends to assert' (Gardiner 2000: 170).

As well as habitus theory, Bourdieu's (1993) **field theory** is a related but somewhat different perspective on media and cultural consumption – although it is principally concerned with media and cultural production. A field is the site of practices, struggles and possibilities enacted in various

arenas of cultural production. For example, there are literary fields, educational fields, media fields, and so on. Each field is characterized by 'the
structure of average chances of access to the different positions ... and the
dispositions of each agent' (Bourdieu 1993: 64). To paraphrase, each field has
its own hierarchy of positions (trainees, executives, managers, directors, and
so on) that function to restrict, regulate and reproduce certain types and
methods of cultural production. However, each field of cultural production
also brings certain dispositions – that is, corresponding habituses – that are
adopted by producers so as to effectively shape what is produced and ultimately consumed. Field (positions) and the habitus (dispositions), in their
'astonishingly close correspondence', constitute a 'sense of social direction
which orients agents' (Bourdieu 1993: 64). For example, risk-taking in fields of
cultural production is rare. The positions and predispositions of producers are
oriented against taking risks so as not to threaten existing consumer uptake of
their products. However, risk-taking – typical of avant-garde production –
tends to produce more daring and original cultural work. Unfortunately, 'The
propensity to move towards the economically most risky positions, and above
all the capacity to persist in them ... seem to depend to a large extent on
possession of substantial economic and social capital' (Bourdieu 1993: 67). So
innovative media and cultural production, in practice, is structured by economic and social constraints. Producers who occupy the more junior positions in a given field, therefore, are not predisposed to 'sacrifice everything'
for a risky venture, given that they do not have the necessary economic
capital to cushion the blow of failure, or the necessary social capital to build
up contacts for the sales and distribution of their products.

How does field theory inform consumer practices? For Bourdieu, the self-
generating, self-regulating fields – and corresponding habituses – of cultural
production tend to mean that consumers are subject to the same products
from the same producers (i.e. large corporations). Even the large corporations
high in economic and social capital, however, take limited risks in what they
produce because their positions of power remain in the balance wherever
there is competition. In the journalistic field, for example, 'competition for
consumers tends to take the form of competition for the newest news
("scoops")' (Bourdieu 1996: 71). Market forces weigh heavily on the journalistic and especially the television fields. In turn, individual journalists feel this
'weight exerted by the journalistic field' which shows how 'the economy
weighs on all fields of cultural production' (Bourdieu 1996: 56). These market
forces are not only felt by journalists either: 'Enslaved by audience ratings,
television imposes market pressures on the supposedly free and enlightened
consumers' (Bourdieu 1996: 67). So consumers – who determine what is
produced in fields such as television – are oppressed by the very logic (i.e.
audience ratings) that Fiske cites as evidence of consumer power. Risks are
generally not taken, so audience ratings are tested out on risk-free practices of

media and cultural production, some of which are inevitably measured as successes and reproduced across all positions within a field. The journalistic field's obsession with audience ratings, likewise, weighs on other fields. For instance, 'Political success increasingly depends on adapting to the demands of the journalistic field' (Bourdieu 1996: 5). Furthermore, the political and journalistic fields effectively collaborate in their 'capacity to impose a way of seeing the world' (Bourdieu 1996: 22). Television is vital for politicians as a means of conveying their positions in struggles with opposition parties. As Herman and Chomsky claim (see Chapter 7), journalists tend to favour mainstream political sources of which they are familiar. Similarly, Bourdieu argues that television consumers are forced to see a rather narrow, mainstream political view of the world as an outcome of fields of cultural production.

Like Bourdieu, Nick Couldry is sceptical of theories that overstate the capacity of consumers to deflect the weight exerted by the media field. For instance, while sharing their interest in the role of media in everyday life, he criticizes Abercrombie and Longhurst's neglect of media power: 'they write sometimes as if underlying issues of power relating to the media had simply disappeared' (Couldry 2000b: 21). By contrast, Couldry is keen to explore 'the inequality in the power of "naming" social reality which the media themselves constitute' (Couldry: 2000b: 22). In *Media Rituals* (2003), Couldry draws on Bourdieu's field theory in his attempt to explain 'how the social world is "mediated" through a media system that has very particular power-effects, and how the actions and beliefs of all of us are caught up in this process' (Couldry 2003: 1–2). However, media power to name and represent social reality is not fixed and centralized. On the contrary, Couldry refers to the myth of the mediated centre – the idea that *the media* (in common phraseology) is concentrated in the hands of dominant ideological interests – and he claims that media rituals are 'condensed forms of action where category distinctions and boundaries related to the myth of the mediated centre are worked upon with particular intensity' (Couldry 2003: 47) in order to naturalize media power. Couldry's theory of media rituals, therefore, demands a broader understanding of media power and its role in our everyday life experiences. An important set of media rituals, for example, seek to reinforce the myth that television and other media present (unmediated) reality. 'Liveness' is a ritual category at work in 'reality TV' because the notion of 'real time', by definition, implicates audiences in the immediacy of what media present to them. As such, liveness 'guarantees a potential connection to our shared social realities as they are happening' (Couldry 2003: 96–7). As well as liveness, Couldry (2003) discusses media pilgrimages – for example, fans visiting filming locations for television shows – and mediated self-disclosure performed, say, in the ritual space of talk shows like *The Oprah Winfrey Show* (1996–), as other categories of media rituals that reveal dynamic social processes at work in power relations between audiences, texts and institutions.

Summary

This chapter has considered:

- Competing definitions and theories of media consumerism and everyday life.
- Fiske's theory of consumer resistance and consumer power, including his comparison between the financial and cultural economies of television.
- De Certeau's theory of everyday consumer tactics, exemplified by speed reading and *la perruque*, along with media literacy approaches that reaffirm the text–reader relationship but nonetheless find sophisticated everyday practices, particularly among young media consumers.
- Theories of fandom as textual poaching and participatory culture (Jenkins).
- Theories of the consumption cycle and mediated experience (Silverstone) that show how media consumption and production inform, and overlap with, each other.
- Theories of the diffused audience and consumer authority (Abercrombie and Longhurst) that call for a paradigm shift away from concepts of media power and resistance (media institutions and texts) to concepts of performance and narcissism (media resources) in unpredictable, changeable authority contexts.
- Bourdieu's habitus and field theories, which when combined suggest that predisposed consumer tastes are shaped by the habitus – a system of classification – and are reproduced in fields of cultural production, including the journalistic field.

Further reading

Benson, R. and Neveu, E. (eds) (2005) *Bourdieu and the Journalistic Field.* Cambridge: Polity.

A valuable edited collection of articles on Bourdieu's field theory and journalism, especially in France and the United States. Included is an article by Bourdieu himself. Accessible to all media students, although some articles are better suited to advanced undergraduates and postgraduates.

Bird, S. E. (2003) *The Audience in Everyday Life: Living in a Media World.* New York: Routledge.

A collection of essays that discuss, for example, news audiences and their responses to media scandals, and the role of the American Indian in popular culture. The value of media ethnography is a consistent claim made by the author. Accessible to all media students, although some essays are better suited to advanced undergraduates and postgraduates.

Brooker, W. and Jermyn, D. (eds) (2003) *The Audience Studies Reader*. London: Routledge.

A diverse selection of historical and contemporary writings on audience research and theory, including sections on fan audiences, screen theory, female audiences and interpretive communities. Useful for all media students.

Laughey, D. (2006) *Music and Youth Culture*. Edinburgh: Edinburgh University Press.

Excuse my indulgence, but this is one of the few empirically-informed accounts of music media consumption and how music interacts with young people's everyday lives (note that this book is also useful in relation to interactionist perspectives discussed in Chapter 5). Accessible to all media students, although some discussion is better suited to advanced under-graduates and postgraduates.

10   Debating media theory

This brief summarizing chapter concludes our discussion of media theory, and points to some key debates and developments – present and future. In the final analysis we have identified, in no particular order, eight distinctive themes or strands in media theory:

- behaviourist media theory
- medium theory (and theories of modernity)
- structuralist media theory
- interactionist media theory
- feminist media theory
- political economy (and postcolonial media theory)
- postmodern media theory
- consumerist media theory.

Each strand has its strengths and weaknesses – there is no such thing as perfect media theory! It would be wrong to suggest that there is not some fuzziness and overlapping across these strands too. Many of the authors discussed previously could feature in more than one chapter (actually some do, such as Stuart Hall, whose work is discussed in Chapters 4 and 7). The work of Ien Ang, for instance, is located within feminist media theory but it would be equally locatable within consumerist – and, to a lesser extent, postmodern – media theory. Moreover, within each strand of media theory is found dialogue and debate. Media theory without dialogue and debate is always sterile and short-lived. For example, in Chapter 2 we encountered different perspectives on behaviourist media theory, from direct effects (the work of Lasswell and Wertham in particular) to uses and gratifications. Nonetheless, all the perspectives that we discussed shared the same behaviourist assumption – that human beings are affected by media stimuli, whether theorized as negative media effects or positive gratifications of prevailing needs.

Of course the really interesting debate, however, is found in the tensions between the strands. The structure–agency debate for instance, located somewhere between the two poles of structuralist and interactionist media theory, continues to provoke fresh and alternative ideas – not least in response to the best efforts of Bourdieu and Giddens at reconciling the debate with theories of structuration. Do media texts and institutions structure our lives? Or are media audiences agents for media, social and political change? The structure–agency debate also informs the debate between political economy and consumerist media theory. Clearly, political economy per-spectives that foreground the economic power of media production are in polar opposition to consumerist perspectives that emphasize consumer power and resistance. Other strands of media theory – such as postmodern media theory – are less straightforwardly placed within the structure–agency debate but are more clearly positioned in relation to other debates. We discussed in Chapter 8 how postmodern media theory and theories of modernity are fundamentally opposed in their view of how far capitalism has advanced into contemporary media and culture. Some theorists of modernity continue to cite processes of rampant capitalism and industrialization in modern-day life; some postmodernists, by contrast, cite the breakdown of the capitalist metanarrative and the rise of media-saturated, post-industrial, information societies. Having said this, McLuhan's medium theory (premised on theories of modernity) and its technological determinism draw parallels with Bau-drillard's postmodern perspective on media simulation. So we return to the point made above about the fuzziness that distinguishes these various strands in media theory.

Instead of attempting a detailed comparative analysis of paradigms in media theory – another book alone would justify such a task – it seems fit as a finale to address some FAQs (frequently asked questions) that media students often want answers to.

1 Which media theory is the best?

That all depends on your point of view. I have my own opinions but have tried to keep opinions firmly away from this book. Perhaps discerning readers will beg to differ and send me emails identifying where my impartial guard has slipped. Essentially, every media student's answer to this question lies in reading and researching widely in relation to each strand of media theory, and then making a convincing case in favour of one particular strand against all the others. It would suffice to say that some theories are more widely criticized than others, but that there is no such thing as a criticism-free the-ory. Indeed, we should be thankful of criticism. Media studies would be a very dull subject if everyone agreed with each other.

2 Which media theory is the easiest to understand?

Again, this is a personal matter. Some students find medium theory an easy option, while others cannot follow a word of McLuhan or Innis. By its nature, theory is never really easy – and no one should panic who finds it difficult. Basing judgements about different theories on degrees of easiness is not a very academic strategy either. This book is designed to make media theory as easy as possible without squeezing all the intellectual substance out of it. If you cannot understand this book, may I suggest a very long gap year? For those who can, base your judgements on the theoretical strand(s) that you most enjoy and sympathize with.

3 I am interested in film/music/video games, etc. – which theory fits my interests?

Each strand of media theory previously discussed can be applied to any medium. Some strands are associated with certain media rather than others – for example, feminist media theory has contributed more to film than popular music studies – but this is merely a coincidental state of affairs. Perhaps you can break the mould?

4 I am interested in media texts/technologies/audiences/institutions – which theory fits my interests?

Although some strands of media theory are focused on one of these dimensions more than the others (e.g. political economy's focus is mostly on institutions, while medium theory's focus is on technologies), there is no divine right for any strand to claim expertise in analysing any of these dimensions. Moreover, the best work in media theory attempts to bridge the unhelpful institution–text–audience divide. Feminist media theory – as we have discussed – contains a range of competing perspectives precisely because it has the virtue of not becoming entrenched in, say, theories of media texts.

5 I have read your book from start to finish – what should I do now?

Read it all again! No, that's a joke. The next thing to do is to read the raw theoretical work that we have discussed. Some of this work is very difficult for anyone to understand – especially if you are new to media theory – but reading, taking notes on and discussing first-hand theory can be a very rewarding and stimulating experience. After that, refer to the further reading lists at the end of each chapter and carry out your own library searches, both of which will uncover useful commentaries and critiques of the raw theory you have already encountered. Remember this fourfold sequence – the more you read, the better you understand, the greater your critical ability, the higher your attainment.

6 Should I discuss examples in my theoretical analysis?

Yes – as we discussed in the introductory chapter, any theory is only as good as its supporting evidence. Use examples both to prove and disprove theories. Your examples provide the tools with which you can carve out your own theoretical path. If you ever need to write a long essay or dissertation, it is well to discuss one or two extended examples – sometimes called 'case studies'. Examples put media theory into practice. Besides, using examples to analyse theories is far more interesting than simply analysing abstract theories.

7 Can I use internet sources?

Sparingly, but remember – the internet is not the best resource for understanding media theory. I have decided not to include a list of web resources not because there are none, but because I would discourage web research as a way into media theory for undergraduate-level students. The internet may provide you with factual information and examples, but the best way to seek out theory and theoretical commentary is to search through academic libraries (i.e. for academic books and journal articles) complemented by online learning resources as provided, for example, by the Athens gateway.

8 Can you point me towards future developments and arguments in media theory?

No student has ever asked me this question, which is good because I do not know the answer. It is simply impossible to forecast the future of media studies and media theory, not least because ideas and theoretical orientations change with the seasons. One thing is certain – the future is bright for media studies. Particularly interesting in forthcoming years will be developments in internet studies (see Livingstone 2005); affect theory and theories of emotion; mediology (see Debray 1996) and its anti-semiotics agenda; media ethics and morality; field theory; theories of celebrity; theories of technological convergence; theories of remediation and new media (see Bolter and Grusin 2000; Manovich 2001); and work that ties media production to consumption practices and vice versa. It is also likely that there will be a narrowing of the – at present – fairly wide gap between media theory and media practice. Some strands of media theory will evolve more rapidly than others, but the interdisciplinary character of media studies should continue to ensure that evolution occurs across all aspects of theory. For example, media psychology is likely to continue its interest in effects and influences, especially in relation to the broad idea of reflexive bodies, while media sociology will remain concerned with social inequalities in relation to, say, political economy and structuralist theories (including questions of media regulation and cultural governance). Feminist media theory seems more distant from postfeminism than ever, appearing to favour the sense of continuation suggested by the third wave rather than a sense of postfeminist completion. Interactionist and postmodern media theories have undergone significant revision in recent years, the latter of which is distinctly out of favour, but – as some folk say –

'what comes around goes around'. Theories of modernity, including medium theory – once distinctly out of fashion – have experienced a widespread revival. This goes to show how the unpredictability of media theory should never be underestimated.

One thing for certain, though, is that media studies and media theory are given a bad name by aberrations like 'Media Studies 2.0'. The accusation that media studies is easy should be resisted at all costs, but a few individuals perpetuate the myth with sweeping generalizations about 'the new media age', as if the sun shone out of their cyber-backsides. Media Studies 2.0 is, with the greatest respect, complete and utter nonsense. It is the malteser of media theory – lightweight and hollow to its core. New media technologies *have* made an impression on our contemporary culture, but to date there has been no digital revolution in media production, distribution and consumption. DIY media of any substance are soon absorbed by corporate interests. The internet can be an alternative medium, but in no sense is it free from established social, economic and political forces. Nor has the internet triggered social and cultural changes on the scale of, say, the telegraph and telephone before it. Of course media studies should look to the future, but it cannot neglect those ghosts of media past that haunt media present.

9 What next?

Go forth, and debate . . .

Glossary

This is a selective and necessarily concise glossary of key terms that should only be referred to in conjunction with the extended discussion of these terms in the main text. Where appropriate, the reader is directed to relevant chapters of the book where discussion can be found. Terms are defined in the context of media theory/media studies – they should not be read as general definitions.

Agenda-setting theory: an 'effects' approach that shows how media influence the agenda of public issues around which political campaigns and other matters of public interest are established (see Chapter 2).

Behaviourism: a theoretical perspective that aims to measure how our thoughts, feelings and actions are affected by media communications.

Chain of communication: 'who, says what, in which channel, to whom, with what effect'. This term is also known as Lasswell's formula (see Chapter 2).

Consumer authority: the notion that audiences can claim ownership of and expertise over the meanings of cultural products – such as media or music texts – during intense phases of consumer-led production (see discussion of Abercrombie and Longhurst in Chapter 9).

Consumer resistance: the concept of audiences being routinely and directly opposed to the profit-making intentions of capitalist production in their uses of media and cultural commodities (see discussion of Fiske in Chapter 9).

Consumerism/consumption: a theoretical perspective that seeks to explore and take complex account of the ways in which media production is received and used by audiences. Consumerism in a general sense also refers to practices of purchasing and using products and services.

Cultivation theory: a longitudinal approach to 'effects' research in which television in particular – although the approach is applicable to other mass media – is assumed to be such an important source of information and entertainment that viewers cannot escape its gradual encroachment into their everyday lives (see Chapter 2).

Cultural resistance: the argument that the power of mass media and cultural institutions is effectively opposed by audiences in cross-cultural contexts of reception.

Diffused audience: the concept of everyday performative consumption of different media resources in such a way as not to consume any singular text or institutional **ideology** (see discussion of Abercrombie and Longhurst in Chapter 9).

Direct effects: an assertion that media texts and technologies impose powerful – and often subliminal – influences on the behaviour and actions of audiences. This perspective is similarly known as the hypodermic syringe, magic bullet or plug-in drug model of **media effects**. It can be compared to perspectives on 'indirect effects' (the idea that media are only one of several influential factors that determine our behaviour and actions) and 'limited effects' (in which media are not considered to have any significant influence on how we think, feel and act).

Discourse: a system of signification (like **language**) governed by rules that structure the ways in which we classify and divide its different meanings. For example, the discourse of television news operates under certain rules and conventions, such as values of newsworthiness and truthfulness. Foucault's theory of discourse is particularly concerned with issues of power and knowledge, and the ways in which particular discourses function to make certain ideas *present* while others are made *absent* (see discussion of Foucault in Chapter 4).

Everyday life: routine, mundane, ordinary contexts of media and cultural consumption and – less often but increasingly common – production.

Femininity: cultural values, ideas and assumptions about female identities. The term 'feminine' describes a **gender** category; the term 'female' is a **sex** category.

Feminisms: a broad term that encompasses different theories of gender and womanhood. No two feminist perspectives are alike but – for the sake of brevity – all feminist theory seeks to analyse and address inequalities between the sexes, not least by politicizing 'the personal' (i.e. what it means to be a woman in contemporary life).

Field theory: an approach to cultural production as structured by social and economic constraints. A field is the site of positions, possibilities and struggles practised in various arenas of cultural – including media – production (see discussion of Bourdieu in Chapter 9). See also: **habitus theory**.

Gender: social and cultural characteristics of **sex** differences, typically categorized as masculinity and femininity.

Gender trouble: the assertion that masculine and feminine identities can be liberated from social norms by being enacted as performances that blur traditional gender lines. Transvestism is an example of troublesome gender performativity (see discussion of Butler in Chapter 6).

Habitus theory: an approach that considers consumer practices to be culturally diverse and actively empowering, but always socially structured. The habitus is a classificatory system that organizes consumer tastes and predispositions from each individual's early years (see discussion of Bourdieu in Chapter 9). See also: **field theory**.

Hegemony: a process of 'give and take' power struggle between ruling elites (e.g. governments) and the masses, in which the rulers offer certain benefits and concessions to their 'subjects' in order to win their consent and maintain the political status quo.

Hyperreality: simulated imagery – for example, media-saturated images of a real entity such as New York City – that becomes more *real* to human experience than the genuinely real entity being simulated (see discussion of Baudrillard in Chapter 8). See also: **simulation/simulacra**.

Ideology: a set of ideas, values, tastes and/or beliefs expounded by a particular social group, organization, religion or culture. For example, the ideology of masculinity – at least in most Western countries – is associated with physical strength and prowess, emotional detachment, hard-nosed business, cars, computers, technological gadgets, and so on.

Information society: a theoretical perspective on advanced capitalism as being predominantly concerned with post-industrial, network economies that have passed through an industrial age into a communications age (see Chapter 8).

Interactionism: a theoretical perspective on the way we, individually and in groups, act in our relation to others in specific co-present and mediated environments.

Intertextuality: the postmodern notion that contemporary media and cultural texts – indeed, all kinds of texts – lack any original, individual style and can only refer back to other, previously produced texts (see discussion of Jameson in Chapter 8).

Labelling theory: an approach to deviance as a social construction in which certain individuals and groups create labels (i.e. names and classifications, such as 'junkies') to exclude or criminalize others (see Chapter 5).

Language: the general meaning is familiar, but in semiotics this term refers specifically to a system of rules (*langue* and *parole*) that structure all the different units of meaning at any particular time. Each and every unit must be different (e.g. in the English language, 'hat' is different to 'bat', 'fat', 'ham', 'hut', and so on) in order for the system to successfully *signify* its meanings (see Chapter 4).

Male gaze, the: a theory about how men in films are represented as 'bearers of the look' which is usually directed at physically desirable, sexually submissive female characters who connote 'to-be-looked-at-ness' and are denied a female gaze (see discussion of Mulvey in Chapter 6).

Masculinity: cultural values, ideas and assumptions about male identities. The term 'masculine' describes a **gender** category; the term 'male' is a **sex** category.

McDonaldization: a feature of advanced modernity in which the corporate structure and practices associated with the fast-food chain (i.e. McDonald's) are symptomatic of wider global production techniques to do with efficiency, calculability, predictability and control (see discussion of Ritzer in Chapter 8).

Media and cultural imperialism: the argument that one nation's media and cultural values are able to infiltrate and potentially colonize the media and cultural infrastructure of other nations (see Chapter 7).

Media effects: a general term that describes the power of media texts and technologies to function as stimuli for audience responses and reactions.

Media literacy: the notion that uses of media texts and technologies enable the learning of critical abilities, skills and competencies.

Mediated quasi-interaction: the non-reciprocal social relations between media producers/personalities and audiences, predominantly monological in character such that the mediated words and actions of public figures reveal themselves to constant scrutiny from 'the public eye' (see discussion of Thompson in Chapter 5).

Medium theory: an approach that emphasizes the importance of media technologies in determining the features of media products and content, as well as determining their social, cultural, political and economic uses (see discussion of Innis and McLuhan in Chapter 3). See also: **technological determinism**.

Metanarrative/grand narrative: a theory or belief-system that emerges – particularly during processes of modernity – to legitimate its claims to truth and knowledge against the sins of ignorance and superstition characteristic of pre-modern societies. However, postmodernity is partly defined by the decline of all-embracing metanarratives, such as communism and feminism (see discussion of Lyotard in Chapter 8).

Minority culture: a modernist notion that describes an elite group of artists and intellectuals capable of appreciating high cultural tastes and values, which they may subsequently transmit to the ill-informed masses.

Modernism: an artistic, literary and critical tradition of experimental work (circa 1890–1940) that cherishes individual creativity in opposition to the hostile consequences of **modernity**.

Modernity: the social, economic, political and technological developments that have characterized the transition from traditional (premodern) to advanced (modern) civilizations (see Figure 3.1 for key characteristics of modernity).

Moral panic: a concept that describes a situation in which an individual, group, event or condition is posited as a threat to society. Politicians, criminal justice institutions and mass media organizations are usually identified as the main sources for such threats, which are more often than not exaggerated and sensationalized (see Chapter 5).

Myth: the social and cultural transformation of linguistic meanings – that is, **language** significations – into a second order of signification (see discussion of Barthes in Chapter 4). For example, 'hat' has a distinct linguistic meaning – as an item of headwear – but it can also be associated with myths, such as the flamboyance of high society at Royal Ascot, or the shady villains of gangster movies.

Orientalism: a cultural-historical perspective on how representations of non-Western peoples and places have been mainly conceived and authorized by Westerners. Generally speaking, Western representations of the Orient, meaning the East and especially the Middle East, have amounted to ethno-centric and racist misconceptions (see discussion of Said in Chapter 7).

Para-social interaction: the illusion of intimacy and familiarity between media personalities (personae) and audiences that can be established through routine use of radio and television (see discussion of Horton and Wohl in Chapter 5).

Pastiche: a postmodern style of imitation that denies the existence of – refuses to acknowledge – the original form it *appears* to be imitating. Pastiche can be contrasted to parody, which is an imitative style that consciously mocks the original form (see discussion of Jameson in Chapter 8).

Patriarchy: a male-dominated social order that expounds masculine values and excludes women from positions of power and authority.

Phenomenistic approach: the argument that media cannot be viewed in isolation from all the other social, cultural, political and economic factors that cause human beings to change their behaviour, attitudes or actions (see Chapter 2).

Placelessness: the idea that people are no longer defined by physical boundaries or places (where we are) but rather by networks of information and knowledge (what we know) – facilitated by new media technologies – that have no sense of place (see discussion of Meyrowitz in Chapter 5).

Political economy: a theoretical approach that analyses the economic and political processes of media ownership and control, with particular emphasis on patterns of economic concentration, conglomeration and globalization.

Postcolonial theory/postcolonialism: an approach that seeks to understand relations between colonizing and colonized peoples that are no longer straightforwardly oppositional, but are still marked by uneven and unequal power relations.

Postfeminism: the term given to a popular strand of feminist theory that emerged in the 1980s as a critique of orthodox **feminisms** and claimed that equality between the sexes had been achieved.

Postmodernism: an artistic, literary and cultural tradition (emerging during the middle of the twentieth century) that has supplanted 'high' **modernism** and embraced 'the popular' (see Chapter 8 for key features of postmodern culture).

Postmodernity: the social, economic, political and technological developments that have characterized the transition from modern to newly-organized ways of life that are typically associated with globalization and the rise of mass culture, media and communications technologies.

Propaganda model: a theory of **hegemony** in which news reporting tends to be sympathetic to government policies and corporate decisions, and at the same time tends to marginalize dissenting voices (see discussion of Herman and Chomsky in Chapter 7). See also: **media and cultural imperialism**.

Public sphere: an inclusive arena of bourgeois intellectual debate that had weighty influence on the politics of eighteenth- and early nineteenth-century Western Europe, but has since declined in importance due in part to commercial expansion of mass media (see discussion of Habermas in Chapter 3).

Race: ethnic characteristics of an individual or group. Historically, **representation** of race in media and cultural texts has been often misguided, at times racist, and always unreflective of 'real' racial experiences and identities (see Chapter 7).

Representation: the construction of reality through **language**. For example, media construct gender realities – such as differences between men and women – through their own 're-presentational' codes and conventions. The stark difference between 'the real' and 'representations of the real' cannot be emphasized too much.

Second wave, the: this term refers to the 1960s Women's Liberation Movement that campaigned for equal rights on issues such as employment, marital relationships and sexual orientation. The second wave follows the first wave of feminist activity typified by the Suffrage Movement that fought to secure the vote for women.

Self-presentation: the dramaturgical techniques deployed by individuals and groups to perform an expression of themselves to others (see discussion of Goffman in Chapter 5).

Semiotics: also known as semiology, this is the study of signs within systems of signification. See also: **language** and **myth**.

Sex: biological distinctions between human beings who are male and female.

Simulation/simulacra: a system of signs that no longer represent real things but serve to mask this absence of reality so as to become a substitute for it (see discussion of Baudrillard in Chapter 8). See also: **hyperreality**.

Standardization: a concept used to characterize the formulaic products of capitalist-driven mass media and mass culture that appeal to the lowest common denominator in pursuit of maximum profit (see discussion of Adorno in Chapter 7).

Structuralism: the theoretical perspective that seeks to understand how systems work to structure their individual parts at any given moment in time.

Structuration theory: the idea that everyday actions – for example, going to work or surfing the web – both produce and reproduce social structures of power (see discussion of Giddens in Chapter 5).

Tactics: everyday consumer practices that win time from and escape the strategies (corporate capitalist structures) of powerful institutions such as mass media (see discussion of de Certeau in Chapter 9).

Technological determinism: the argument that technologies significantly affect and shape people's lives independent of social, political and economic factors that may affect how these technologies are invented and adopted. See also: **medium theory**.

Third wave, the: while it continues to engage in feminist politics and issues associated with **the second wave**, the third wave – emerging in the 1990s – foregrounds the realization of genuine female pleasure and desire, as well as guarding against the idea of complete feminine autonomy celebrated by **postfeminism**.

Two-step flow: a behaviourist model of how ideas travel from mass media to opinion leaders (step one), and then from opinion leaders to more passive individuals in a given society (step two) (see Chapter 2).

Uses and gratifications: a behaviourist perspective on how individuals engage with media texts and technologies in order to satisfy certain social and psychological needs (see Chapter 2).

Bibliography

Abercrombie, N. (1991) The privilege of the producer, in R. Keat and N. Abercrombie (eds) *Enterprise Culture*. London: Routledge: 171–85.

Abercrombie, N. (1994) Authority and consumer society, in R. Keats, N. Whiteley and N. Abercrombie (eds) *The Authority of the Consumer*. London: Routledge: 43–57.

Abercrombie, N. and Longhurst, B. (1998) *Audiences: A Sociological Theory of Performance and Imagination*. London: Sage.

Adorno, T. W. (1990) On popular music, in S. Frith and A. Goodwin (eds) *On Record: Rock, Pop and the Written Word*. London: Routledge: 301–14.

Adorno, T. W. (1991) On the fetish character in music and the regression of listening, in *The Culture Industry: Selected Essays on Mass Culture*. London: Routledge: 26–52.

Adorno, T. W. and Horkheimer, M. (1973) *Dialectic of Enlightenment*. London: Allen Lane.

Akass, K. and McCabe, J. (2004) *Reading Sex and the City*. London: I. B. Tauris.

Althusser, L. (1971) *Lenin and Philosophy*. London: New Left Books.

Alvarado, M., Gutch, R. and Wollen, T. (1987) *Learning the Media*. London: Macmillan.

Anderson, B. (1991) *Imagined Communities: Reflections on the Origin and Spread of Nationalism*. London: Verso.

Ang, I. (1989) *Watching Dallas: Soap Opera and the Melodramatic Imagination*. London: Routledge.

Ang, I. (1996) *Living Room Wars: Rethinking Media Audiences for a Postmodern World*. London: Routledge.

Appadurai, A. (1993) Disjuncture and difference in the global cultural economy, in B. Robins (ed.) *The Phantom Public Sphere*. Minneapolis: University of Minnesota Press.

Atkinson, P. and Housley, W. (2003) *Interactionism: An Essay in Sociological Amnesia*. London: Sage.

Bacon-Smith, C. (1992) *Enterprising Women: Television Fandom and the Creation of Popular Myth*. Philadelphia, PA: University of Pennsylvania Press.

Bandura, A. and Walters, R. H. (1969) *Social Learning and Personality Development*. London: Holt, Rinehart and Winston.

Barker, M. and Petley, J. (eds) (2001) *Ill Effects: The Media/Violence Debate*, 2nd edn. London: Routledge.

Barthes, R. (1993) *Mythologies*. London: Vintage Books.

Baudrillard, J. (1983) *Simulations*. New York: Semiotext(e).

Baudrillard, J. (1985) The ecstasy of communication, in H. Foster (ed.) *Postmodern Culture*. London: Pluto Press: 126–34.

Baudrillard, J. (1994) *Simulacra and Simulation*. Ann Arbor, MI: University of Michigan Press.

Baudrillard, J. (1995) *The Gulf War Did Not Take Place*. Sydney: Power Publications.

Baudrillard, J. (2002) *The Spirit of Terrorism, and Requiem for the Twin Towers*. London: Verso.

Bauman, Z. (1992) *Intimations of Postmodernity*. London: Routledge.

Bauman, Z. (1996) From pilgrim to tourist – or a short history of identity, in S. Hall and P. du Gay (eds) *Questions of Cultural Identity*. London: Sage: 18–36.

Bayton, M. (1990) How women become musicians, in S. Frith and A. Goodwin (eds) *On Record: Rock, Pop and the Written Word*. London: Routledge: 238–57.

BBC Online (2006) Call to bridge West–Muslim divide, 13 November, http:// news.bbc.co.uk/1/hi/world/europe/6142308.stm

Becker, H. S. (1951) The professional dance musician and his audience, *American Journal of Sociology*, 57: 136–44.

Becker, H. S. (1982) *Art Worlds*. Berkeley: University of California Press.

Becker, H. S. (1991) *Outsiders: Studies in the Sociology of Deviance*. New York: The Free Press.

Bell, D. (1999) *The Coming of Post-industrial Society: A Venture in Social Forecasting*. New York: Basic Books.

Benjamin, W. (1973a) The work of art in the age of mechanical reproduction, in *Illuminations*. London: Fontana Press: 211–44.

Benjamin, W. (1973b) What is epic theatre?, in *Illuminations*. London: Fontana Press: 144–51.

Bennett, T. (1982a) Theories of the media, theories of society, in M. Gurevitch, T. Bennett, J. Curran and J. Woollacott (eds) *Culture, Society and the Media*. London: Routledge: 30–55.

Bennett, T. (1982b) Media, 'reality', signification, in M. Gurevitch, T. Bennett, J. Curran and J. Woollacott (eds) *Culture, Society and the Media*. London: Routledge: 287–308.

Benson, R. and Neveu, E. (eds) (2005) *Bourdieu and the Journalistic Field*. Cambridge: Polity.

Benwell, B. (ed.) (2003) *Masculinity and Men's Lifestyle Magazines*. Oxford: Blackwell.

Berger, J. (1972) *Ways of Seeing*. London: Penguin and the BBC.

Berman, M. (1988) *All That Is Solid Melts into Air: The Experience of Modernity*. Harmondsworth: Penguin.

Beynon, J. (2002) *Masculinities and Culture*. Buckingham: Open University Press.

Bignell, J. (2002) *Media Semiotics: An Introduction*, 2nd edn. Manchester: Manchester University Press.

Bird, S. E. (2003) *The Audience in Everyday Life: Living in a Media World*. New York: Routledge.

Blumer, H. (1969) *Symbolic Interaction: Perspective and Method*. Berkeley, CA: University of California Press.

Blumler, J. G. and Katz, E. (eds) (1974) *The Uses of Mass Communications: Current Perspectives on Gratifications Research*. London: Sage.

Bolter, J. D. and Grusin, R. (2000) *Remediation: Understanding New Media*. Cambridge, MA: MIT Press.

Boorstin, D. J. (1992) *The Image: A Guide to Pseudo-events in America*. New York: Vintage.

Bourdieu, P. (1977) *Outline of a Theory of Practice*. Cambridge: Cambridge University Press.

Bourdieu, P. (1984) *Distinction: A Social Critique of the Judgement of Taste*. London: Routledge and Kegan Paul.

Bourdieu, P. (1986) Forms of capital, in J. G. Richardson (ed.) *Handbook of Theory and Research for the Sociology of Education*. New York: Greenwood Press: 241–58.

Bourdieu, P. (1993) *The Field of Cultural Production: Essays on Art and Literature*. Cambridge: Polity.

Bourdieu, P. (1996) *On Television and Journalism*. London: Pluto Press.

Boyd-Barrett, O. (1988) Cultural dependency and the mass media, in M. Gurevitch, T. Bennett, J. Curran and J. Woollacott (eds) *Culture, Society and the Media*. London: Routledge: 174–95.

Boyd-Barrett, O. (1995) The political economy approach, in O. Boyd-Barrett and C. Newbold (eds) *Approaches to Media: A Reader*. London: Arnold: 186–92.

Boyle, K. (2005) Feminism without men: feminist media studies in a post-feminist age, in J. Curran and M. Gurevitch (eds) *Mass Media and Society*, 4th edn. London: Hodder Arnold: 29–45.

Brecht, B. (1979) Introduction, *The Threepenny Opera*. London: Methuen.

Briggs, A. (1966) *The Communications Revolution*, Third Mansbridge Memorial Lecture. Leeds: Leeds University Press.

Brooker, W. and Jermyn, D. (eds) (2003) *The Audience Studies Reader*. London: Routledge.

Brown, M. E. (1994) *Soap Opera and Women's Talk: The Pleasure of Resistance*. London: Sage.

Brunsdon, C. (1989) Text and audience, in E. Seiter, H. Borchers, G. Kreutzner and E-M. Warth (eds) *Remote Control: Television, Audiences and Cultural Power*. London: Routledge.

Brunsdon, C. (1997) *Screen Tastes: Soap Opera to Satellite Dishes*. London: Routledge.

Brunsdon, C. (2000) *The Feminist, the Housewife, and the Soap Opera*. Oxford: Oxford University Press.

Bryant, J. and Thompson, S. (2002) *Fundamentals of Media Effects*. New York: McGraw-Hill.

Buckingham, D. (1987) *Public Secrets: EastEnders and its Audience*. London: BFI.

Buckingham, D. (1993) *Children Talking Television: The Making of Television Literacy*. London: The Falmer Press.

Buckingham, D. (2000) *After the Death of Childhood: Growing Up in the Age of Electronic Media*. Cambridge: Polity.

Butler, J. (1990) Performative acts and gender constitution: an essay in phenomenology and feminist theory, in S. Ellen (ed.) *Performing Feminisms: Feminist Critical Theory and Theatre*. Baltimore, MD: The Johns Hopkins Press: 270–82.

Butler, J. (1999) *Gender Trouble: Feminism and the Subversion of Identity*. New York: Routledge.

Butler, J. (2004) *Undoing Gender*. New York: Routledge.

Cantril, H. and Allport, G. W. (2004) The influence of radio upon mental and social life from *The Psychology of Radio* (1935), in J. D. Peters and P. Simonson (eds) *Mass Communication and American Social Thought: Key Texts, 1919–1968*. Lanham, MD: Rowman and Littlefield: 110–15.

Cantril, H., Gaudet, H. and Herzog, H. (1947) *The Invasion from Mars: A Study in the Psychology of Panic with the Complete Script of the Famous Orson Welles Broadcast*. Princeton, NJ: Princeton University Press.

Carey, J. and Kreiling, A. L. (1974) Popular culture and uses and gratifications: notes toward an accommodation, in J. G. Blumler and E. Katz (eds) *The Uses of Mass Communications: Current Perspectives on Gratifications Research*. London: Sage: 225–48.

Carter, C., Branston, G. and Allan, S. (eds) (1998) *News, Gender and Power*. London: Routledge.

Cashmore, E. (1994) *... And There Was Television*. London: Routledge.

Cashmore, E. (2004) *Beckham*, 2nd edn. Cambridge: Polity.

Castells, M. (1997) An introduction to the Information Age, *City*, 7: 6–16.

Castells, M. (2000) *The Rise of the Network Society*, 2nd edn. Oxford: Blackwell.

Castells, M. (2004) *The Power of Identity*, 2nd edn. Oxford: Blackwell.

Chomsky, N. (2002) *Media Control: The Spectacular Achievements of Propaganda*, 2nd edn. New York: Seven Stories Press.

Clare, A. (2001) *On Men: Masculinity in Crisis*. London: Arrow Books.

Clarke, G. (1990) Defending ski-jumpers: a critique of theories of youth subcultures, in S. Frith and A. Goodwin (eds) *On Record: Rock, Pop, and the Written Word*. London: Routledge: 81–96.

Cohen, S. (ed.) (1971) *Images of Deviance*. Harmondsworth: Penguin.

Cohen, S. (2002) *Folk Devils and Moral Panics: The Creation of the Mods and Rockers*, 3rd edn. London: Routledge.

Cohen, S. and Young, J. (eds) (1973) *The Manufacture of News: Social Problems, Deviance and the Mass Media*. London: Constable.

Connell, R. W. (1995) *Masculinities*. Cambridge: Polity.

Cornell, D. (ed.) (2000) *Feminism and Pornography*. Oxford: Oxford University Press.

Corner, J. (1998) *Studying Media: Problems of Theory and Method*. Edinburgh: Edinburgh University Press.

Corrigan, P. (1997) *The Sociology of Consumption: An Introduction*. London: Sage.

Couldry, N. (2000a) *Inside Culture: Re-imagining the Method of Cultural Studies*. London: Sage.

Couldry, N. (2000b) *The Place of Media Power: Pilgrims and Witnesses of the Media Age*. London: Routledge.

Couldry, N. (2003) *Media Rituals: A Critical Approach*. London: Routledge.

Critcher, C. (2003) *Moral Panics and the Media*. Buckingham: Open University Press.

Cumberbatch, G. and Howitt, D. (1989) *A Measure of Uncertainty: The Effects of the Mass Media*. London: John Libbey.

Curran, J. and Park, M-J. (eds) (2000) *De-Westernizing Media Studies*. London: Routledge.

Curran, J. and Seaton, J. (2003) *Power without Responsibility: The Press and Broadcasting in Britain*, 6th edn. London: Routledge.

Davies, M. M. (1989) *Television is Good for Your Kids*. London: Hilary Shipman.

Dayan, D. and Katz, E. (1992) *Media Events: The Live Broadcasting of History*. Cambridge, MA: Harvard University Press.

de Beauvoir, S. (1989) *The Second Sex*. New York: Vintage.

Debord, G. (1994) *The Society of the Spectacle*. New York: Zone Books.

Debray, R. (1996) *Media Manifestos: On the Technological Transmission of Cultural Forms*. London: Verso.

de Certeau, M. (1984) *The Practice of Everyday Life*. Berkeley, CA: University of California Press.

DeNora, T. (2000) *Music in Everyday Life*. Cambridge: Cambridge University Press.

Doane, M. A. (2000) Film and the masquerade: theorizing the female spectator, in E. A. Kaplan (ed.) *Feminism and Film*. Oxford: Oxford University Press: 418–36.

Dworkin, A. (1981) *Pornography: Men Possessing Women*. London: The Women's Press.

Dyer, R. (1997) *White*. London: Routledge.

Easthope, A. and McGowan, K. (eds) (1992) *A Critical and Cultural Theory Reader*. Buckingham: Open University Press.

Eco, U. (1973) Social life as a sign system, in D. Robey (ed.) *Structuralism: An Introduction*. Oxford: Oxford University Press: 57–72.

Eisenstein, E. L. (1979) *The Printing Press as an Agent of Change: Communications and Cultural Transformations in Early-Modern Europe*, vols I and II. Cambridge: Cambridge University Press.

Eldridge, J. (ed.) (1995) *Glasgow Media Group Reader*, vol. 1: *News Content, Language and Visuals*. London: Routledge.

Eldridge, J., Kitzinger, J. and Williams, K. (1997) *The Mass Media and Power in Modern Britain*. Oxford: Oxford University Press.

Eliot, T. S. (1951) *Selected Essays*. London: Faber and Faber.

Elliott, P. (1974) Uses and gratifications research: a critique and a sociological alternative, in J. G. Blumler and E. Katz (eds) *The Uses of Mass Communications: Current Perspectives on Gratifications Research*. London: Sage: 249–68.

Elliott, P. (1995) Intellectuals, the 'information society' and the disappearance of the public sphere, in O. Boyd-Barrett and C. Newbold (eds) *Approaches to Media: A Reader*. London: Arnold: 260–2.

Faludi, S. (1992) *Backlash: The Undeclared War Against Women*. London: Chatto and Windus.

Faludi, S. (2000) *Stiffed: The Betrayal of the American Man*. New York: Perennial.

Featherstone, M. (1991) *Consumer Culture and Postmodernism*. London: Sage.

Fejes, F. (1981) Media imperialism: an assessment, *Media, Culture and Society*, 3: 281–9.

Fiske, J. (1987) *Television Culture*. London: Methuen.

Fiske, J. (1989) *Understanding Popular Culture*. Boston: Unwin Hyman.

Fiske, J. (1991a) *Reading the Popular*. London: Routledge.

Fiske, J. (1991b) Postmodernism and television, in J. Curran and M. Gurevitch (eds) *Mass Media and Society*. London: Arnold: 55–67.

Fiske, J. (1993) *Power Plays, Power Works*. London: Verso.

Fiske, J. (1996) *Media Matters: Race and Gender in US Politics*, rev. edn. Minneapolis: University of Minnesota Press.

Foucault, M. (1989) *The Archaeology of Knowledge*. London: Routledge.

Foucault, M. (1995) *Discipline and Punish: The Birth of the Prison*. New York: Vintage.

Frazer, E. (1987) Teenage girls reading Jackie, *Media, Culture and Society*, 9: 407–25.

Friedan, B. (1992) *The Feminine Mystique*. London: Penguin.

Frith, S. (1983) *Sound Effects: Youth, Leisure and the Politics of Rock*. London: Constable.

Frith, S. (1996) *Performing Rites: Evaluating Popular Music*. Oxford: Oxford University Press.

Gamble, S. (2001) Postfeminism, in S. Gamble (ed.) *The Routledge Companion to Feminism and Postfeminism*. London: Routledge: 43–54.

Gardiner, M. E. (2000) *Critiques of Everyday Life*. London: Routledge.

Garnham, N. (1990) *Capitalism and Communication*. London: Sage.

Garnham, N. (1995) Contribution to a political economy of mass communication, in O. Boyd-Barrett and C. Newbold (eds) *Approaches to Media: A Reader*. London: Arnold: 216–21.

Garnham, N. (2000) *Emancipation, the Media and Modernity: Arguments About the Media and Social Theory*. Oxford: Oxford University Press.

Gauntlett, D. (1996) *Video Critical: Children, the Environment and Media Power*. Bedfordshire: University of Luton Press.

Gauntlett, D. (2005) *Moving Experiences: Media Effects and Beyond*, 2nd edn. Eastleigh: John Libbey.

Genosko, G. (1999) *McLuhan and Baudrillard: The Masters of Implosion*. London: Routledge.

Geraghty, C. (1991) *Women and Soap Opera: A Study of Prime Time Soaps*. Cambridge: Polity.

Gerbner, G. (1973) Cultural indicators: the third voice, in G. Gerbner, L. P. Gross and W. H. Melody (eds) *Communications Technology and Social Policy: Understanding the New 'Cultural Revolution'*. New York: John Wiley and Sons: 555–73.

Gerbner, G., Gross, L., Morgan, M. and Signorielli, N. (1980) The 'mainstreaming' of America: violence profile no. 11, *Journal of Communication*, 30(3): 10–29.

Gerbner, G., Gross, L., Morgan, M. and Signorielli, N. (1986) Living with television: the dynamics of the cultivation process, in J. Bryant and D. Zillmann (eds) *Perspectives on Media Effects*. New Jersey: Lawrence Erlbaum Associates: 17–40.

Gibbs, J. L., Ellison, N. B. and Heino, R. D. (2006) Self-presentation in online personals: the role of anticipated future interaction, self-disclosure, and perceived success in internet dating, *Communication Research*, 33(2): 152–77.

Giddens, A. (1984) *The Constitution of Society: Outline of a Theory of Structuration*. Cambridge: Polity.

Giddens, A. (1990) *The Consequences of Modernity*. Cambridge: Polity.

Giddens, A. (1991) *Modernity and Self-identity: Self and Society in the Late Modern Age*. Cambridge: Polity.

Gill, R. (2003) Power and the production of subjects: a genealogy of the New Man and the New Lad, in B. Benwell (ed.) *Masculinity and Men's Lifestyle Magazines*. Oxford: Blackwell: 34–56.

Gilroy, P. (1987) *'There Ain't No Black in the Union Jack': The Cultural Politics of Race and Nation*. London: Hutchinson.

Gilroy, P. (1993) *The Black Atlantic: Modernity and Double Consciousness*. London: Verso.

Glasgow Media Group (1976) *Bad News Volume 1*. London: Routledge and Kegan Paul.

Glasgow Media Group (1980) *More Bad News: Volume 2 of Bad News*. London: Routledge and Kegan Paul.

Glasgow Media Group – G. Philo, J. Hewitt, P. Beharrell and H. Davis (1982) *Really Bad News*. London: Writers and Readers.

Glassner, B. (1990) Fit for postmodern selfhood, in H. S. Becker and M. M. McCall (eds) *Symbolic Interaction and Cultural Studies*. Chicago: University of Chicago Press: 215–43.

Goffman, E. (1979) *Gender Advertisements*. New York: Harper and Row.

Goffman, E. (1981) *Forms of Talk*. Oxford: Blackwell.

Goffman, E. (1990) *The Presentation of Self in Everyday Life*. Harmondsworth: Penguin.

Golding, P. and Murdock, G. (2000) Culture, communications and political economy, in J. Curran and M. Gurevitch (eds) *Mass Media and Society*, 3rd edn. London: Arnold: 70–92.

Gorton, K. (2004) (Un)fashionable feminists: the media and *Ally McBeal*, in S.

Gillis, G. Howie and R. Munford (eds) *Third Wave Feminism: A Critical Exploration.* Basingstoke: Palgrave: 154–63.

Gramsci, A. (1971) *Selections from the Prison Notebooks.* London: Lawrence and Wishart.

Gray, A. (1992) *Video Playtime: The Gendering of a Leisure Technology.* London: Routledge.

Greer, G. (2000) *The Whole Woman.* London: Anchor.

Gunter, B. and McAleer, J. (1997) *Children and Television,* 2nd edn. London: Routledge.

Habermas, J. (1985) Modernity – an incomplete project, in H. Foster (ed.) *Postmodern Culture.* London: Pluto Press: 3–15.

Habermas, J. (1989) *The Structural Transformation of the Public Sphere: An Inquiry into a Category of Bourgeois Society.* Cambridge: Polity.

Hall, S. (1975) Television as a medium and its relation to culture, *CCCS Stencilled Paper No. 34.* Birmingham: University of Birmingham.

Hall, S. (1977) Culture, the media and the 'ideological effect', in J. Curran, M. Gurevitch and J. Woollacott (eds) *Mass Communication and Society.* London: Arnold: 315–48.

Hall, S. (1978) The treatment of 'football hooliganism' in the press, in R. Ingham, S. Hall, J. Clarke, P. Marsh and J. Donovan (eds) *'Football Hooliganism': The Wider Context.* London: Inter-Action Imprint: 15–36.

Hall, S. (1980) Encoding/decoding, in S. Hall, D. Hobson, A. Lowe and P. Willis (eds) *Culture, Media, Language: Working Papers in Cultural Studies, 1972–79.* London: Hutchinson: 128–38.

Hall, S. (1982) The rediscovery of 'ideology': return of the repressed in media studies, in M. Gurevitch, T. Bennett, J. Curran and J. Woollacott (eds) *Culture, Society and the Media.* London: Routledge: 56–90.

Hall, S. (1995) The whites of their eyes: racist ideologies and the media, in G. Dines and J. M. Humez (eds) *Gender, Race and Class in Media: A Text-Reader.* London: Sage: 18–22.

Hall, S. (1996a) The problem of ideology: marxism without guarantees, in D. Morley and K-H. Chen (eds) *Stuart Hall: Critical Dialogues in Cultural Studies.* London: Routledge: 25–46.

Hall, S. (1996b) When was 'the post-colonial'? Thinking at the limit, in I. Chambers and L. Curti (eds) *The Post-Colonial Question.* London: Routledge: 242–60.

Hall, S. (ed.) (1997) *Representation: Cultural Representations and Signifying Practices.* London: Sage and The Open University.

Hall, S., Critcher, C., Jefferson, T., Clarke, J. and Roberts, B. (1978) *Policing the Crisis: Mugging, the State, and Law and Order.* Basingstoke: Macmillan.

Handleman, D. (2003) Towards the virtual encounter: Horton and Wohl's 'Mass Communication and Para-Social Interaction', in E. Katz, J. D. Peters, T. Liebes and A. Orloff (eds) *Canonic Texts in Media Research: Are There Any? Should There Be? How about These?* Cambridge: Polity: 137–51.

Hartley, J. (ed.) (2005) *Creative Industries*. Oxford: Blackwell.

Harvey, D. (1989) *The Condition of Postmodernity: An Enquiry into the Origins of Cultural Change*. Oxford: Blackwell.

Hebdige, D. (1979) *Subculture: The Meaning of Style*. London: Routledge.

Hebdige, D. (1989) Towards a cartography of taste 1935–1962, in B. Waites, T. Bennett and G. Martin (eds) *Popular Culture: Past and Present*. London: Routledge: 194–218.

Herman, E. S. and Chomsky, N. (1994) *Manufacturing Consent: The Political Economy of Mass Media*. London: Vintage.

Hermes, J. (1995) *Reading Women's Magazines: An Analysis of Everyday Media Use*. Cambridge: Polity.

Hesmondhalgh, D. (2002) *The Cultural Industries*. London: Sage.

Hesmondhalgh, D. (2005) Subcultures, scenes or tribes? None of the above, *Journal of Youth Studies*, 8(1): 21–40.

Heywood, L. and Drake, J. (1997) Introduction, in L. Heywood and J. Drake (eds) *Third Wave Agenda: Being Feminist, Doing Feminism*. Minneapolis: University of Minnesota Press: 1–20.

Hillis, K., Petit, M. and Epley, N. S. (eds) (2006) *Everyday eBay: Culture, Collecting and Desire*. New York: Routledge.

Hills, M. (2002) *Fan Cultures*. London: Routledge.

Himmelweit, H. T., Oppenheim, A. N. and Vince, P. (1958) *Television and the Child: An Empirical Study of the Effect of Television on the Young*. London: Oxford University Press.

Hobson, D. (1980) Housewives and the mass media, in S. Hall, D. Hobson, A. Lowe and P. Willis (eds) *Culture, Media, Language: Working Papers in Cultural Studies, 1972–79*. London: Hutchinson: 105–14.

Hodkinson, P. (2002) *Goth: Identity, Style and Subculture*. Oxford: Berg.

Hoggart, R. (1958) *The Uses of Literacy: Aspects of a Working-class Life with Special Reference to Publications and Entertainments*. London: Pelican.

Hoggart, R. (1972) *Only Connect: On Culture and Communication*. London: Chatto and Windus.

Hoggart, R. (2004) *Mass Media in a Mass Society: Myth and Reality*. London: Continuum.

Hollows, J. and Moseley, R. (eds) (2005) *Feminism in Popular Culture*. Oxford: Berg.

hooks, b. (1992) *Black Looks: Race and Representation*. Boston, MA: South End Press.

Horton, D. and Wohl, R. R. (2004) Mass communication and para-social interaction: observations on intimacy at a distance (first published 1956), in J. D. Peters and P. Simonson (eds) *Mass Communication and American Social Thought: Key Texts, 1919–1968*. Lanham, MD: Rowman and Littlefield: 373–86.

Howe, M. J. A. (1977) *Television and Children*. London: New University Education.

Innis, H. A. (1951) *The Bias of Communication*. Toronto: University of Toronto Press.

Innis, H. A. (1986) *Empire and Communications*. Victoria: Press Porcepic.

Jackson, P., Stevenson, N. and Brooks, K. (2001) *Making Sense of Men's Magazines*. Cambridge: Polity.

Jameson, F. (1991) *Postmodernism or, The Cultural Logic of Late Capitalism*. London: Verso.

Jameson, F. (1998) *The Cultural Turn: Selected Writings on the Postmodern 1983–1998*. London: Verso.

Jenkins, H. (1992) *Textual Poachers: Television Fans and Participatory Culture*. New York: Routledge.

Kaplan, E. A. (1993) Madonna politics: perversion, repression, or subversion? Or masks and/as master-y, in C. Schwichtenberg (ed.) *The Madonna Connection: Representational Politics, Subcultural Identities, and Cultural Theory*. Boulder, CO: Westview Press: 149–65.

Kaplan, E. A. (2000) *Feminism and Film*. Oxford: Oxford University Press.

Katz, E., Blumler, J. G. and Gurevitch, M. (1974) Utilization of mass communication by the individual, in J. G. Blumler and E. Katz (eds) *The Uses of Mass Communications: Current Perspectives on Gratifications Research*. London: Sage: 19–32.

Katz, E. and Lazarsfeld, P. F. (1955) *Personal Influence: The Part Played by People in the Flow of Mass Communications*. Illinois: The Free Press.

Kitzinger, J. (1993) Understanding AIDS: media messages and what people know about AIDS, in J. Eldridge (ed.) *Getting the Message: News, Truth and Power*. London: Routledge: 271–304.

Klapper, J. T. (1960) *The Effects of Mass Communication*. New York: The Free Press.

Klein, M. (1997) Duality and redefinition: young feminism and the alternative music community, in L. Heywood and J. Drake (eds) *Third Wave Agenda: Being Feminist, Doing Feminism*. Minneapolis: University of Minnesota Press: 207–25.

Kroker, A. and Cook, D. (1988) *The Postmodern Scene*. London: Macmillan.

Kuhn, A. (2000) Women's genres, in E. A. Kaplan (ed.) *Feminism and Film*. Oxford: Oxford University Press: 437–49.

Lacan, J. (1993) The mirror stage, in A. Easthope (ed.) *Contemporary Film Theory*. London: Longman: 33–9.

Lasswell, H. D. (1971a) *Propaganda Technique in World War 1*. Cambridge, MA: MIT Press.

Lasswell, H. D. (1971b) The structure and function of communication in society, in W. Schramm and D. F. Roberts (eds) *The Processes and Effects of Mass Communication*. Chicago: University of Illinois Press: 84–99.

Laughey, D. (2006) *Music and Youth Culture*. Edinburgh: Edinburgh University Press.

Lazarsfeld, P. F. and Merton, R. K. (2004) Mass communication, popular taste, and organized social action from *The Communication of Ideas* (1948), in J. D. Peters and P. Simonson (eds) *Mass Communication and American Social Thought: Key Texts, 1919–1968*. Lanham, MD: Rowman and Littlefield: 230–41.

Leavis, F. R. (1930) *Mass Civilization and Minority Culture*. Cambridge: The Minority Press.

Leavis, Q. D. (1932) *Fiction and the Reading Public*. London: Chatto and Windus.

Lee, M. J. (1993) *Consumer Culture Reborn: The Cultural Politics of Consumption*. London: Routledge.

Levinson, P. (1999) *Digital McLuhan: A Guide to the Information Millennium*. London: Routledge.

Leyshon, A., Webb, P., French, S., Thrift, N. and Crewe, L. (2005) On the reproduction of the musical economy after the internet, *Media, Culture and Society*, 27(2): 177–209.

Liebes, T. and Katz, E. (1990) *The Export of Meaning: Cross-Cultural Readings of Dallas*. New York: Oxford University Press.

Lippmann, W. (1922) *Public Opinion*. New York: Macmillan.

Livingstone, S. (2002) *Young People and New Media: Childhood and the Changing Media Environment*. London: Sage.

Livingstone, S. (2005) Critical debates in internet studies: reflections on an emerging field, in J. Curran and M. Gurevitch (eds) *Mass Media and Society*, 4th edn. London: Hodder Arnold: 9–28.

Longhurst, B. (2007) *Cultural Change and Ordinary Life*. Maidenhead: Open University Press.

Longhurst, B. and Savage, M. (1996) Social class, consumption and the influence of Bourdieu: some critical issues, in S. Edgell, K. Hetherington and A. Warde (eds) *Consumption Matters: The Production and Experience of Consumption*. Oxford: Blackwell: 274–301.

Luhmann, N. (2000) *The Reality of the Mass Media*. Cambridge: Polity.

Lury, C. (1996) *Consumer Culture*. Cambridge: Polity.

Lynd, R. S. and Lynd, H. M. (1929) *Middletown: A Study in American Culture*. New York: Harcourt, Brace and Company.

Lyon, D. (1988) *The Information Society: Issues and Illusions*. Cambridge: Polity.

Lyon, D. (1999) *Postmodernity*, 2nd edn. Buckingham: Open University Press.

Lyon, D. (2001) *Surveillance Society: Monitoring Everyday Life*. Buckingham: Open University Press.

Lyotard, J-F. (1984) *The Postmodern Condition: A Report on Knowledge*. Manchester: Manchester University Press.

MacInnes, J. (1998) *The End of Masculinity: The Confusion of Sexual Genesis and Sexual Difference in Modern Society*. Buckingham: Open University Press.

MacKay, H. (ed.) (1997) *Consumption and Everyday Life*. London: Sage.

Macklin, M. C. and Carlson, L. (eds) (1999) *Advertising to Children: Concepts and Controversies*. London: Sage.

Madge, C. and Harrisson, T. (1937) *Mass-Observation*. London: Frederick Muller.

Madge, C. and Harrisson, T. (1939) *Britain by Mass-Observation*. Penguin: Harmondsworth.

Manovich, L. (2001) *The Language of New Media*. Cambridge, MA: MIT Press.

McCombs, M. (2004) *Setting the Agenda: The Mass Media and Public Opinion*. Cambridge: Polity.

McCombs, M. and Gilbert, S. (1986) News influence on our pictures of the world, in J. Bryant and D. Zillmann (eds) *Perspectives on Media Effects*. New Jersey: Lawrence Erlbaum Associates: 1–15.

McCombs, M. and Shaw, D. (1972) The agenda-setting function of mass media, *Public Opinion Quarterly*, 36: 176–87.

McCourt, T. and Burkart, P. (2003) When creators, corporations and consumers collide: Napster and the development of on-line music distribution, *Media, Culture and Society*, 25(3): 333–50.

McCracken, G. (1990) *Culture and Consumption: New Approaches to the Symbolic Character of Consumer Goods and Activities*. Bloomington: Indiana University Press.

McGuigan, J. (1992) *Cultural Populism*. London: Routledge.

McGuigan, J. (2006) *Modernity and Postmodern Culture*, 2nd edn. Maidenhead: Open University Press.

McLuhan, M. (1964) *Understanding Media: The Extensions of Man*. London: MIT Press.

McLuhan, M and Fiore, Q. (2001) *War and Peace in the Global Village*. London: Gingko.

McNair, B. (2002) *Striptease Culture: Sex, Media and the Democratization of Desire*. London: Routledge.

McQuail, D. (1977) The influence and effects of mass media, in J. Curran, M. Gurevitch and J. Woollacott (eds) *Mass Communication and Society*. London: Edward Arnold: 70–94.

McQuail, D. and Windahl, S. (1993) *Communication Models for the Study of Mass Communications*, 2nd edn. Harlow: Pearson.

McRobbie, A. (1994) *Postmodernism and Popular Culture*. London: Routledge.

McRobbie, A. (1996) *More!*: new sexualities in girls' and women's magazines, in J. Curran, D. Morley and V. Walkerdine (eds) *Cultural Studies and Communications*. London: Arnold: 172–94.

McRobbie, A. (2000) *Feminism and Youth Culture*, 2nd edn. Basingstoke: Macmillan.

McRobbie, A. (2006) Post-feminism and popular culture: Bridget Jones and the new gender regime, in J. Curran and D. Morley (eds) *Media and Cultural Theory*. London: Routledge: 59–69.

Merrin, W. (2005) *Baudrillard and the Media: A Critical Introduction*. Cambridge: Polity.

Meyrowitz, J. (1985) *No Sense of Place: The Impact of Electronic Media on Social Behaviour*. New York: Oxford University Press.

Meyrowitz, J. (1994) Medium theory, in D. Crowley and D. Mitchell (eds) *Communication Theory Today*. Cambridge: Polity: 50–77.

Miege, B. (1989) *The Capitalization of Cultural Production*. New York: International General.

Miller, D. and Williams, K. (1993) Negotiating HIV/AIDS information: agendas, media strategies and the news, in J. Eldridge (ed.) *Getting the Message: News, Truth and Power*. London: Routledge: 126–42.

Modleski, T. (1990) *Loving with a Vengeance: Mass-produced Fantasies for Women*. New York: Routledge.

Moores, S. (2000) *Media and Everyday Life in Modern Society*. Edinburgh: Edinburgh University Press.

Moores, S. (2005) *Media/Theory: Thinking about Media and Communications*. Abingdon: Routledge.

Morley, D. (1980) Texts, readers, subjects, in S. Hall, D. Hobson, A. Lowe and P. Willis (eds) *Culture, Media, Language: Working Papers in Cultural Studies, 1972–79*. London: Hutchinson: 163–73.

Morley, D. (1986) *Family Television: Cultural Power and Domestic Leisure*. London: Comedia.

Morley, D. (1992) *Television, Audiences and Cultural Studies*. London: Routledge.

Morley, D. (2007) *Media, Modernity and Technology: The Geography of the New*. Abingdon: Routledge.

Morley, D. and Brunsdon, C. (1999) *The Nationwide Television Studies*. London: Routledge.

Morley, D. and Chen, K-H. (eds) (1996) *Stuart Hall: Critical Dialogues in Cultural Studies*. London: Routledge.

Mosco, V. (1996) *The Political Economy of Communication: Rethinking and Renewal*. London: Sage.

Muggleton, D. (2000) *Inside Subculture: The Postmodern Meaning of Style*. Oxford: Berg.

Mulvey, L. (1989) Visual pleasure and narrative cinema, in *Visual and Other Pleasures*. Basingstoke: Macmillan: 14–26.

Murdock, G. and Golding, P. (1977) Capitalism, communication and class relations, in J. Curran, M. Gurevitch and J. Woollacott (eds) *Mass Communication and Society*. London: Arnold: 12–43.

Murdock, G. and Golding, P. (1995) For a political economy of mass communications, in O. Boyd-Barrett and C. Newbold (eds) *Approaches to Media: A Reader*. London: Arnold: 201–15.

Neale, S. (1980) *Genre*. London: BFI.

Nederveen Pieterse, J. (2004) *Globalization and Culture: Global Melange*. Lanham, MD: Rowman and Littlefield.

Negrine, R. (1994) *Politics and the Mass Media in Britain*, 2nd edn. London: Routledge.

Negroponte, N. (1995) *Being Digital*. London: Hodder and Stoughton.

Negus, K. (1996) *Popular Music in Theory: An Introduction*. Cambridge: Polity.

Negus, K. and Pickering, M. (2004) *Creativity, Communication and Cultural Value*. London: Sage.

Nixon, S. (1997) Exhibiting masculinity, in S. Hall (ed.) *Representation: Cultural Representations and Signifying Practices*. London: Sage and The Open University: 291–330.

Ong, W. J. (1993) *Orality and Literacy: The Technologizing of the Word*. London: Routledge.

Ouellette, L. (2002) Victims no more: postfeminism, television and *Ally McBeal*, *The Communication Review*, 5: 315–35.

Petley, J. (1997) In defence of 'video nasties', in T. O'Sullivan and Y. Jewkes (eds) *The Media Studies Reader*. London: Arnold: 188–95.

Poole, E. (2002) *Reporting Islam: Media Representations of British Muslims*. London: I. B. Tauris.

Postman, N. (1983) *The Disappearance of Childhood*. London: W. H. Auden.

Postman, N. (1987) *Amusing Ourselves to Death: Public Discourse in the Age of Show Business*. London: Methuen.

Postman, N. (1993) *Technopoly: The Surrender of Culture to Technology*. New York: Vintage Books.

Qualter, T. H. (1997) The social role of advertising, in T. O'Sullivan and Y. Jewkes (eds) *The Media Studies Reader*. London: Arnold: 154–64.

Radway, J. A. (1984) *Reading the Romance: Women, Patriarchy, and Popular Literature*. Chapel Hill, NC: University of North Carolina Press.

Riesman, D. (1990) Listening to popular music, in S. Frith and A. Goodwin (eds) *On Record: Rock, Pop, and the Written Word*. London: Routledge: 5–13.

Riesman, D. with N. Glazer and R. Denney (1961) *The Lonely Crowd: A Study of the Changing American Character*. New Haven, CT: Yale University Press.

Ritzer, G. (1993) *The McDonaldization of Society: An Investigation into the Changing Character of Contemporary Social Life*. Thousand Oaks, CA: Pine Forge Press.

Ritzer, G. (1998) *The McDonaldization Thesis: Explorations and Extensions*. London: Sage.

Rose, T. (1994) *Black Noise: Rap Music and Black Culture in Contemporary America*. London: Wesleyan University Press.

Said, E. (1994) *Culture and Imperialism*. London: Vintage.

Said, E. (1995) *Orientalism: Western Conceptions of the Orient*. Harmondsworth: Penguin.

Sandvoss, C. (2005) *Fans: The Mirror of Consumption*. Cambridge: Polity.

Saussure, F. de (1966) *Course in General Linguistics*. New York: McGraw-Hill.

Scannell, P. (ed.) (1991) *Broadcast Talk*. London: Sage.

Scannell, P. (1996) *Radio, Television and Everyday Life: A Phenomenological Approach*. Oxford: Blackwell.

Schiller, H. I. (1977) The free flow of information – for whom?, in G. Gerbner (ed.) *Mass Media Policies in Changing Cultures*. New York: John Wiley and Sons: 105–15.

Schiller, H. I. (1992) *Mass Communications and American Empire*, 2nd edn. Oxford: Westview Press.

Schiller, H. I. (1997) Not yet the post-imperialist era, in T. O'Sullivan and Y. Jewkes (eds) *The Media Studies Reader*. London: Arnold: 360–72.

Schlesinger, P. (1978) *Putting 'Reality' Together: BBC News*. London: Constable.

Schramm, W., Lyle, J. and Parker, E. B. (1961) *Television in the Lives of Our Children*. Stanford, CA: Stanford University Press.

Scollon, R. (1998) *Mediated Discourse as Social Interaction: A Study of News Discourse*. London: Longman.

Sigman, A. (2005) *Remotely Controlled: How Television is Damaging Our Lives – and What We Can Do about It*. London: Vermilion.

Silverstone, R. (1994) *Television and Everyday Life*. London: Routledge.

Silverstone, R. (1999) *Why Study the Media?* London: Sage.

Silverstone, R. (2007) *Media and Morality: On the Rise of the Mediapolis*. Cambridge: Polity.

Silverstone, R., Hirsch, E. and Morley, D. (1992) Information and communication technologies and the moral economy of the household, in R. Silverstone and E. Hirsch (eds) *Consuming Technologies: Media and Information in Domestic Spaces*. London: Routledge: 15–31.

Skeggs, B. (1993) A good time for women only, in F. Lloyd (ed.) *Deconstructing Madonna*. London: Batsford: 60–73.

Slevin, J. (2000) *The Internet and Society*. Cambridge: Polity.

Sreberny, A. (2000) The global and the local in international communications, in J. Curran and M. Gurevitch (eds) *Mass Media and Society*, 3rd edn. London: Arnold: 93–119.

Stevenson, N., Jackson, P. and Brooks, K. (2003) Reading men's lifestyle magazines: cultural power and the information society, in B. Benwell (ed.) *Masculinity and Men's Lifestyle Magazines*. Oxford: Blackwell: 112–31.

Stone, G. and McCombs, M. (1981) Tracing the time lag in agenda setting, *Journalism Quarterly*, 58: 151–5.

Strinati, D. (1995) *An Introduction to Theories of Popular Culture*. London: Routledge.

Sturrock, J. (ed.) (1979) *Structuralism and Since: From Lévi-Strauss to Derrida*. Oxford: Oxford University Press.

Tagg, P. (1989) Open letter: 'Black Music', 'Afro-American Music' and 'European Music', *Popular Music*, 8(3): 285–98.

Taylor, P. M. (1997) *Global Communications, International Affairs and the Media since 1945*. London: Routledge.

Thompson, J. B. (1990) *Ideology and Modern Culture: Critical Social Theory in the Era of Mass Communication*. Cambridge: Polity.

Thompson, J. B. (1994) Social theory and the media, in D. Crowley and D. Mitchell (eds) *Communication Theory Today*. Cambridge: Polity: 27–49.

Thompson, J. B. (1995a) *The Media and Modernity: A Social Theory of the Media*. Cambridge: Polity.

Thompson, J. B. (1995b) The theory of the public sphere, in O. Boyd-Barrett and C. Newbold (eds) *Approaches to Media: A Reader*. London: Arnold: 252–9.

Thompson, J. B. (1996) Tradition and self in a mediated world, in P. Heelas, S. Lash and P. Morris (eds) *Detraditionalization: Critical Reflections on Authority and Identity*. Oxford: Blackwell: 89–108.

Thompson, J. B. (2000) *Political Scandal: Power and Visibility in the Media Age*. Cambridge: Polity.

Thornham, S. (2000) *Feminist Theory and Cultural Studies: Stories of Unsettled Relations*. London: Arnold.

Thornton, S. (1995) *Club Cultures: Music, Media and Subcultural Capital*. Cambridge: Polity.

Toffler, A. (1981) *The Third Wave*. London: Pan.

Toffler, A. and Toffler, H. (1995) *Creating a New Civilization: The Politics of the Third Wave*. Atlanta, GA: Turner Publishing.

Tolson, A. (2005) *Media Talk: Spoken Discourse on TV and Radio*. Edinburgh: Edinburgh University Press.

Tuchman, G. (1978) Introduction: the symbolic annihilation of women by the mass media, in G. Tuchman, A. K. Daniels and J. Benet (eds) *Hearth and Home: Images of Women in the Mass Media*. New York: Oxford University Press: 3–38.

Tudor, A. (1999) *Decoding Culture: Theory and Method in Cultural Studies*. London: Sage.

Tunstall, J. (1977) *The Media Are American: Anglo-American Media in the World*. London: Constable.

Tunstall, J. and Machin, D. (1999) *The Anglo-American Media Connection*. Oxford: Oxford University Press.

Turner, B. S. (1990) Periodization and politics in the postmodern, in B. S. Turner (ed.) *Theories of Modernity and Postmodernity*. London: Sage: 1–13.

Walter, N. (1999) *The New Feminism*. London: Virago.

Warshow, R. (1957) Paul, the horror comics, and Dr. Wertham, in B. Rosenberg and D. M. White (eds) *Mass Culture: The Popular Arts in America*. Glencoe, ILL: The Free Press: 199–211.

Wasko, J. (1994) *Hollywood in the Information Age: Beyond the Silver Screen*. Cambridge: Polity.

Wasko, J. (2001) *Understanding Disney: The Manufacture of Fantasy*. Cambridge: Polity.

Wasko, J. (2003) *How Hollywood Works*. London: Sage.

Watney, S. (1997) Moral panics, in T. O'Sullivan and Y. Jewkes (eds) *The Media Studies Reader*. London: Arnold: 124–33.

Webster, F. (2002) *Theories of the Information Society*, 2nd edn. London: Routledge.

Wertham, F. (1955) *Seduction of the Innocent*. London: Museum Press.

Whannel, G. (2002) *Media Sport Stars: Masculinities and Moralities*. London: Routledge.

Whelehan, I. (1995) *Modern Feminist Thought: From the Second Wave to 'Post-Feminism'*. Edinburgh: Edinburgh University Press.

White, H. (1979) Michel Foucault, in J. Sturrock (ed.) *Structuralism and Since: From Lévi-Strauss to Derrida*. Oxford: Oxford University Press: 81–115.

Whiteley, S. (2000) *Women and Popular Music: Sexuality, Identity and Subjectivity*. London: Routledge.

Wilkins, L. T. (1964) *Social Deviance: Social Policy, Action and Research*. London: Tavistock.

Williams, R. (1965) *The Long Revolution*. Harmondsworth: Penguin.

Williams, R. (1980) Base and superstructure in marxist cultural theory, in *Problems in Materialism and Culture: Selected Essays*. London: Verso Editions and NLB: 31–49.

Williams, R. (1983a) *Keywords: A Vocabulary of Culture and Society*. London: Flamingo.

Williams, R. (1983b) *Towards 2000*. London: Chatto and Windus.

Williams, R. (2003) *Television: Technology and Cultural Form*. London: Routledge.

Williamson, J. (1978) *Decoding Advertisements: Ideology and Meaning in Advertising*. London: Marion Boyars.

Willis, P. E. (1978) *Profane Culture*. London: Routledge.

Willis, P. with Jones, S., Canaan, J. and Hurd, G. (1990) *Common Culture: Symbolic Work at Play in the Everyday Cultures of the Young*. Milton Keynes: Open University Press.

Winship, J. (1987) *Inside Women's Magazines*. London: Pandora.

Winston, B. (1998) *Media Technology and Society – A History: From the Telegraph to the Internet*. London: Routledge.

Wolf, N. (1993) *Fire with Fire: The New Female Power and How It Will Change the Twenty-First Century*. New York: Random House.

Woodworth, G. M. (2004) Hackers, users, and suits: Napster and representations of identity, *Popular Music and Society*, 27(2): 161–84.

Yahoo! News UK (2007) Casino Royale premieres in China, 30 January, http://uk.news.yahoo.com/30012007/356/casino-royale-premieres-china.html

Young, J. (1971a) *The Drugtakers: The Social Meaning of Drug Use*. London: Paladin.

Young, J. (1971b) The role of the police as amplifiers of deviancy, negotiators of reality and translators of fantasy: some consequences of our present system of drug controls as seen in Notting Hill, in S. Cohen (ed.) *Images of Deviance*. Harmondsworth: Penguin: 27–61.

Young, J. (1973) The myth of the drug taker in the mass media, in S. Cohen and J. Young (eds) *The Manufacture of News: Social Problems, Deviance and the Mass Media*. London: Constable: 314–22.

Zoonen, L. van (1991) Feminist perspectives on the media, in J. Curran and M. Gurevitch (eds) *Mass Media and Society*. London: Arnold: 33–54.

Zoonen, L. van (1994) *Feminist Media Studies*. London: Sage.

Index